ALSO BY JAMES D. TABOR

Why Waco?: Cults and the Battle for
Religious Freedom in America
(with Eugene Gallagher)

A Noble Death: Suicide and Martyrdom
Among Ancient Jews and Christians
(with Arthur Droge)

Things Unutterable: Paul's Ascent to
Paradise in its Greco-Roman, Judaic,
and early Christian Contexts

The

JESUS DYNASTY

The Hidden History of Jesus, His Royal Family,
and the Birth of Christianity

JAMES D. TABOR

SIMON & SCHUSTER
New York London Toronto Sydney

SIMON & SCHUSTER
Rockefeller Center
1230 Avenue of the Americas
New York, NY 10020

Designed by Ruth Lee Mui
Maps by Paul Pugliese

Manufactured in the United States of America

ISBN: 0-7432-8723-1

Ad memoriam Albert Schweitzer (1875–1965).
Missionary, philosopher, historian extraordinaire.
In whose shadow we all stand.

Contents

Part Four: Entering the Lion's Den

Part Five: Waiting for the Son of Man

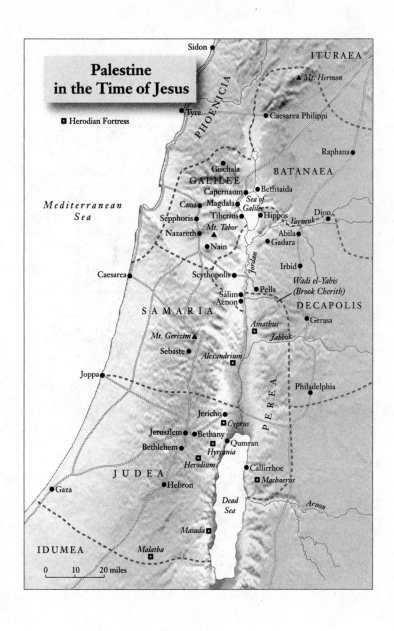

Palestine in the Time of Jesus

■ Herodian Fortress

ITURAEA

Sidon

Mt. Hermon

PHOENICIA

Tyre

Caesarea Philippi

Raphana

Gischala

BATANAEA

GALILEE

Capernaum ● Bethsaida

Cana ● Magdala ● Sea of Galilee

Sepphoris ● Tiberius ● Hippos

Dion

Nazareth ● Mt. Tabor

Yarmuk

Mediterranean Sea

Nain

Abila ● Gadara

Jordan

Irbid

Caesarea

Scythopolis

Wadi el-Yabis (Brook Cherith)

Sálim ● Pella

Aenon

DECAPOLIS

SAMARIA

Amathus

Gerasa

Mt. Gerizim

Jabbok

Sebaste

Alexandrium

Joppa

PEREA

Philadelphia

Jericho

Cyprus

Jerusalem ● Bethany

Bethlehem

Qumran

Hyrcania

Herodium

Callirrhoe

JUDEA

Machaerus

Gaza ● Hebron

Dead Sea

Arnon

Masada

IDUMEA

Malatha

0   10   20 miles

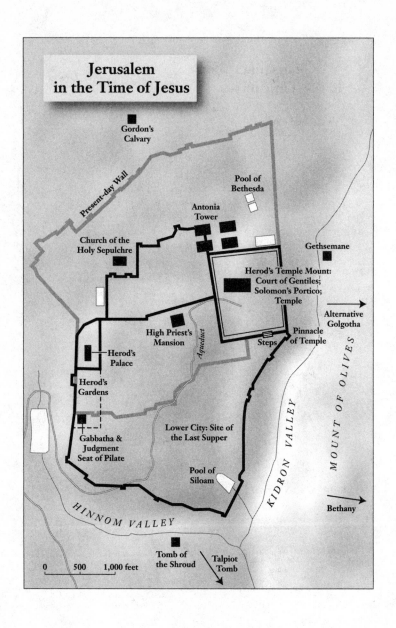

Jerusalem in the Time of Jesus

Gordon's Calvary

Present-day Wall

Pool of Bethesda

Antonia Tower

Church of the Holy Sepulchre

Gethsemane

Herod's Temple Mount: Court of Gentiles; Solomon's Portico; Temple

Alternative Golgotha

High Priest's Mansion

Aqueduct

Steps

Pinnacle of Temple

Herod's Palace

Herod's Gardens

Lower City: Site of the Last Supper

KIDRON VALLEY

MOUNT OF OLIVES

Gabbatha & Judgment Seat of Pilate

Pool of Siloam

Bethany

HINNOM VALLEY

Tomb of the Shroud

Talpiot Tomb

0   500   1,000 feet

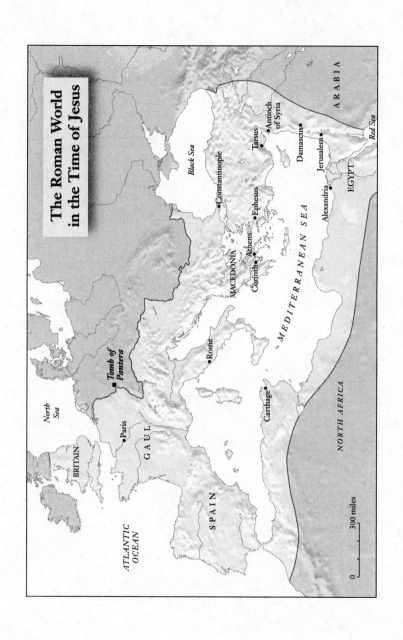

The Roman World in the Time of Jesus

ATLANTIC
OCEAN

North Sea

BRITAIN

Paris

GAUL

SPAIN

Tomb of
Pantera

Rome

Carthage

NORTH AFRICA

MEDITERRANEAN SEA

MACEDONIA

Corinth

Athens

Ephesus

Constantinople

Black Sea

Tarsus

Antioch
of Syria

Damascus

Jerusalem

Alexandria

EGYPT

ARABIA

Red Sea

0   300 miles

The
JESUS
DYNASTY

DISCOVERING
THE JESUS DYNASTY

IT is a rare book that is forty years in the making. In some sense this is the case with *The Jesus Dynasty*. Over forty years ago, as a teenager, I made my first visit to the Holy Land with my parents and my sister. It was that experience that set me on my own lifelong "quest for the historical Jesus." This is the phrase scholars use to describe historical research over the past two hundred years related to Jesus and the origins of early Christianity.

What do we *really* know about Jesus and how do we know it? Forty years ago I had not even formulated the question with any sophistication. I knew nothing of archaeology, the Dead Sea Scrolls and other ancient texts, or historical research. But I had begun to read the Bible, particularly the New Testament, and had become fascinated with the figure of Jesus. On that Holy Land trip this interest began to develop into a more intense desire to know what could be known about him and to somehow *touch* that past.

I vividly remember walking around the Old City of Jerusalem. The city was thick with tourists, all Christians, no Jews or Israelis. This was before the 1967 Six Day War when the Old City of east Jerusalem was still ruled by Jordan. We were shown around by one of the hundreds of would-be resident guides who could be hired on the spot pressing upon anyone who looked like a tourist. We saw all the sites typically shown to Christian pilgrims—the Church of the Holy Sepulchre, the Mount of Olives, the Garden of Gethsemane, the Upper Room of the Last Supper, and the Dome of the Rock, where the ancient Jewish Temple once stood. On such a tour one enters dozens of churches, all built centuries after the time of Jesus but supposedly at the precise place where this or that event took place.

Over the three days we were there I began to experience a growing sense of disappointment. I was having difficulty connecting, even in my imagination, 20th-century Jerusalem with the city in the time of Jesus as described in the New Testament. Even if the names and places were the same, and correctly identified, what I saw before me were Turkish, Crusader, and Byzantine remains, with little if anything from the 1st century A.D. visible. Even the modern street level, I learned, was twelve to fifteen feet above that of Roman times. I had purchased a tourist guidebook entitled *Walking Where Jesus Walked*, and somehow, in my naiveté, I wanted to do just that.

We stayed in a small hotel on top of the Mount of Olives just to the east of the Old City. About midnight, restless, I got out of bed, Bible in hand, and decided to walk to the Garden of Gethsemane at the foot of the mountain. The steep path down is now paved, but I could see bedrock cut or worn along the way on both sides, indicating this was the narrow road from ancient times. I imagined Jesus riding the donkey down that very path into the Old City, hailed by the crowds as Messiah, a week before he was crucified. In those days, unlike today, you could enter the Garden of Gethsemane at any hour, day or night, as the gate was always open. Visitors were also allowed to walk among the centuries-old olive trees. I was the only one there that night, at that hour. My reading had convinced me that this was the spot where Jesus spent the last night of his life in prayer. For the first time on our tour, on that path and in the garden, I felt that I was able to reach back and connect with the past that I sought. I stayed there for the longest time, trying to imagine it all. I kept thinking to myself—this is the place. It happened here. The "historian" in me was awakening and I think a bit of the "archaeologist" as well. In some way I had begun what would become a lifelong quest to discover and to understand the life of Jesus as he lived it.

There is something in all of us that thrills to this experience of touching the past. It could be an old letter, a genealogical record, a battlefield, a cemetery, or fragments of an ancient text. Today in Israel you can visit the Shrine of the Book at the Israel Museum and view the Dead Sea Scrolls, which date to around the time of Jesus. I think many visitors experience the same feeling I did the first time I saw the displays. There, under glass, just a few inches away, are the *actual* ancient documents written over two thousand years ago. I remember pausing for long minutes before each exhibit, trying to take in the reality of what I was viewing. There one is looking at the very parchment or papyrus from that long-ago time, with words in Hebrew and Aramaic that could have been read by Jesus or his followers.

Many other sites in Jerusalem have now been excavated. You can walk or sit on the very steps that led up to the Jewish Temple built in the time of Herod the Great. When I first visited Jerusalem in 1962 these steps were twenty-five feet below the present surface, completely lost to modern eyes. In various places the paving stones of the streets of the Roman city have been exposed. Twelve feet below the modern street level, in the Jewish Quarter, you can walk in the ruins of a wealthy mansion, one that likely belonged to the family of high priests who presided over the trial of Jesus. In the summer of 2004 the pool of Siloam, mentioned in the New Testament, was uncovered, after being forgotten and hidden from view for centuries. All over the country the past is being exposed to the present by the spade of the archaeologist and equally by the deciphering of ancient texts by the historian.

I have since been back to Israel and Jordan dozens of times as a researcher and scholar. Whether I am digging an archaeological site, researching in a library, or studying firsthand a given area or location, my focus remains the same—to recreate a past that has important relevance to our present. *The Jesus Dynasty* is a new historical investigation of Jesus, his royal family, and the birth of Christianity. At the same time it is a reflection of my own personal quest, integrating the results of my own discoveries and insights over the course of my professional career.

The Jesus Dynasty presents the Jesus story in an entirely new light. It is history, not fiction. And yet it differs considerably, sometimes radically, from the standard portrait of Jesus informed by theological dogma. *The Jesus Dynasty* proposes an original version of Christianity, long lost and forgotten, but one that can be reliably traced back to the founder, Jesus himself. The impact and implications of this book are far-reaching and potentially revolutionary. There is a sense in which one might call it "the greatest story *never* told." It will thrill and excite many, upset and anger others, but also challenge its readers, of whatever persuasion, to honestly weigh evidence and consider new possibilities.

The Jesus Dynasty has no connection to the recently popularized notions that Jesus married and fathered children through Mary Magdalene. While gripping fiction, this idea is long on speculation and short on evidence. But as is so often the case, the truth is even stranger than fiction—and every bit as intriguing.

In *The Jesus Dynasty* you will discover that Jesus was the firstborn son of a *royal family*—a descendant of King David of ancient Israel. He really was proclaimed "King of the Jews," and was executed by the Romans for this claim. Rather than a church, or a new religion, as commonly understood, he established a royal dynasty drawn from his own brothers and immediate family. *Rather than being the founder of a church, Jesus was claimant to a throne.* According to the Hebrew Prophets, the Messiah, the scion of David, who would lead the nation of Israel in the last days, was to spring from this specific lineage. Recently released portions of the Dead Sea Scrolls have shed further light on the concrete nature of this expectation. This coveted royal bloodline, the family of David, with its radical revolutionary potential, was well known to the Herod family, the native rulers of Palestine at the time, but also to the Roman officials who ruled the country, including the emperors themselves. These "royals" were not only watched, but also at critical times even hunted down and executed.

Shortly before he died, Jesus set up a provisional government with twelve regional officials, one over each of the twelve tribes or districts of Israel, and he left his brother James at the head of this fledgling government. James became the uncontested leader of the early Christian movement. This significant fact of history has been largely forgotten, or as likely, hidden. Properly understood, it changes everything we thought we knew about Jesus, his mission, and his message. Everyone has heard of Peter, Paul, and John—but the pivotal place of James, the beloved disciple and younger brother of Jesus, has been effectively blotted from Christian memory.

The Jesus Dynasty explores how and why Christians gradually lost the recognition that Jesus was part of a large family, the members of which exercised dynastic leadership among his followers. This critical, alternative, story, which survives even in our New Testament records and in bits and pieces of later Christian tradition, can be effectively recovered. A combination of recent archaeological discoveries and the surfacing of texts long forgotten has given us a new perspective from which to view the birth of Christianity. Understanding the origins of this largest global religion not only offers us insights about the past, it also opens up whole new ways of seeing Christianity in our own day. We now have a sharper and more historically reliable understanding of Jesus as he was in his own time and place.

THE AMERICAN COLONY HOTEL, JERUSALEM

JUNE 7, 2005

Introduction

A TALE OF TWO TOMBS

MANY of the great archaeological discoveries of our time have been accidental. It is as if there is some mysterious hidden axiom at work—what we most hope to discover we seldom find, and what we least expect can suddenly appear. This seems to be particularly true when it comes to the historical study of Jesus and the movement he founded, subsequently known as Christianity. One thinks of the appearance of the Dead Sea Scrolls in 1947 from caves in the Judean desert, or the uncovering of the 1st-century A.D. skeleton of a crucified man by a road-building crew in Jerusalem in 1968, or the chance discovery in 2000 of the tomb of the high priest Caiaphas, who presided over the trial of Jesus.[1] When it comes to archaeology it seems that time and chance are equal partners with careful planning and method.

A LATE NIGHT DISCOVERY IN JERUSALEM

I learned this firsthand late one Wednesday afternoon on June 14, 2000, while hiking with five of my students in the Hinnom Valley, just south of the Old City of Jerusalem in an area known as Akeldama.[2] We had been in Israel for two weeks excavating a newly discovered cave a few miles west of Jerusalem at a place called Suba, which has the earliest drawings related to John the Baptizer ever found. The University of North Carolina at Charlotte, where I am a professor, is the academic sponsor of the dig. Dr. Shimon Gibson and I are co-directors of the excavation. It had been an exciting trip, our second season at the "Cave of John the Baptist," as we had come to call it. We had decided to do a bit of archaeological sightseeing as a break from a hard day of digging in the summer heat. The Hinnom Valley is an area thick with ancient rock-hewn tombs, just a stone's throw from the Arab village of Silwan. Many of the tombs are open, having been robbed and emptied centuries ago. But a significant number are still sealed and intact, covered with topsoil and preserved for the past two thousand years. On that late evening Gibson, who is an Israeli archaeologist, had offered to take us into some of the open tombs to give us an idea of what Jewish burial was like in the time of Jesus.

None of us had the slightest inkling of the exciting discovery just ahead, or the stealth operation that was about to begin. I certainly had no idea that we were about to stumble onto something that would relate to my lifelong research regarding the historical Jesus, and more specifically to the Jesus dynasty itself. We finished our tour of half a dozen tombs about 7 P.M. It was beginning to get dark and we needed to head back to Jerusalem to the British School of Archaeology where we were staying so we could get some rest. As it turned out, none of us were to sleep at all that night.

As we were making our way back to our cars, Jeff Poplin, one of my students, pointed down the hillside below where we had parked. The entrance to a freshly opened tomb was visible in the setting sunlight. Moist soil was piled about the entrance and we could see fragments of broken ossuaries scattered all about. These were the stone bone boxes that Jews of the 1st century used to hold the bones of the deceased. As we approached closer the rectangular entrance to the tomb was clearly exposed, measuring about a square meter. We stuck our heads inside. It was pitch dark, but the damp musty smell of such a space, sealed from outside air for thousands of years, filled our nostrils. It is not an unpleasant smell, but one like no other, and something one never forgets.

Tomb robberies in this area are relatively rare—perhaps two or three occur over the span of a decade. The Israelis have a special armed unit responsible for protecting antiquities, and the desecrating of an ancient tomb is a serious crime. Judging from the broken ossuaries at the entrance and the fresh soil piled around, the tomb in front of us had most likely just been robbed the night before.

Gibson alerted the Israeli authorities on his cell phone and with their permission he, his assistant Rafi Lewis, and a couple of my students went inside to survey the damage while the authorities were on their way. I waited outside with the others, standing watch. It was rapidly growing dark. The tomb had more than one chamber or level. The group inside disappeared and after a while we could not hear them anymore. The Israelis took much longer to arrive than we expected. The minutes ticked by. After about twenty minutes, and hearing and seeing nothing, those of us outside began to wonder if we should go in and find the others.

Suddenly we heard the excited shouting of Lee Hutchinson, another of my students, muffled at first, then more distinct, as he scrambled toward the upper chamber. He was yelling, "Dr. Tabor! Dr. Tabor! Dr. Gibson has found something very important!" He was so excited he could hardly talk. With his head sticking out of the entrance and his body still inside, he told us that the tomb had three chambers or levels, and in the lowest chamber, in a burial niche carved into the wall, there were the remains of a skeleton with portions of its cloth burial shroud still intact.

Gibson eventually surfaced and explained to us the remarkable implications of this discovery. Jewish burial at the time of Jesus was carried out in two distinct stages—a primary and a secondary "burial." First the body was washed and anointed with oils and spices and wrapped in a burial shroud. It was then placed on a stone shelf or in a niche known as a *loculus* carved into the bedrock wall of the tomb. The body was allowed to decompose and desiccate for as long as a year. When mostly bones were left, the remains were gathered and placed into an ossuary or "bone box" usually carved from limestone.[3] Often the name of the deceased was carved or scratched on the side into the stone. Some ossuaries hold the bones of more than one individual, and some are inscribed with more than one name. These rectangular lidded boxes vary in size but typically they are 20 by 10 by 12 inches, long enough for the femur or thigh bone, and wide enough to hold the skull.

Photo with cutaway drawing of the Tomb of the Shroud

Ossuaries were commonly used in Jewish burials in and around Jerusalem from about 30 B.C. to A.D. 70, a hundred-year period surrounding the lifetime of Jesus. They regularly turn up through foiled tomb robberies, or accidentally as a result of construction projects. When a tomb has been so violated the archaeologists are called in on an emergency, or rescue, basis to record what they can. The artifacts, including the ossuaries, are catalogued and stored, and the bones are promptly turned over to the Orthodox Jewish community for reburial.

Thousands of ossuaries have been found in Israel, especially in the rock-hewn tombs outside Jerusalem. But finding a skeleton still laid out in a loculus and wrapped in its burial shroud was a first. For some reason the family of the deceased had not returned after the primary burial to place their loved one more permanently in an ossuary.

Organic materials, such as cloth, normally could not survive outside a desert area, and with Jerusalem in the mountains, with its damp winters and rainfall, such a find seemed unbelievable. The tomb had probably been undisturbed since the 1st century A.D. Most of the tombs in this area of Akeldama dated to the time of Jesus, and only a few of them had been opened or robbed over the centuries. We could see no evidence to think this one was any different from the others. However, Gibson did allow the possibility that maybe this particular skeleton with the burial shroud had been placed there from a later period—perhaps from the Crusades—thus accounting for its preservation. There are cases where ancient tombs were reused in later periods. But Gibson was of the view that we might well have stumbled across the only example of a 1st-century burial shroud ever found. Only carbon-14 testing of the fabric could tell us for certain. The whole scene reminded me of the initial examination of the Dead Sea Scrolls. At that time scholars found it hard to believe they could have survived for two thousand years. The Scrolls had been preserved in the dry heat of the Judean desert, but we were in the mountains of Jerusalem where the winter weather is rainy and damp. So we were quite prepared to accept a late medieval or Crusades date for the fabric.

The Israelis arrived with supervisor Boaz Zissu of the Israel Antiquities Authority. We spent the rest of the night removing and labeling every bit of the fragile remaining cloth. Boaz told us that thieves had initially opened this very tomb in 1998 but that he and Amir Ganor, who is in charge of protecting tombs in the area, had been able to block it back up and prevent its total looting.[4] No one at that time had noticed the shrouded skeletal remains in the lower chamber.

Since my students were trained in archaeology they were allowed to participate. Gibson spent several hours bent over on his hands and knees, squeezed into the narrow loculus. The students photographed, labeled, and recorded each stage of the retrieval. We finished close to daybreak and our carefully packaged cargo was taken to the laboratory of the Israel Antiquities Authority at the Rockefeller Museum, just north of the Old City.

Our team returned to the States a few days later and a precious sample of the cloth, hastily licensed for scientific export, was shipped off to the Accelerator Mass Spectrometry Laboratory at the University of Arizona in Tucson for carbon-14 dating. It was in this lab, back in 1988, that the "Shroud of Turin" had been dated to A.D. 1300, demonstrating it to be a medieval forgery. As fate would have it, the scientist I contacted in Tucson, Dr. Douglas Donahue, was the individual who supervised the C-14 tests on the Turin shroud. I did not tell Donahue anything about the provenance of our sample—only that we knew it was not modern and we wanted it to be rushed if possible. As the days passed I found it hard to think of anything else or to concentrate on my other work.

Just after noon on August 9, Donahue reached me by phone at my office at the university. He had the results of the tests. His voice was matter-of-fact and subdued. He asked me if I was sitting down and as he began to read aloud his report I detected a hint of excitement. *The Akeldama shroud had been scientifically dated to the first half of the 1st century A.D.*—precisely to the time of Jesus!

Donahue faxed me a copy of his report and I sent it immediately to Gibson in Jerusalem. In his cover letter Donahue closed with an interesting observation: "Our friends from Shroud of Turin days would certainly have appreciated a result like this. I will be interested to know the ramifications of this result." At the time we had just begun to study the tomb and what remained of its contents. None of us could have imagined the far-reaching ramifications that would come to light.

The tomb itself had been strewn with hundreds of fragments of broken ossuaries and scattered bones. Only one large heavy ossuary was left intact, but it had no inscription. What the tomb robbers typically do is remove only a few of the finest ossuaries, preferably some with clear or interesting inscriptions, so as not to flood the antiquities market where they hope to carry out clandestine illegal sales to collectors. They purposely break the rest and carry out only the pieces that have the inscriptions, since such fragments can be easily sold and draw little attention.

Gibson put together an impressive team of experts to begin scientific analysis of the remains of the Tomb of the Shroud, including forensic anthropologists, textile experts, DNA specialists, paleobiologists, and epigraphers. The fragmented ossuaries had to be restored, the cloth of the shroud analyzed, and DNA and other biological tests done on the skeletal remains. In the end twenty ossuaries were restored and three of

Broken ossuary fragments from the Tomb of the Shroud

them had inscriptions that had been missed by the thieves. The clearest one has the name "Maria" or Mary written in Aramaic. A second one possibly is the name "Salome."

The DNA tests done on the various bone samples were quite successful, even after two thousand years. We were able to establish a network of sibling and maternal links between the individuals buried in the tomb. Typically families and extended families used the same rock-hewn tomb over several generations. As for our shrouded individual, we were able to determine that "he" was indeed an adult male, probably of aristocratic birth, that he suffered from leprosy (Hanson's disease), and, microbiological tests indicated, that he most likely died of tuberculosis.

Gibson and I began to comb the ancient literature for evidence related to the use of burial shrouds and ossuaries among the Jews of Judea and Galilee in the Roman period. As it turns out, the references in the New Testament to the shrouded burial of Jesus provide us with some of our

Restored ossuaries from the Tomb of the Shroud

most valuable evidence related to the Jewish customs in use in the early 1st century A.D. in Jerusalem—the very time of our man of the shroud. After all, Jesus' body was washed and wrapped in a two-piece linen shroud and laid out with spices on a stone shelf or slab in a rock-hewn

The name "Mary" inscribed on a fragment from the Tomb of the Shroud

family tomb just outside the walls of the Old City of Jerusalem. Our man of the shroud must have been similarly prepared for burial. We had no reason to speculate that our tomb was in any way connected with the one in which Jesus was initially taken, but as Gibson once remarked to me, our "man of the shroud" lived and died in Jerusalem in the time of Jesus and as a member of the upper classes, very likely might have observed the fateful events of that Passover weekend when Jesus was crucified.

The following year, in the summer of 2001, when I returned to Israel to continue our work at the "John the Baptist" cave, I still had the Tomb of the Shroud much on my mind. I began to make some discreet inquiries in the Old City of Jerusalem among some trusted contacts I had made in the antiquities business. I was able to determine that the missing inscribed fragments from our ossuaries had made it onto the illegal market and could possibly be recovered. At one point the principal person with whom I was dealing asked me if there would be a "bonus" payment if *all* the missing inscriptions were retrieved. I tried to be calm and matter of fact at this implied disclosure, excited to think that the stolen material from our shroud tomb might still be retrieved. On the other hand, I knew that making payments for stolen goods is something we could not do. I simply replied that we would discuss the matter further when I could see the fragments. I felt it was important to stress the scientific aspects of our quest. After all, my university would now be responsible for publishing the academic study of the shroud tomb and we were not collectors wanting to get hold of some new artifacts. I got the distinct impression that if no one would be prosecuted some type of "exchange" could be worked out. To recover these inscribed fragments would have been invaluable to our study of the Tomb of the Shroud because we would be able to assemble the names of the deceased and match them by DNA with the slight residue of human remains that still clung to the insides of our restored ossuaries. Gibson and I were exploring how that might legally be done when the Intifada or Palestinian uprising reached such a level that we felt it was too dangerous to carry out our plan. At one point that summer, after a series of three bombings over one weekend, we were told not even to go into the city of Jerusalem at all. We had set up our excavation at the "John the Baptizer" cave at Kibbutz Suba near the site, outside the dangerous areas.

On my next visit to Jerusalem I resumed my investigative efforts to recover our missing ossuary fragments through my contacts in the antiquities market. I quickly discovered that everything had changed. Even those I had talked to before began to act as though we never had spoken. What had changed was the dramatic announcement in October 2002 that an ossuary inscribed "James son of Joseph brother of Jesus" had suddenly come to light. Its appearance and the resulting controversy it stirred had caused everyone who deals with antiquities in the Old City to completely clam up.

THE BURIAL BOX OF JAMES THE BROTHER OF JESUS?

It was noon on Monday, October 21, 2002, when Hershel Shanks, editor of *Biblical Archaeology Review*, announced at a press conference in Washington, D.C., that a limestone ossuary or "bone box" inscribed in ancient Aramaic with the phrase "James son of Joseph brother of Jesus" had surfaced in Jerusalem. The Associated Press flashed the story around the world that afternoon, and the next morning there were front-page stories about the James ossuary in the *New York Times*, the *Washington Post*, and practically every other newspaper in the world. That evening all the major television networks carried the news. Feature stories followed in *Time*, *Newsweek*, and *U.S. News & World Report*. Even though the ossuary had once held the bones of James, not Jesus, most of the stories emphasized that the inscription was the only physical artifact ever found from the 1st century A.D. that mentioned Jesus. The writers had to scramble a bit to deal with the "James" side of the story since it quickly became obvious that few people, whether in media or the general public, were even aware that Jesus had a brother named James.

We were told that an undisclosed private collector, later revealed to be an Israeli named Oded Golan, had bought the ossuary fifteen years earlier from a Jerusalem antiquities dealer who said it came from the area of Silwan, just south of the Old City of Jerusalem. Golan had not paid much attention to the inscription nor realized its significance. In April 2002 he had shown a photo of the ossuary to André Lemaire, professor of Semitic languages at the Sorbonne, who was on a visit to Jerusalem.

The James Ossuary on display at the Royal Ontario Museum

Lemaire was immediately intrigued, recognizing that the combination of names and relationships very likely pointed to not just any James but to *the* James, brother of Jesus in Christian tradition. He could hardly believe his eyes. Golan allowed him to study the actual ossuary shortly thereafter. After careful examination Lemaire was convinced based on his expertise in ancient scripts that the inscription was authentic. Later in interviews Golan was asked why he had not recognized the potential importance of such an artifact when he first bought it. He explained that as a Jew he was of course familiar with the Christian teaching of Mary's virginity but had never imagined that Jesus, the "son of God," could have had a brother. Obviously, he was not alone in that assumption.

Lemaire told Shanks about the ossuary when Shanks was on a visit to Jerusalem in May 2002. Shanks was duly cautious, since this particular ossuary had not come from any authorized archaeological excavation, and thus its authenticity could be questioned. He asked Lemaire to prepare a detailed article about the new find to be published in the upcoming issue of *Biblical Archaeology Review*, and he insisted that the ossuary be tested scientifically. Golan agreed, and arrangements were made for experts at the Geological Survey of Israel in Jerusalem to examine it.

Inscriptions on ossuaries can of course be forged, but modern cuts into ancient limestone will not contain the ancient patina that naturally coats the surface of the stone over time. In the meantime Shanks brought in several other expert paleographers to give their opinions on the authenticity of the script itself. The ossuary passed all the authenticity tests with flying colors. The scientists concluded that the patina inside the letters was ancient, adhering firmly to the stone, despite the fact that someone had done a bit of cleaning of the inscription. No signs of the use of any modern tool or instrument were evident. The paleographers agreed with Lemaire's analysis that the script was authentic and wholly consistent with that of the 1st century A.D. There seemed little doubt that the ossuary once held the bones of "a" James, son of "a" Joseph, with a brother named "Jesus," who had died and been buried in the 1st century A.D.

Shimon Gibson's drawing of the James Ossuary inscription

Shanks was ready to go to press and he went into high gear. He knew that next to the discovery of the Dead Sea Scrolls this was perhaps the most sensational archaeological find in modern times. He engaged the services of Emmy Award–winning producer Simcha Jacobovici to produce a documentary for the Discovery Channel on the James Ossuary that would air on Easter Sunday of 2003. He also worked out a deal to publish a co-authored book with biblical scholar Ben Witherington to coincide with the release of the film.[5] The discovery was hailed in both the book and film as "the first archaeological link to Jesus and his family."

With Golan's permission Shanks arranged a special exhibit for the ossuary at the Royal Ontario Museum in Toronto. It would open in late
November 2002. The city of Toronto and the month of November were
not accidental choices. Toronto was slated to be the host city for the annual meeting of thousands of biblical scholars, archaeologists, and academics in the study of religion the weekend before Thanksgiving. The
Society of Biblical Literature quickly arranged for a special session devoted to a discussion of the authenticity and potential significance of the
James Ossuary.

The Israel Antiquities Authority (IAA) had to approve the temporary
export license but at that point no one recognized the potentially explo-
sive attention that the ossuary would generate. When the ossuary suddenly made world headlines following Shanks's press conference on
October 21 in Washington, D.C., the Israeli authorities were taken completely unawares and were duly embarrassed. But all the arrangements for
the Toronto exhibit were already in place. The Israelis immediately initiated an investigation into the circumstances of Golan's acquisition of the
ossuary but they did allow it to leave the country. According to Israeli law,
if Golan had acquired it after 1978, the ossuary would have been sold il-
legally and subject to confiscation by the state.

When the ossuary arrived in Toronto it had been cracked in transit
and the scientific team at the Royal Ontario Museum took on the task of
repairing it for the exhibit. One of the cracks ran through part of the inscription, allowing the scientific team at the museum to more closely examine the way the letters were cut into the limestone. They agreed with
the Israeli scientists that ancient patina was present in the letters, it was
firmly adhering to the stone and consistent with the rest of the ossuary.

Even before the Toronto gatherings, questions were being raised about
the conclusions of Lemaire and Shanks. No one questioned the authenticity of the ossuary itself—it was clearly a genuine artifact from the time
of Jesus. Some objected to any discussion of the ossuary at all since it was
a "black market" item lacking an archaeological context. Others had argued that the phrase "brother of Jesus" appeared to be written in a different hand than "James son of Joseph," and might have been added by a
forger. Still others maintained that even if genuine we would never be

able to *prove* that the "James son of Joseph" of the ossuary was the brother of Jesus of Nazareth since all three names were common in the period.

I first viewed the ossuary at the November meeting in Toronto at a private after-hours gathering of scholars at the Royal Ontario Museum. About twenty-five of us were invited—historians, archaeologists, epigraphers, and New Testament scholars. I stood next to Shanks and heard firsthand three of the top experts on ancient scripts in the world all agree that the inscription was authentic. The feeling in the room was contagious and electrifying yet strangely sober and subdued. I think most of us were convinced that we were standing before the actual 2,000-year-old stone box that had once held the bones of James the brother of Jesus of Nazareth.

When the James Ossuary was returned to Israel in February 2003, the Israel Antiquities Authority confiscated it and appointed a team of fifteen experts to make a judgment as to the authenticity of all or part of the inscription. The committee was divided into epigraphers who were experts in ancient scripts and physical scientists who were to test the geochemistry of the artifact. In June 2003 the IAA committee declared the ossuary genuine but the inscription a partial forgery. A month later Golan was arrested on suspicion of forging antiquities. He has since been formally indicted and charged with adding the phrase "brother of Jesus" to an otherwise genuine ossuary that was inscribed with "James son of Joseph," attempting to coat the letters with a fake baked-on patina, and lying about when he acquired the ossuary—all for purposes of generating worldwide publicity and financial gain. Both the IAA committee conclusions and the indictment against Oded Golan were widely reported in the media, giving the public the impression that the experts had now concluded that the James Ossuary was a forgery.[6] Such is hardly the case, and the authenticity issue is far from settled.[7]

André Lemaire, the Sorbonne epigrapher, continues to strongly defend the authenticity of the inscription and has offered detailed responses to the ossuary detractors. Ada Yardeni, not on the IAA committee but one of Israel's leading experts in ancient writing, agrees. She points out unique features about the Aramaic phrasing in the inscription that no forger could have possibly known. She even offered a concluding comment, "If it is a forgery then I quit."[8] To date not a single qualified epigrapher or pale-ographer has pointed out any evidence of forgery. In fact one member of the IAA committee who, against his better judgment, went along with the original vote now says he thinks the inscription is authentic. Other qualified experts have questioned the IAA geochemical tests on the patina. The IAA geologists have had to back down from their initially pro-posed theories as to how the allegedly fake patina was produced. One member of the IAA committee has said that she saw ancient patina in the last two letters of the inscription—the very part that is supposed to be forged. The geologists from the Geological Survey of Israel who initially found the inscription to be authentic have not changed their position, nor has the scientific team at the Royal Ontario Museum that examined the ossuary after it was broken.[9]

The James Ossuary inscription is likely authentic. There is also reli-able circumstantial evidence that it was looted from our Tomb of the Shroud either when it was first robbed in 1998, or perhaps just before we discovered it looted a second time in June 2000. *Was it possible that we had unknowingly stumbled upon the Jesus family tomb?*

The main inconsistency in Oded Golan's story has to do with when he acquired the ossuary. When the story first broke in October 2001 he told Shanks that he had had it for about fifteen years. He later gave a number of interviews in which he said he acquired it in the "mid-1970s" or about twenty-five years earlier. That would put the date back before 1978, when it was legal to buy such items. At one point he said he acquired it in 1967, just after the Six Day War, which would mean he had owned it for thirty-five years. But the rest of his story is consistent. He says that he bought it from an Arab antiquities dealer in the Old City of Jerusalem who in turn said it came from the area of Silwan, an Arab village south of the Old City where the Kidron and Hinnom valleys meet.

Oded Golan expanded upon his "Silwan" in an informal social conver-sation with Rafi Lewis at Golan's apartment in December 2002. (In June 2000, Rafi Lewis was Shimon Gibson's assistant and was with us the night we found our looted tomb.) Rafi had asked Golan whether "Silwan" included the Hinnom Valley and he replied yes, explaining that in fact the James Ossuary came from the Hinnom Valley. Of course Akeldama, in Hinnom, is the precise location of our Shroud tomb.[10]

According to Shimon Gibson, only two tombs were looted in the Hinnom Valley area in the 1990s. The first was not excavated and was re-sealed. There is no evidence that ossuaries were taken from that one. The second was our shroud tomb. Recall that my inquiries in the Old City shortly after we found the tomb indicated that the black market had been suddenly "flooded" with new ossuary materials.

There is one ossuary in particular from our shroud tomb that caught the attention of Gibson and me. It has a simple incised border running around the edges of the side panels that is precisely the style found on the James Ossuary. Ossuaries come in a wide variety of styles and decora-tions, and many have borders, but I have not seen another ossuary with that exact style of border. To get a firsthand look, Gibson and I recently visited the warehouse in Bet Shemesh where our ossuaries are stored. This particular one is smaller than the James Ossuary; it was likely in-tended for a child, but judging from its similarity it may well have been made by the same stonecutter. As we looked through the vast rows of shelves holding the enormous os-suary collection of the State of Is-rael we saw no other examples matching these two. It seemed to us another piece of the puzzle. It makes sense that a single family might buy two ossuaries from the same artisan—and thus the styles would be matched.

A Tomb of the Shroud ossuary that resembles the James Ossuary

There is one way this matter might be settled. The James Os-suary had significant bone materials still in it when it was first shown to Hershel Shanks and the filmmaker Simcha Jacobovici. Simcha, an Or-thodox Jew, was quoted by the *New Yorker* as saying, "I looked in the box, there were still some bone fragments. I thought, Oh my gosh, if this is real, then Jesus' DNA is there!"[11] Oded Golan later cleaned out these fragments before shipping the ossuary to Toronto, and at one point he showed a *Time* magazine reporter a Tupperware container that he said was full of those bones. Presumably the Israelis who raided his apartment are in possession of those remains. Since we have already done extensive

DNA tests on the skeletal remains of the inhabitants of our Tomb of the Shroud, why not test the bones from the James Ossuary to see if there is any possible match of mitochondrial DNA? That would tell us whether the deceased of the James Ossuary had any sibling relations in the tomb, or perhaps that one of the females was his mother. Or we might come up with no match at all. It would be particularly interesting to look at the DNA sequence of the James Ossuary remains and our "Maria" or Mary from the shroud tomb.

On November 17, 2003, Gibson and I made a formal request by letter to Shuka Dorfman, director of the Israel Antiquities Authority, that we be allowed to carry out such DNA tests on these skeletal fragments from the James Ossuary. Our thinking was that whether the inscription on the ossuary is authentic or forged—and Dorfman is convinced it is forged— it is nonetheless of scientific value to determine *where* the ossuary itself originated. Given the circumstantial evidence that it might have come from our Tomb of the Shroud, a DNA match or the lack thereof could help advance our knowledge, no matter what position one might hold about the inscription itself.

Our request was promptly denied on the grounds that the bones in the ossuary had been added by Golan to camouflage the forgery and have no connection to the original, thus rendering any tests unnecessary. We know that is not the case. But doing DNA tests on the bones of a "James" and a "Maria," particularly if that James had a brother named Jesus, means moving from the realm of science to that of theology. Our hope is that when the trial of Golan is completed and some of the emotions die down, we will still be able to pursue these scientific tests. But there is another intriguing side to this unfinished story.

THE MYSTERY OF THE TALPIOT TOMB

The "James Ossuary" story was not the first to generate worldwide headlines about ancient ossuaries and their possible relation to Jesus. Shortly before Easter in 1996 another dramatic story broke: "Jesus Family Tomb Discovered." It was reported that a tomb discovered back in 1980, but never brought to public attention, contained a significant cluster of names associated with the Jesus family, including a Mary, a Joseph, a second Mary, a Jude son of Jesus, a Matthew, and most significantly, a Jesus son of Joseph. The London *Sunday Times* paraded the story in a full front-page feature article under the title "The Tomb That Dare Not Speak Its Name" on March 31. On Easter morning the BBC aired a feature documentary on the tomb titled *The Body in Question*. The Associated Press, Reuters, and Gannett quickly cobbled stories from this initial in-depth treatment, and supplemented them with their own reports filed by correspondents who descended in droves upon unsuspecting officials of the IAA in the Old City of Jerusalem and clamored to know more. As with the James Ossuary, the Israelis were caught in the middle of things.

The questions mounted: When had the tomb been discovered? Why had it not immediately been reported to the public? Was there some type of cover-up due to the shocking contents of the tomb?[12]

In 1995, the year before the story broke, a BBC/CTVC British film crew led by Ray Bruce and Chris Mann was in Jerusalem filming a documentary on the Resurrection for their upcoming Easter special. Their aim was to bring to the British public the latest and best historical and archaeological evidence related to the reports of Jesus' empty tomb and his resurrection. They intended their program to be provocative and challenging, but they could not have imagined the surprise that awaited them.

They arrived at the archaeological warehouse of the Israel Antiquities Authority in Romemma, a rundown suburb of Jerusalem, where they had arranged for some routine filming of a few 1st-century "ossuaries." Ray Bruce and his fellow producer Chris Mann had done a bit of homework. They had learned from a catalogue published in 1994 by L. H. Rahmani[13] that of the thousand or more ossuaries stored and catalogued in various Israeli collections, six bore the name "Jesus" (Yeshu, Yeshua, or Yehoshua in Hebrew), and of those six, *two were inscribed with the designation "Jesus son of Joseph."*

The first, found in 1926, is beautifully carved and clearly legible.[14] The second, found in 1980, is nearly illegible, with the inscription scratched into the stone as if with a nail or sharp pointed object. As luck would have it, both were housed in the Romemma warehouse. The curator, Baruk Brendel, was willing to show the British crew both items.[15] The crew was understandably pleased to be able to film an intact ossuary with such an inscription from the very period of Jesus' lifetime. Still, things at this point were fairly routine, since even an ossuary with the name of "Jesus son of Joseph," however fascinating to the public, was not considered particularly noteworthy by the experts because both names were exceedingly common in that period. But then the excitement began.

Chris and Ray asked Baruk whether any of the other ossuaries in the collection were related to either of the "Jesus son of Joseph" ossuaries. The catalogue and tags were examined and it turned out five others were shelved nearby that had all been found in the same tomb as the "Jesus son of Joseph" ossuary. The tomb was in East Talpiot, just south of Jerusalem's Old City. The tomb had been uncovered when TNT was detonated by a construction crew putting up a new apartment complex. Israeli archaeologist Joseph Gath, now deceased, excavated it quickly so the construction could proceed.

Out of curiosity, Ray and Chris asked about the names on the other five ossuaries. Chris later commented that as Brendel ticked off the names "it felt like the balls of the national lottery coming up and approaching the jackpot." In addition to the "Jesus son of Joseph" ossuary there was a Joseph; a Mary, presumably his wife; another Mary; a Jude son of Jesus; and a Matthew.[16]

For the crew this was a journalistic moment made in heaven. The traditional tomb where Jesus was buried after his crucifixion is just outside the Old City to the north, the site today of the Church of the Holy Sepulchre. Jesus had been placed hastily in a tomb near the crucifixion site by an aristocratic and influential sympathizer, Joseph of Arimathea, and not in his own family tomb. Even the gospels imply that he was only temporarily put there, due to the rush of the Passover holiday. Although the family was from Nazareth, a town to the north in Galilee, the New Testament indicates that Mary as well as Jesus' brothers and sisters had taken up residence in Jerusalem. Tradition has it that Mary, mother of Jesus, did in fact die and was buried in Jerusalem, not Galilee, and there are no fewer than two sites shown today to tourists that lay claim to

A Talpiot ossuary inscribed "Jesus son of Joseph"

being the spot. Needless to say, this Talpiot tomb had not been put on any tourist map.

Was it possible that Jesus' mortal remains were finally buried with those of his father and mother? Might the other Mary be either a sister or his close companion Mary Magdalene? Could the "Jude son of Jesus" be his biological son? The possibilities were as intriguing as they were shocking and heretical.

The producers interviewed various Jewish and Christian archaeologists and historians familiar with the tomb. Everyone seemed to agree that although the names were interesting, they were so common in this period to make even such a grouping as this unique but inconclusive. Several pointed out that the name Mary was the most common female name in the period and the name Joseph the second most common male name, after Simon. Amos Kloner, who subsequently published the official report on the Talpiot excavation, maintained that the "possibility of it being Jesus' family [is] very close to zero."[17] Motti Neiger, spokesperson for the Israel Antiquities Authority, agreed "that chances of these being the actual burials of the holy family are almost nil."[18]

But it was the "almost" that interested the producers. And everyone did seem to acknowledge that this particular *cluster* of names, among the hundreds of ossuaries catalogued, was unparalleled, however common the individual names might have been. Joe Zias, curator at the Rockefeller Museum and perhaps as familiar with Jewish tombs in the area as anyone, seemed to be the only expert that thought the grouping might be statistically significant and at least deserved further investigation. He commented: "Had it not been found in a tomb I would have said 100 percent of what we are looking at are forgeries. But this came from a very good, undisturbed archaeological context. It is not something that was invented."[19]

The only way anything else could be done scientifically would be to carry out mitochondrial DNA tests on the bone samples to at least ascertain how the individuals buried there might be maternally related. Such tests, no matter what the results, could not "prove" that this particular Jesus was the one who became known as Christ, but they could show whether any of these individuals were offspring of either of the two Marys, or had a sibling relationship to one another.

If neither of the Marys turned out to be mother to this "Jesus," it would at least eliminate the possibility that this was the mother and son of Christian faith. But one of the Marys could also be a sister. Since Joseph was such a common male name we should not assume that the ossuary with the name "Joseph" was necessarily for the father of the one called "Jesus son of Joseph." He could easily be related in another way, or not at all. For example, Jesus of Nazareth also had a brother named Joseph.

Neil Silberman once quoted David Flusser, the late and great professor of ancient Judaism and early Christianity at Hebrew University, on this subject:

> Many years ago a man from the BBC came to me and he asked
> me if the Dead Sea Scrolls will harm Christianity. I said to him

that nothing can harm Christianity. The only thing which could be dangerous to Christianity would be to find a tomb with the sarcophagus or ossuary of Jesus—still containing his bones. And then I said I surely hope that it will not be found in the territory of the State of Israel.[20]

This is the stuff of which novels are made and there have been several published about "finding the bones of Jesus," but in the real world of archaeology such things smack of sensationalism. Biblical scholar Father Jerome Murphy O'Connor of Jerusalem's Ecole Biblique commented that although there was no way to prove the ossuary inscribed "Jesus son of Joseph" had contained the bones of Christ, if such proof could be made "the consequences for the faith would be disastrous."[21]

The Israelis are very sensitive to the Christian world and maintain official diplomatic relations with the Vatican. They are pleased to fill the role of the welcoming custodians for Christian tourism of the Holy Land. The last thing in which they want to be involved is some archaeological find that would spark controversy or provoke Christian theological debates. A Jesus "family tomb" would be problem enough, but one that contained an ossuary marked "Jesus son of Joseph" would surely place them in the most delicate situation imaginable.

Although it is impossible to prove that this particular tomb was related to Jesus of Nazareth, what made the tomb remarkable was not only the grouping of the names, but the fact that these ossuaries came from a documented and controlled archaeological context. The tomb and its remains could be scientifically studied. Perhaps there was more to learn from a careful reexamination of all the evidence related to the tomb or maybe even from a further investigation of the site itself. After all, Joseph Gath, the original excavator, was dead, and the official report on the tomb had not yet been published.

The media had reported, however, that an apartment building had been built over the site of the tomb shortly after its excavation in 1980, obliterating the site and foreclosing any possibility of further direct investigation. Until the official report on the tomb was published, there seemed to be little more to learn.

I had not the slightest inkling back in 1996 that this Talpiot tomb would become part of my own firsthand investigation in future years, nor how it might relate to my research on the Jesus dynasty. Shimon Gibson and I had not even met. Nearly a decade later, in early 2004, I learned that Gibson had assisted Gath in the excavation of this 1980 tomb and had done the official drawings for publication. Time and time again Shimon Gibson turns up as the right man at the right time, fortuitously linking discoveries that one would not suspect to be linked at all.

Ray Bruce and his crew had been told that the ossuaries were "empty" of bones, indicating that the tomb had likely been robbed at an earlier time and the bones lost or scattered. We now know that this was not the case. According to the official report on the Talpiot tomb published in 1996 by Amos Kloner, these ossuaries definitely held bones.[22] By Israeli law, all human remains from the tomb have to have been turned over to the Orthodox Jewish authorities for reburial, apparently precluding the possibility of DNA or any other kinds of scientific tests. I say "appar-

The mysterious façade over the entrance to the Talpiot tomb

ently" because most ossuaries, even those in the Israeli state archive collection, still contain slight residues of human remains and fragments of bone material. Unless the ossuaries are scrubbed clean, which is not the normal practice, modern sophisticated DNA tests can yield evidence from the tiniest sample.

I asked Gibson about the Talpiot tomb on a visit to Israel in 2004. He recalled two very unusual things about that particular tomb in addition to the interesting cluster of family names. The front of the tomb had a strange decoration carved into the façade over the entrance—a circle with an inverted pyramid over it. No one seemed to know what it might mean or symbolize. Also there were three skulls placed curiously on the floor of the tomb, each directly in front of a loculus or shaft holding ossuaries. Gibson pulled an old photo of the entrance to the tomb from his files. He also spread out in front of me his detailed original drawing of the plan of the tomb. The skulls were clearly visible, included in his plan just as he had seen them.

Curiously, in the official report on the tomb that Amos Kloner published in 1996, Gibson's drawing appears but with the skulls carefully air-

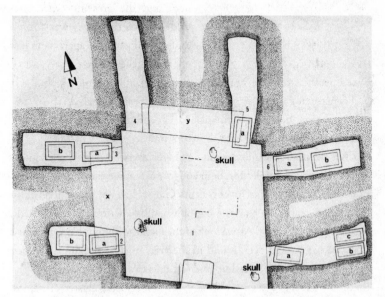

Shimon Gibson's original drawing of the Talpiot tomb with the skulls

James Tabor standing over the
ventilation pipes to the Talpiot tomb

brushed away. Gibson and I decided to do a bit of sleuthing. I think we might have been the first archaeologists in history to go looking for an ancient tomb by going out knocking on doors.

We went back to the neighborhood, to the very street, where the tomb had once been visible nearly twenty-five years earlier. An apartment complex had indeed been built on the site. We began asking around and to our surprise long-term residents knew the location of an "apartment of the tomb." Many thought that apartment was jinxed, and it had become the subject of local ghost stories. We knocked on the door and the present owner confirmed for us that there was a tomb under the floor of his apartment, just off the kitchen, where there was a raised porch area. Two ventilation vents marked the spot. The builders had constructed things so that the tomb had been preserved. The owner told us that he had bought the place at a good price, despite the stories, and he was not a believer in such superstitions.

Over the next year Gibson and I gathered every bit of published information about the Talpiot tomb. In 2005 we examined the original excavation files in the Israeli archives because Gibson had been the surveyor on the original team. We read the unpublished handwritten notes of Gath, the deceased excavator. As we looked through the Talpiot file we learned that two tombs had been found in the area, in close proximity to each other. One had been sealed up and left unexcavated. The other was the tomb Gibson had drawn—the one with the unusual cluster of names. Whether they might be related we had no idea, but that possibility did occur to us. We were not sure which of the two tombs was under the apartment. The only way to know would be to try and drop a robot camera down the ventilation pipes to see whether the tomb had been excavated or not. It was not clear that we would find anything of importance if we ever did go back into the excavated tomb, but our interest was piqued. The strange insignia on the front of the tomb, the skulls that had been ceremonially placed in front of the ossuaries, and the interesting cluster of names all begged for an explanation.

We decided to drive out to Bet Shemesh just outside Jerusalem to take a look at the Talpiot ossuaries firsthand. They are now stored, along with hundreds of other archaeological artifacts, in the new warehouse built there by the Israel Antiquities Authority. There one sees shelf after shelf, floor to ceiling, of neatly stacked and stored materials, all carefully catalogued and labeled. Most of the ossuaries in the State of Israel collection are housed there. There was one major surprise.

THE MISSING OSSUARY

Shimon Gibson's original drawing of the excavation of the Talpiot tomb clearly shows a total of *ten* ossuaries. In the official publication of the excavation Amos Kloner also confirms that ten ossuaries were recovered and retained by the Israel Antiquities Authority. Kloner carefully goes through them one by one in his report and describes them in detail as to size, decoration, and inscriptions. When he comes to the last, the tenth, he offers a single-word description: plain. Nothing more. Apparently he had nothing in his files regarding this *tenth* ossuary other than its dimensions: 60 by 26 by 30 centimeters. With each description he includes a photo of the ossuary under discussion—all except the tenth. Since Kloner was not the original excavator he is merely writing up his report based on the notes of the now-deceased Gath.

But the official catalogue of ossuaries in the State of Israel collection, published by Rahmani in 1994, also includes just *nine* ossuaries from this tomb. And yet we know that the tenth was definitely given a catalogue number by the IAA: 80.509.

As we arrived at the Bet Shemesh warehouse the curator told us even before we were taken to the area where the Talpiot ossuaries were shelved that there was a minor problem—*one ossuary was missing*. IAA 80.509, number ten in Kloner's report, was nowhere to be found. It had disappeared.

I have no idea what to make of this. In the vast collection of antiquities now held by the State of Israel things do get misplaced. But no one seems to have any explanation for this particular case and as far as I know we were the first to recognize the problem and inquire about it. Since the Talpiot tomb contained ten ossuaries, three with no inscriptions, but six with such an interesting cluster of names, one would surely like to confirm somehow whether the single-word description of "plain" is all that can be said of the missing tenth ossuary. If it could be located and it did have a name inscribed, it would be of the greatest interest to see what that name might be.

Just recently I noticed that the dimensions of the missing tenth ossuary are precisely the same, to the centimeter, to those of the James Ossuary. Is it remotely possible that Oded Golan did acquire his ossuary many years ago—maybe not in the "mid-'70s" as he now says, but not that long thereafter—in 1980 or thereabouts, when the Talpiot tomb was discovered? Was that tenth ossuary stolen after it was catalogued but before the excavation of the tomb was completed? Gibson did recall that when he arrived to do his drawings, some days after the excavation began, some but not all the ossuaries were in place. Several had been moved to facilitate the excavation work. He drew them in their original locations as the director of the excavation, Joseph Gath, indicated. Gibson told me that he is not sure if all ten were on site at that time or not.

For now, pending further evidence, whether through DNA tests or retrieval of the missing ossuary, this is where the Tale of Two Tombs must end. But it is where our story of the Jesus dynasty begins. These two rock-hewn family tombs located just outside the Old City of Jerusalem reveal more vividly than any scriptural source what family burial was like at the time of Jesus. And it is here that we begin to learn about Jesus' life and the dynasty that he established before his death, for his death was certainly not the end of his mission or his legacy. The gripping story of the Jesus dynasty that follows in no way depends on the authenticity of the James Ossuary inscription, nor whether either of these two tombs was indeed the Jesus family tomb. What we can say is that Mary, the mother of Jesus, was likely buried with her family in a tomb near the Old City of Jerusalem very much like one of these. There is something about a tomb of this type, with the ossuaries, preserved bones, and the inscribed names so familiar to us after two thousand years, that brings chills up the spine as we try to imagine and connect with the past. And what is most exciting is that we never know what new evidence might emerge at any point to allow us to put more pieces of our story together. After all, as we have seen, things that are least expected seem often to turn up and surprise us all.

Part One

IN THE BEGINNING
WAS THE FAMILY

I

A VIRGIN SHALL
CONCEIVE

WHEN I think of Mary the mother of Jesus I think of the forgotten city of Sepphoris. According to tradition Mary was the firstborn daughter of an older couple named Joachim and Anna who lived there.[1] Few today have heard of Sepphoris. It is not mentioned in the New Testament. Until fairly recently it was not even included on those maps of the Holy Land found in the back of many Bibles. It had become a lost city to us—until very recently.

I first took my students to excavate at Sepphoris in the summer of 1996. We returned in 1999 and 2000 to participate in two more seasons of excavations. We joined one of the teams, led by Professor James Strange of the University of South Florida, who had begun digging there in 1983. After more than two decades of excavations by several teams of archaeologists, not even one-tenth of the ancient Roman city has been exposed. Yet enough has been done to begin to offer us a glimpse of the splendor of the place in the time of Mary and her son Jesus.

When Jesus was growing up in Nazareth, Sepphoris was the dominant city of the entire region. Built on a hill rising four hundred feet above the flat plain below, it is still visible from miles around. Jesus' well-known saying that a "city set on a hill cannot be hid" surely came to him

growing up in Nazareth and looking north at the gleaming city of Sepphoris four miles away. It could not be missed. Nazareth was hardly anything. Nestled in the hills, just to the southeast by a spring, the total
population was probably not more than 200. It was one of dozens of
small villages that dotted the plain around the huge and impressive capital city.

Today things are reversed. Nazareth is the largest Arab city in Israel
with a population of over 60,000, half Christian, half Muslim. It literally
fills the hills and valleys around its center with impressive suburbs and
magnificent churches. Christian tours invariably include it as a major
stop on their itinerary. Sepphoris is merely a bare hill dotted with ancient
ruins in the distance. Every day at our excavations we would sit on
the southern slopes of the ruins of Sepphoris and eat our lunch, gazing
across the valley at the bustling city of Nazareth gleaming in the late
morning sun. We tried to imagine how different things must have been
in Jesus' day, with the prominence of the two locations reversed. Though
living in a small village, Jesus grew up just outside the urban capital of
Galilee. The implications of this geographical fact are enormous as we
seek to historically recapture hidden or forgotten aspects of the early
life of Jesus.

The ruins of Sepphoris viewed from Nazareth today

When Mary was born, around the year 18 B.C., the Romans occupied the northern area of Palestine called Galilee. Sepphoris was a Jewish city, but the Romans had made it the administrative center for the entire region. Herod the Great ruled the country. He had been an intimate friend of Antony and Cleopatra. The Roman general Octavian, later to reign as Caesar Augustus, confirmed him as "King of the Jews." And yet Herod lacked the vital Davidic bloodline that would have entitled him to such a throne.[2] Herod had a Jewish mother but an Idumean father. He was sensitive about his half-Jewish origins, which many Jews considered a disqualification for legitimate rule over Israel. Out of jealousy and fear he ordered the public genealogical records of the leading Israelite families destroyed. He also married Mariamne, a princess of the priestly Hashmoneans, in a vain effort to placate Jewish opposition to his base origins. The Hashmonean line is the one that produced the Maccabees, who had ruled the country for a century before the Romans invaded Palestine. In a fit of rage Herod later murdered her and their two sons. Josephus, the 1st-century Jewish historian, tells us that Herod went so far as to equip the desert fortress Masada as a place to flee should the population depose

The child Mary with Joachim and Anna by Strozzi

him and restore a ruler of David's royal line.[3] The Roman emperors Vespasian and Domitian would search out and execute members of the royal "house of David" family in the late decades of the 1st century.[4] In those times power was one thing, but pedigree—particularly that of the native royal family—was quite another. And this matter of pedigree takes us right back to Nazareth.

In 4 B.C. when Mary would have been about fourteen, Herod the Great died. Shortly after his death, a certain Judas son of Ezekias broke into the royal palace at Sepphoris. After seizing all the arms that were stored there, he and his followers began to rampage throughout Galilee. Pockets of revolt and opposition to Rome broke out all over the country.[5] Josephus wrote that at that time "anyone might make himself king as the head of a band of rebels," and he named several others who tried.[6] The Romans reacted quickly and with overwhelming force. The Roman governor of Syria, the infamous Publius Quintilius Varus, led three legions from Syria to brutally crush opposition to Roman rule.[7] Including auxiliary forces as many as twenty thousand troops poured into the country from the north, burnt Sepphoris to the ground, and sent its inhabitants into slavery as punishment for their participation in the outbreaks. Varus rounded up rebels all over the country and crucified two thousand men who had participated in the revolt.[8] The trauma that gripped Galilee must have been dreadful, with dying men nailed to crosses at intervals up and down the main roads or on hillsides visible to all who passed.

Following the revolt the Romans divided Palestine into three districts, each ruled by a son of Herod the Great. Archelaus received Judea, which was in the south and included the mountainous territory to the north called Samaria. Philip was given charge of the region east of the Jordan, around the Sea of Galilee. Herod Antipas received the territory of Galilee, north of Judea, as well as Perea, east of the Jordan River. This was the same Herod that later beheaded John the Baptizer and participated in the trial of Jesus. Herod Antipas chose to fortify and rebuild the city of Sepphoris, making it his palatial capital, and he did it in high Greco-Roman style. It occupied a strategic location overlooking the Bet Netofa Valley with major roads intersecting. Though it remained a Jewish city it had a 4,000-seat theater (as impressive as the one his father had built at

Caesarea on the Mediterranean coast), colonnaded streets and markets, elaborate civic buildings, an elaborate water system, and public baths. Josephus, who was eyewitness to its splendor, writes that Sepphoris became the "ornament of all Galilee."[9] But as Herod Antipas consolidated his hold over his bequeathed territories, his legitimacy to the throne was suspect. Who was the rightful King of Israel?

Drawing of Sepphoris viewed from Nazareth in the time of Jesus

Sometime before the conflagration of Sepphoris, Mary and her family moved to the little village of Nazareth, just four miles southeast. We have no record of what happened to her parents, Joachim and Anna, or whether they were still alive at the time, but we do know what became of their daughter.[10]

At the time of the revolt and brutal suppression, Mary, age fourteen or fifteen, was already considered a woman and was pledged in marriage to a local artisan named Joseph. It was there in Nazareth at this time that she had her own troubles—she got pregnant before the marriage and Joseph was not the father. Luke says that when the couple went to Bethlehem for the birth of Jesus Mary was still his "betrothed" (Luke 2:5). The Greek word he uses is very clear.[11] It means they were still only engaged yet she was ready to deliver the child. After the birth of her child in Bethlehem the couple returned to Nazareth, right in the aftermath of the disaster, with the smoke of Sepphoris scarcely cleared.[12]

With an understanding of the history of Sepphoris a whole new set of images is added to the "Christmas story": crucified corpses rotting on crosses, the nearby capital city in flames, and fellow citizens either killed or exiled into slavery. The future of this family and the child that they carried was hardly certain.

GOSPEL SOURCES

As we begin to reconstruct the birth, life, and teachings of Jesus our best and earliest sources are the four gospels, Matthew, Mark, Luke, and John, contained in the New Testament. For the past two hundred years scholars have analyzed and compared these texts and their relationship to one another. The results of this painstaking research have allowed us to read them more carefully, and to use them responsibly as we do other ancient historical sources, even though they are included in the New Testament canon as sacred texts of Scripture. All four New Testament Gospels are written in Greek though we have an ancient tradition that the gospel of Matthew was originally composed in Hebrew or Aramaic. The names associated with these gospels are traditional and the authors, whoever they might have been, never identify themselves by name. Mark is our earliest gospel, even though it comes second in the New Testament. Mark was written around A.D. 70, and it provides us with the basic narrative framework of the career of Jesus. Matthew was written next, likely around A.D. 80, and the author uses Mark as his main source but edits it freely, as we will see. As I will explain more fully later, the author of Matthew also had access to a collection of the teachings of Jesus that we call Q, which Mark did not have. He incorporates that material into his work as well. Luke was written around A.D. 90 and the author uses both Mark and the Q source, but he has a considerable amount of his own material with which he supplements his story. These three gospels, Mark, Matthew, and Luke, are called the Synoptics, because of the tight literary relationship between them. One simple way of putting this is that Mark provides the basic story line, and both Matthew and Luke use Mark but incorporate Q and some of their own materials. John is our latest gospel, written toward the close of the 1st century, and it has no literary connection to the three Synoptic gospels. The author of John offers us an entirely independent tradition focusing on Jesus as a divine and exalted Son of God. In that sense John is more theologically oriented but that is not to say his account is devoid of valuable historical information. As we shall see, without John's independent record we would lack many important geographical and chronological details.

There are other gospels than these four, such as the *Gospel of Thomas*, written in Coptic and discovered in 1945 in Egypt; a Hebrew version of Matthew passed down within rabbinic circles; and a half-dozen so-called "Apocryphal" gospels that were composed in the 2nd and 3rd centuries A.D. These will be introduced and discussed as we encounter them in our investigation. But it remains the case that our most reliable sources for reconstructing what we can know about Jesus are the New Testament gospels themselves. As we shall see, when they are read carefully and critically many new and fascinating insights emerge. We begin our investigation with what we can know about Mary's pregnancy and the birth of her firstborn son, Jesus.

TROUBLE IN NAZARETH

One can try to imagine the stir Mary's pregnancy must have caused in a village the size of Nazareth. To say that tongues were wagging would be an understatement. Both families were well known.[13] Houses were close together, with married children often living in extensions of the main house of their parents, sharing a common courtyard. Village life was intensely interdependent both economically and socially, a fact driven home to me when I first visited "Nazareth Village." There, at a site in the modern city of Nazareth, archaeologists are reconstructing an authentic version of a 1st-century Jewish village.[14] One can enter the small rooms of the houses, walk in the common courtyards and narrow streets, and sense the unavoidable intertwining that must have involved every aspect of life. There were not many secrets in Nazareth.

Joseph had a serious problem that no fiancé wants even to imagine.

He was engaged to Mary, their families had agreed to a marriage, but his bride-to-be "was found to be with child" before the wedding (Matthew 1:18). According to the Gospel of Matthew, Joseph was the one who had discovered the pregnancy, and he resolved to break off plans for the marriage while keeping things quiet so as not to shame her. Perhaps he planned to help her leave town and bear her child in secret. We are not told. One thing he knew for certain: he was not the father of the unborn child. With or without his help Mary left town hastily and, according to tradition, went south to the little village of Ein Kerem, four miles west of Jerusalem in the hill country of Judea. There Mary stayed for three months with close family relatives, an older couple, Elizabeth and Zechariah (Luke 1:39). Elizabeth was pregnant herself at the time, in her sixth month, with the child we know as John the Baptist or, more literally, John the Baptizer. How Mary and Elizabeth were related we don't know, whether cousins, or perhaps niece and aunt, but given these circumstances the two families were likely very close. And this means that Jesus and John the Baptizer were related as well.

According to Luke the birth took place in Bethlehem in response to a Roman tax census. Bethlehem, just outside of Jerusalem, in Judea, is in the south of the country, while Nazareth is in the north in Galilee, about a three-day journey apart. Luke tells us that the couple, finding the city overcrowded and all guest rooms booked, lodged in a stable, where Jesus was born. It is common to find cavelike structures from that time hollowed out of the rock and attached to dwellings, used to shelter domestic animals. Since, according to Luke, Joseph and his betrothed Mary were not yet married, we don't know when the wedding took place, but it had to be after the birth of the child (Luke 2:5). Luke later refers to Jesus as "a son of Joseph" yet he clearly does not believe that Joseph is the father. He implies by this language that the couple married and Joseph became the legal adoptive father of Jesus (Luke 4:22). Matthew says that Joseph "took his wife," but he does not say when. He adds a fascinating note—that the couple only had sexual relations after the birth of the child (Matthew 1:25).[15] This would fit with Luke's implication that the marriage took place after the birth. In Jewish culture the sexual act of "knowing" the woman is what consummated the marriage.[16]

That is the bare outline presented in the first chapters of the gospels of Matthew and Luke.[17] The other two gospels, Mark and John, begin their accounts with Jesus as an adult and tell us nothing at all about his birth.[18]

Matthew and Luke both agree on the source of Mary's pregnancy. In Matthew's account Joseph had a dream shortly after finding out about the pregnancy. In this dream an angel told him that her pregnancy was "by a holy spirit" and that he was to go ahead with the marriage regardless.[19] He was to name her child Jesus. By marrying a pregnant woman who carried a child that was not his, and legally naming that child, he was in effect "adopting" Jesus as his legal son. The phrase "by a holy spirit" implies that the pregnancy came from the agency of God's spirit but falls short of saying, outright, that God was the father of Jesus in the sense that, say, Zeus was said to be the father of Hercules by his seduction of his mother, Alkmene. In that sense the account is different from those miraculous birth stories so common in Greco-Roman mythology.

The seduction of Alkmene by Zeus on an ancient Greek vase

Matthew also alludes to an ancient saying of the Hebrew prophet Isaiah, "A young woman shall conceive and bear a son and shall call his name Immanuel," as if to say that Mary's pregnancy was a fulfillment of prophecy (Isaiah 7:14).[20] But Isaiah was speaking of a child to be born in *his own day*, the 8th century B.C., and whose birth would be a sign for King Hezekiah, who ruled at that time. The Hebrew word (*'almah*) that Matthew puts as "virgin" in his Greek translation means a "young woman" or "maiden" and carries no miraculous implications whatsoever.[21] The child is given the unusual name of Immanuel, meaning "God with us," and Isaiah assures King Hezekiah that before this special child was old enough to know "right from wrong" the Assyrians who threatened Jerusalem and Judea would be removed from the land. Hezekiah would not have long to wait. Matthew implies that Isaiah's prophecy was "fulfilled" by the miraculous virgin birth of Jesus—but the original text clearly carries no such meaning.

In Luke's account it is Mary who had a dream. The angel Gabriel told her that she would become pregnant, bear a son, and name him Jesus. The name Jesus in Hebrew is the same as the name Joshua and was quite common among Jews at that time. This child was to be great. He would be called "the son of the Most High" and sit on the throne of his father David, ruling over the nation of Israel forever. Mary responded, "How will this be since I don't know a man?" This biblical expression definitely means to have sex. The angel replied that "a holy spirit will come upon you and power of the Most High will overshadow you, so the holy thing begotten will be called the son of God" (Luke 1:35).

The earliest Christian creeds affirm, based on these texts, that Jesus was "conceived of the Holy Spirit, born of the virgin Mary."[22] It is easy to confuse the "immaculate conception" with the "virgin birth." The Immaculate Conception, as taught by the Roman Catholic Church, refers to the conception of Mary by her mother Anna, not to the conception of Jesus. This teaching holds that Mary was born without "original sin," inherited by every human being since Adam. This allowed her to give birth to Jesus in a special state of moral purity. The "virgin birth" is a further teaching— that Mary, without a man, became pregnant through the agency of the Holy Spirit. It refers more to the source of the pregnancy than to the

The Assumption of Mary by Poussin

"birth" itself.[23] One might refer to the idea as the "virginal conception," since the focus is on the cause of her pregnancy.

A further Catholic dogma holds that Mary remained a perpetual virgin (*semper virgine*, "ever-virgin") her entire life.[24] Even Protestant leaders such as Luther, Calvin, Zwingli, and John Wesley shared this view, though it is less common among Protestants today.[25] Mary was idealized over time as the divine-like holy "Mother of God." She was so far removed from her culture and her time that the very idea that she had sexual relations, bore additional children, and lived a normal life as a married Jewish woman seemed unthinkable for centuries. She was quite literally "exalted to heaven," and her actual humanity was lost, as was the importance of her forefathers.

2

A SON OF DAVID?

MATTHEW calls Jesus a "son of David" in the opening line of his gospel. In Luke the angel predicted to Mary that her son Jesus would "sit on the throne of *his father* David" (Luke 1:32).¹ The two concepts are intertwined. Not every descendant of David occupied David's throne, but no one occupied the throne who was not a descendant of David. King David, reputed author of many of the Psalms and father of King Solomon, was the most renowned of Israel's ancient kings. Shortly before David's death God promised him that his "throne" would last forever and that only those of his "seed" could occupy it as rulers over the nation of Israel (2 Samuel 7:12–16). The Hebrew prophets took up this promise and made it the basis for their prediction that in the "Last Days" the Christ or Messiah would sit on David's throne as an ideal ruler over Israel. He then, of necessity, had to have the right pedigree.

This promise was seen as an unbreakable covenant. In the book of Jeremiah God declares that if you can break the fixed order of the heavens "then I will reject the seed of Jacob and David my servant and will not choose *one of his seed* to rule over the seed of Abraham, Isaac, and Jacob" (Jeremiah 33:25–26). This promise to David, of royal descendants reigning over Israel, was likened to a fixed law of nature.

Others might rule the land of Israel, whether Greeks or Romans, but they were regarded as foreign and illegitimate occupiers whom God would rightfully remove when the true Messiah came. There was a brief period of Jewish independence from 165–63 B.C., just before the Romans took over the country. A native Jewish family known as the Maccabees or the Hashmoneans ruled the country, establishing a priestly dynasty, but were unable to claim Davidic lineage.[2] As we have noted, Herod the Great, despite his title "King of the Jews," feared that a true descendant of David's ancestry might arise and threaten his power.

So the obvious question is *how was* Jesus a "son of David"? What do we know of his lineage that might support this claim that he was a part of the royal family of David?

Luke and Matthew give Jesus no human father yet they give different genealogical accounts of his ancestry. Genealogies, or what many Bible readers remember as the lists of "begats," do not usually make gripping reading, but Jesus' genealogies are full of surprises.

JESUS' LEGAL LINEAGE AND AN ANCIENT CURSE

Matthew begins his book with this genealogy: "Abraham begat Isaac, and Isaac begat Jacob, and Jacob begat Judah," and so forth. Since Matthew is the first book of the New Testament, more than a few eager Bible readers have had good intentions dampened by this technical beginning. But let's look again. Matthew lists forty male names, all the way from Abraham, who lived a thousand years before David, through David, and down to Joseph, husband of Mary.

Any standard Jewish genealogy at the time was based solely on the male lineage, which was of primary importance. One's father was the significant factor in the cultural world in which Jesus was born. Yet in Matthew we find four women mentioned, connected to four of the forty male names listed. This is completely irregular and unexpected. Matthew records:

Judah fathered Perez and Zerah *from Tamar* (v. 3)
Salmon fathered Boaz *from Rahab* (v. 5)
Boaz fathered Obed *from Ruth* (v. 5)
David fathered Solomon *from Uriah's wife* (v. 5)

These are all women's names, or in the case of Uriah's wife, an unnamed woman. But even more surprising, each of these four women was a foreigner who had a scandalous sexual reputation in the Old Testament.[3] The first, Tamar, a widow desperate for a child, purposely got pregnant by dressing up as a roadside prostitute and enticing her own father-in-law. Rahab was a tavern keeper or "prostitute." Ruth was a Moabite woman, which was bad enough since Israelites were forbidden to have anything to do with Moabites because of their reputation as sexual temptresses. But Ruth crawled into the bed of Boaz, her future husband, after getting him drunk one night, in order to get him to marry her. Uriah's wife—her name is not even given here for the disgrace of it all—was the infamous Bathsheba. She had an adulterous affair with King David and ended up pregnant, blending his fame with shame ever after. And yet, Matthew is otherwise giving us the revered royal lineage of King David himself! Something very important is going on here. The regular drumming pattern of a list of male names is jarred by mention of these women, each of whom was well known to Jewish readers. They don't belong in a formal genealogy of the royal family. The stories of these women in the Bible stand out because of their shocking sexual details. It is clear that Matthew is trying to put Jesus' own potentially scandalous birth into the context of his forefathers—and foremothers. He is preparing the reader for what is to come.

At the end of the list, the very last name in the very last line, the other shoe drops. Matthew surely intends to startle, catching the reader unawares. He writes:

> *Jacob fathered Joseph, the husband of Mary;*
> from her was fathered *Jesus called Christ.*

What one would expect in any standard male genealogy would be:

> *Jacob fathered Joseph;*
> *Joseph* fathered *Jesus, called the Christ.*

Matthew uses the verb "fathered" or "begot" (Greek *gennao*) thirty-nine times in the active voice with a masculine subject. But when he comes to Joseph he makes an important shift. He uses the same verb in the passive voice with a feminine object: *from her was fathered* Jesus. So a *fifth* woman unexpectedly slips into the list: Mary herself.

And yet this is definitely not Mary's bloodline. This is Joseph's genealogy. So why is she included? Matthew is setting the reader up for the story that immediately follows, in which Mary, an engaged woman, is pregnant by a man who is not her husband. It is as if he is silently cautioning any overly pious or judgmental readers not to jump to conclusions. In the most revered genealogy of that culture, the royal line of King David himself, there are stories of sexual immorality involving both men and women who were nonetheless honored in memory.

But there is yet another remarkable feature of this lineage of Joseph that is vital to the story and should not be missed. Joseph's branch of David's family, even though it had supplied all the ancient kings of Judah, had been put under a ban or curse by the prophet Jeremiah. In those last dark days just before the Babylonians destroyed Jerusalem in 586 B.C. Jeremiah had made a shocking declaration about Jechoniah, the final reigning king of David's line: "Write this man down as stripped . . . for *none of his seed* shall succeed in sitting on the throne of David and ruling in Judah again" (Jeremiah 22:30).[4] Joseph was a direct descendant of this ill-reputed Jechoniah (Matthew 1:11–12).[5]

In effect, it was as if Jeremiah were declaring the covenant that God made with David null and void. At least it might appear that way. Psalm 89, written in the aftermath of these developments, laments: "You have renounced the covenant with your servant; you have defiled his crown in the dust" (Psalm 89:39). Or so it seemed. After all, Jechoniah was the last Jewish king of the royal family of David to occupy the throne in the land of Israel. Joseph was of this same line, but as the *legal* father of Jesus, rather than the *biological* father, Joseph's ancestry did not disqualify Jesus' potential claim to the throne if Jesus could claim descent from David through another branch of the Davidic lineage. But how many "branches" of the Davidic family were there?

A HIDDEN BRANCH OF THE ROYAL FAMILY

Luke's genealogy provides us with the missing key to understanding how Jesus could claim Davidic descent with no biological connection to his adoptive father Joseph. Luke records his genealogy of Jesus in his third chapter. Jesus was thirty years old and had just been baptized by John. Whereas Matthew begins with Abraham and follows the line down to Joseph, Jesus' adoptive father, Luke *begins* with Jesus and works backward—all the way back to Adam! Rather than forty names, as in Matthew, we have seventy-six. There are three striking features in this genealogy.

First, it begins with a surprising qualification. Literally translated it says: "And Jesus was about thirty years [old] when he began, being a son as was supposed of Joseph, of Heli" (Luke 3:23). The Greek is quite terse, but what jumps off the page is the phrase "as was supposed."[6] Luke is telling his readers two things: that Joseph was only the "supposed" or "legal" father of Jesus and that Jesus had a grandfather named Heli. According to Matthew, Joseph's father was named Jacob. So who was Heli? The most obvious solution is that he was Mary's father.[7] One seldom hears anything about the grandparents of Jesus, but Jesus had *two* grandfathers, one from Joseph and the other from Mary. Two grandfathers means two separate family trees. What we have in Luke 3:23–38 is the other side of Jesus' family, traced through his actual bloodline from his mother Mary. The reason Mary is not named is that Luke abides by convention and includes only males in his list. Since Luke acknowledges no biological father for Jesus he begins with Joseph as a "stand-in" but qualifies things with the phrase "as was supposed." A freely paraphrased translation would go like this: "And Jesus was about thirty years old when he began his work, *supposedly* being a son of Joseph but *actually* being of the line of Heli." If Mary's parents were indeed named Joachim and Anna, as early Christian tradition holds, it is possible that Heli is short for the name Eliakim, which in turn is a form of the traditional name Joachim.

It is unlikely that Luke simply concocted such a detailed record. Jewish families were quite zealous about genealogical records—all the more so if one was descended from the line of David. Josephus, the Jewish historian of that period, traces his own priestly genealogy with obvious pride and mentions archival records that he had consulted.[8] Julius Africanus, an early 3rd-century Jewish-Christian writer who lived in Palestine, reports that leading Jewish families kept private genealogical records, since Herod and his successors had sought to destroy those that were public.

Africanus specifically notes the practice of keeping clandestine family genealogies as characteristic of Jesus' descendants.[9] Since the Davidic lineage of Jesus was so important to the early Christians it is likely that Luke had one of these records available to him.

Luke's genealogy also reveals another important bit of information. Mary, like her husband Joseph, was of the lineage of King David—but with a vital difference. Her connection to David was *not* through the cursed lineage running back through Jechoniah to David's son Solomon. Rather she could trace herself back through another of David's sons, namely Nathan, the brother of Solomon (Luke 3:31). Nathan, like Solomon, was a son of David's favored wife Bathsheba, but Nathan never occupied the throne and his genealogy accordingly became obscure. He is listed in the biblical record but no descendants are mentioned, in contrast to his brother Solomon (1 Chronicles 3:5–10). So, according to Luke, Jesus could claim a direct ancestry back to King David through his mother Mary as well. He did not have the "adoptive" claim through his legal father Joseph alone, but also that of David's actual bloodline.

THE TWO BRANCHES OF THE
ROYAL FAMILY OF DAVID

The lineage on the left is provided by Matthew as the lineage of Joseph, Jesus' legal father. It is shorter and abbreviated after Jeconiah. The names in italics are those who reigned as kings of Israel and Judah. The lineage on the right is provided by Luke as the biological line of Jesus' mother Mary.

⟋ **David** ⟍

Solomon	Nathan
Rehoboam	Mattatha
Abijah	Menna
Asa	Melea
Jehoshaphat	Eliakim
Joram	Jonam
Uzziah	Joseph
Jotham	Judah
Ahaz	Simeon

THE TWO BRANCHES OF THE
ROYAL FAMILY OF DAVID (*Cont.*)

Hezekiah	Levi
Manasseh	Matthat
Amon	Jorim
Josiah	Eliezer
Jechoniah	Joshua
	Er
	Elmadam
	Cosam
	Addi
	Melchi
	Neri
	Shealtiel
	Zerubbabel
	Rhesa
	Joanan
	Joda
	Josech
	Semein
	Mattathias
	Maath
Shealtiel	Naggai
Zerubbabel	Esli
Abiud	Nahum
Eliakim	Amos
Azor	Mattathias
Zadok	Joseph
Achim	Jannai
Eliud	Melchi
Eleazar	Levi
Matthan	Matthat
Jacob	Heli (Eliakim)
Joseph	Mary

The name Nazareth, the town where Mary lived, comes from the Hebrew word *netzer* meaning "branch" or "shoot."[10] One could loosely translate Nazareth as "Branch Town." But why would a town have such a strange name? As we have seen, in the time of Jesus it was a tiny village. Its claim to fame was not size or economic prominence but something potentially even more significant. In the Dead Sea Scrolls, written before Jesus' lifetime, we regularly find the future Messiah or King of Israel described as the "branch of David."[11] The term is taken from Isaiah 11, where the Messiah of David's lineage is called a "Branch." The term stuck. The later followers of Jesus were called Nazarenes or "Branchites."[12] The little village of Nazareth very likely got its name, or perhaps its nickname, because it was known as the place where members of the royal family had settled and were concentrated. It is no surprise that both Mary and Joseph lived there, as each represented different "branches" of the "Branch of David." The gospels mention other "relatives" of the family that lived there (Mark 6:4). It is entirely possible that most of the inhabitants of "Branch Town" were members of the same extended "Branch" family. The family's affinity for this area of Galilee continued for centuries. North of Sepphoris, about twelve miles from Nazareth, was a town called Kokhaba or "Star Town." The term "Star," like "Branch" is a coded term for the Messiah that is also found in the Dead Sea Scrolls.[13] Both Nazareth and Kokhaba were noted well into the 2nd century A.D. as towns in which families related to Jesus, and thus part of the "royal family," were concentrated.[14]

Finally, the names in Luke that run from King David down to Heli, Mary's father, offer us some very interesting clues that further explain why this particular Davidic line was uniquely important. There are listed no fewer than six instances of the name we know as Matthew: Matthat (twice), Mattathias (twice), Maath, and Mattatha. What is striking is that the name Matthew was one invariably associated with a priestly, not a kingly or royal, lineage. One of Jesus' Twelve Apostles was named Matthew, but he was also called Levi.[15] Two of the six "Matthews" in Jesus' lineage were sons of fathers named "Levi." Josephus records that his own father, grandfather, great-grandfather, and brother were all named Matthias, and they were all priests of the tribe of Levi from the distinguished priestly family of the Hashmoneans or Maccabees. Ancient Israel was divided into twelve tribes, descendants of the twelve sons of Jacob, the grandson of Abraham. The priests of Israel had to be descendants of Aaron, brother of Moses, who was from the tribe of Levi. The kings had to be of the royal lineage of King David, who was of the tribe of Judah. These positions, king and priest, gave the tribes of Judah and Levi special prominence. But why would there be so many priestly names in a Davidic dynasty?

Remember, when Mary became pregnant and left Nazareth to stay with Elizabeth, mother of John the Baptizer, Luke notes that they were *relatives*, though he does not say how (Luke 1:36). But he also records that Elizabeth and her husband Zechariah were of the priestly lineage (Luke 1:5). This is further confirmation of the link between Mary's Davidic family and the priestly tribe of Levi.

It is inconceivable that such a heavy prevalence of Levite or priestly names would be part of Mary's genealogy unless there was a significant influence from the tribe of Levi merging into this particular royal line of the tribe of Judah. What appears likely is that Mary was of mixed lineage. Luke only names the male line from David down to Mary. But the large number of priestly names indicates that there were likely important Levite women marrying into this Davidic line along the way. It is a pattern that goes all the way back to Aaron, brother of Moses, the very first Israelite priest. Aaron of the tribe of Levi married a princess of the tribe of Judah named Elisheva or Elizabeth (Exodus 6:23).

What is all the more amazing is that this mixing of these two tribes in a single family was verified in the Talpiot tomb that I discussed in the Introduction. It contained five names common to the family of Jesus—two Marys, a Joseph, a Jesus, and a Jude—and also a *Matya* or Matthew. These were all in the same family tomb. The "Jude" who was buried there is surely of the tribe of Judah, and the Matthew is certainly of the tribe of Levi—yet they had lain side by side for two thousand years, waiting to tell us something important. Whether this is the Jesus family tomb or not, the combination of these names demonstrates that the genealogy of Luke, with its mixing of these two tribes, is historically plausible within a single Jewish family of the times.

The name "Matthew" on one of the Talpiot ossuaries

When I was able to view these Talpiot ossuaries recently in the Israel Antiquities warehouse in Bet Shemesh, I was glad to see our Matya, or Matthew, shelved with the other members of his family around him, as if giving mute testimony to Luke's genealogy. I ran my gloved hand gently over the "Matthew" inscription and then over the others, trying somehow through touch to connect to the past that these names represent. But is there any special significance to such a mixed ancestry of Davidic and Levite lineage? The Dead Sea Scrolls provide us with the surprising answer.

ONE, TWO, OR THREE MESSIAHS:
A NEW REVELATION

Christians and Jews subsequently have come to focus on *the* Messiah—a single figure of David's line who was to rule as King in the last days. And yet, in the Dead Sea Scrolls we encounter a devoutly religious community, usually identified with the Essenes, who expected the coming of three figures—a *prophet* like Moses and the *messiahs* of Aaron and of Israel.[16] The "Messiah of Israel" is clearly the Davidic king, but the "Messiah of Aaron" refers to a priest figure—*also* called a messiah. This insight fills a gap in our understanding of the Jesus dynasty. Various texts begin to make more sense and fit together in a way that has been previously overlooked.

The English word "messiah" comes from the Hebrew word *moshiach*, which simply means "an anointed one." The equivalent Greek word, *christos*, also means "anointed" and from that we have derived our more familiar term "Christ," meaning Messiah. The word refers to a sacred ritual in which oil was poured on the head of a chosen individual to officially confirm him as either priest or king. A prophet typically carried out the installation on the one chosen by God. But in either case, whether priest or king, the candidate had to have the proper bloodline to qualify. Most people are surprised to learn that the very first Messiah in the Bible was Aaron. He was "anointed" as a priest by his brother Moses and is referred to in the Hebrew text as a *"moshiach"* or "messiah" (Exodus 40:12–15). This was hundreds of years before the prophet Samuel anointed David as king of Israel (1 Samuel 16:13). An anointed priest had to be a descendant of Aaron, and the anointed king had to be a descendant of David. Mary, the mother of Jesus, was a direct descendant of King David but she also had bloodline ties to a Levite or priestly lineage descended from Aaron. This is evidenced both by her genealogy and her kinship with the family of Elizabeth, mother of John the Baptizer. In later centuries, after the biblical era, the father determined one's tribal affiliation, while the mother was seen as the guarantor of a child's "Jewishness." Things were not so settled in biblical times. Women in the Bible are spoken of as bearing "seed" and the same Hebrew word *zara'* (literally "seed") is used to refer to the offspring of either men or women.[17] Accordingly, Jesus could make claim to being from the "seed of David" through the lineage of his mother.[18] But what do we know about Jesus' father? If Joseph was only his adoptive father, then who might his biological father have been? For those who accept by faith the accounts of the "virgin birth" in Matthew and Luke the question is moot—*Jesus had no human father*. But is there any evidence in our records that might offer us a more historically based alternative?

3

AN UNNAMED FATHER
OF JESUS?

ALTHOUGH only Matthew and Luke assert the "virgin birth" of Jesus, and the teaching is found nowhere else in the New Testament, the belief that Mary's pregnancy resulted from a divine act of God without any male involvement developed into a fundamental theological dogma in early Christianity. For millions of Christians any suggestion that Jesus was conceived through the normal process of human sexual reproduction, even if somehow sanctified by God, is viewed as scandalous if not outright heresy. But history, by its very nature, is an open process of inquiry that cannot be bound by the dogmas of faith. Historians are obligated to examine whatever evidence we have, even if such discoveries might be considered shocking or sacrilegious to some. The assumption of the historian is that all human beings have both a biological mother and father, and that Jesus is no exception. *That leaves two possibilities—either Joseph or some other unnamed man was the father of Jesus.* Is it possible that a more historical reading of these two birth stories in the light of all our surviving evidence might reveal to us a profoundly human Jesus that dogmatic faith has obscured? Could such a revelation end up being as spiritually meaningful as the belief in the "virgin birth"—a teaching that many sincere Christians have problems accepting literally?[1]

Scholars who question the literal truth of Matthew and Luke's birth stories have suggested that they are a way of affirming the divine nature of Jesus as "Son of God" by giving him an extraordinary supernatural birth. This idea of humans being fathered by gods is quite common in Greco-Roman culture.[2] There was a whole host of heroes who were said to be the product of a union between their mother and a god—Plato, Empedocles, Hercules, Pythagoras, Alexander the Great, and even Caesar Augustus. In text after text we find the idea of the *divine man* (*theios aner*) whose supernatural birth, ability to perform miracles, and extraordinary death separate him from the ordinary world of mortals. These heroes are not "eternal" gods, like Zeus or Jupiter. They are mortal human beings who have been exalted to a heavenly state of immortal life. In the time of Jesus their temples and shrines filled every city and province of the Roman Empire.[3] It is easy to imagine that early Christians who believed Jesus was every bit as exalted and heavenly as any of the Greek and Roman heroes and gods would appropriate this way of relating the story of his birth. It was a way of affirming that Jesus was both human and divine. Modern interpreters who view the stories in this way usually maintain that Joseph was likely the father and that these supernatural accounts were invented later by Jesus' followers to honor Jesus and to promote his exalted status in a manner common to that culture.

But there is another possibility; an alternative explanation as to what might be behind these "virgin birth" accounts. And it has some very compelling evidence in its favor. When you read the account of Mary's unsuspected pregnancy, what is particularly notable in both texts is an underlying tone of realism that runs through the narratives. These seem to be real people, living in real times and places. In contrast, the birth stories common in Greco-Roman literature have a decidedly legendary flavor to them. For example, in Plutarch's account of the birth of Alexander the Great, mother Olympias got pregnant from a snake; it was announced by a bolt of lightning that sealed her womb so that her husband Philip could not have sex with her.[4] Granted, both Matthew and Luke include dreams and visions of angels but the core story itself—that of a man who discovers that his bride-to-be is pregnant and knows he is not the father—has a realistic and thoroughly human quality to it. The narrative, despite its miraculous elements, "rings true."

What if the virgin birth stories were created, not to present Jesus as a divine Greco-Roman style hero, but to address a shockingly real situation—Mary's pregnancy before her marriage to Joseph? All four women that Matthew mentions in his genealogy had sex out of wedlock and at least two of them became pregnant. By naming these particular women Matthew seems to be implicitly addressing Mary's situation.

There are some indications in our gospels that the charge of illegitimacy was circulating behind the scenes. Mark is our earliest gospel, written around A.D. 70. He includes an important scene in which Jesus returns home to Nazareth as an adult. There is a buzz about him among the townsfolk. Notice carefully their language:

Is not this the carpenter, *the son of Mary* and brother of James,
and Joses, and Judas and Simon? And are not his sisters here with us?
(Mark 6:3)

Matthew uses Mark as a source and includes the same story, but notice how he very cleverly rephrases things:

Is not this *the carpenter's son*? Is not his mother called Mary?
And are not his brothers James and Joseph and Simon and Judas?
And are not all his sisters with us? (Matthew 13:55)

This subtle but critical shift in wording is absolutely telling:

Is not this the *carpenter*, the *son of Mary*? (Mark)

Is not this the *carpenter's son*? Is not his mother called Mary? (Matthew)

Calling Jesus "the son of Mary" indicates an unnamed father. In Judaism children are invariably referred to as sons or daughters of the father—*not* the mother. Mark never refers to Joseph at all, by name or otherwise. He avoids the paternity issue altogether. There has to be some good reason for this silence. Matthew, in contrast, is quick to reshape Mark's wording so that the illegitimacy issue is not even hinted at. We even find that later Greek manuscripts of Mark's gospel try to "fix" the scandal by altering the text to read "the son of Mary *and Joseph*." Here we have evidence of a progressive move to mute or play down the scandal that had been familiar in the hometown village of Nazareth decades earlier. Rumors and gossip die hard and seldom completely disappear.

In the gospel of John things are even more explicit. At one point Jesus was in Jerusalem sparring with his Jewish critics. The conversation became very heated and almost turned violent. One of their responses to Jesus was the startling assertion—"*We* were not born of fornication," as if to imply, as *you* were (John 8:41). Something is clearly going on here. This was a very low blow: an obvious attempt to undermine Jesus' standing by reference to a rumor about his illegitimate birth. In a 4th-century A.D. Christian text called the *Acts of Pilate*, which might have origins reaching back to the late 2nd century, there is an account of Jesus' trial before Pilate. One of the charges of his enemies is "you were born of fornication." No one takes the text as a historical record of the trial, but it does witness to the longevity of the illegitimacy charge. Whoever wrote the text found it necessary to construct a trial scene that addressed the same charge we encounter in the 1st-century gospel of John.

John mentions Joseph only twice, and he provides no birth story at all (John 1:45; 6:42). Why such reluctance to openly refer to someone's father? In a passage roughly equivalent to Mark's we read:

Is not this Jesus, the son of Joseph? *Do we not know his father and mother?* (John 6:42)

Once again, there appears to be the slightest hint of something irregular. Why name Joseph—then redundantly add, "Do we not know his father and mother"? Coupled with the other text about being "born of fornication," the illegitimacy charge is more than implicit.

Surely it is no accident that Mark and John, the two gospels that say nothing about Jesus' birth, and little or nothing about his father, seem to preserve for us these subtle hints of the charge of illegitimacy. Both Matthew and Luke try to mitigate the issue by claiming Jesus was conceived by the "holy spirit," but both of them freely admit that Joseph was not the father. And that is the point. The notion of illegitimacy is a consistent element found in all four New Testament gospels. Each seems to agree—*Joseph was not the father of Jesus.*

This charge of illegitimacy is not limited to these four gospels. The *Gospel of Thomas* was discovered in upper Egypt at a place called Nag Hammadi by an Arab farmer who was digging in the area for fertilizer. It had been sealed in a clay jar and buried in a field, along with a dozen other lost Christian texts, all written on papyri in ancient Coptic. It was likely hidden in the late 4th century to protect it from orthodox Christians who would have destroyed it as "heretical." Many scholars date it as early as the 2nd century A.D. It is clearly the most precious lost Christian document discovered in the last two thousand years. It contains 114 sayings of Jesus. Some have called it a "fifth gospel" in that it supplies so many missing pieces of Jesus' teaching—otherwise lost and forgotten. Toward the end of the collection, in Saying 105, Jesus tells his disciples:

> One who knows his father and his mother will be called *the son of a whore.*[5]

Many scholars have found in this cryptic saying an echo of the ugly label that Jesus had faced throughout his life—namely that his mother Mary had become pregnant out of wedlock. The *Gospel of Thomas* has no birth stories or references to Joseph or to the virgin birth but here in this text we appear to have some reflection of the illegitimacy story. The implication is that the charge was unjust and that Jesus knew the circumstances of his birth as well as the identity of his unnamed and absent father.

So, if Jesus' father was not Joseph, who might it possibly have been? And what circumstances led to Mary being accused of fornication and labeled a "whore"? In terms of any historical certainty we probably will never know. If we were filling out Jesus' birth certificate we would have to put down "father unknown." But the case is not entirely closed. There are stories and rumors that circulated quite early, and there is a name—*Pantera*—that seems to crop up here and there with some consistency.

THE MYSTERY OF
PANTERA SOLVED

The earliest version of the Pantera story comes from a Greek philosopher named Celsus. In an anti-Christian work titled *On the True Doctrine*, written around A.D. 178, he relates a tale that Mary "was pregnant by a Roman soldier named Panthera" and was driven away by her husband as an adulterer.[6] It is unlikely that Celsus invented this name or the occupation of the man he insists was the biological father of Jesus. He is repeating what he has heard circulating in Jewish circles. The name itself appears even earlier. The prominent rabbi Eliezer ben Hyrcanus, who lived around the end of the 1st century A.D., relates a teaching told to him by a Galilean follower of Jesus named Jacob of Sikhnin in the city of Sepphoris.[7] Some have identified this Jacob as the grandson of Jesus' youngest brother, Judas. Jacob passes on the teaching "in the name of Jesus the son of Panteri."[8] There is a dispute among these early rabbis, also involving this same follower of Jesus named Jacob, as to whether it is permissible or not to heal a snakebite in the "name of Jesus son of Panter."[9] These early sources say nothing of why Jesus would be called "son of Pantera," nor do they identify Pantera as a Roman soldier, but they do show that Jesus is identified by this name quite early in Galilee and that the name could be used without explanation or qualification.[10] Various Christian scholars have suggested that Pantera was a term of abusive slang, a play on the Greek word *parthenos*, which means "virgin," but the two words don't match very closely. Others have suggested that Jesus is slanderously called "son of a Panther" in reference to the wild and lustful nature of his real father. The problem with these suggestions is that the earliest references to Jesus as "son of Pantera" are not polemical. In Judaism when you want to identify a person you attach the name of the father. That is the clear sense of these earliest references. They are intended to identify, not to malign.

The evidence shows that the early Christians took this tradition seriously and were not able to easily dismiss it as slanderous rumor. The 4th-century orthodox Christian Epiphanius assumes there is some degree of authenticity in the "Jesus son of Panthera" tradition but explains it by claiming that Joseph's father was known as Jacob Panthera—thus making the name a part of the family.[11] Remarkably, as late as the 8th century A.D. similar attempts to "domesticate" the Panthera tradition were cropping up. John of Damascus passes on a tradition that Mary's great-grandfather was named Panthera. These far-fetched attempts to legitimize the name "Pantera" as part of Jesus' ancestry show that the designation of "Jesus son of Pantera" could not simply be dismissed as a malicious fabrication of Jewish opponents.[12]

We now know that Pantera/Panthera was a Greek name that shows up in a number of Latin inscriptions from the period, *especially as a surname for Roman soldiers.* Of one thing we can be sure—Pantera is a real name, not a concocted term of slander.

In 1906 the great German historian Adolf Deissmann published a short article titled "Der Name Panthera." In his study Deissmann detailed the various ancient inscriptions that used the name Pantera/Panthera in and around the 1st century A.D.[13] He showed conclusively that the name was in use during that time and was especially favored by Roman soldiers. One particular example he cited stood out. It was the inscribed tombstone of one *Tiberius Julius Abdes Pantera,* discovered in a Roman cemetery in 1859 at Bingerbrück, just twelve miles north of Bad Kreuznach, where the Nahe River meets the Rhine. Deissmann included a photo showing the carved figure of a Roman soldier with the neck and head broken off and a clearly preserved Latin inscription under his feet that read:

Tiberius Julius Abdes Pantera
of Sidon, aged 62
a soldier of 40 years service,
of the 1st cohort of archers,
lies here[14]

Deissmann noted that this particular "Pantera" had died in the middle of the 1st century A.D. and had come to Germany from Palestine. I was intrigued with this unlikely convergence of name, date, and place. I decided that I would try to track down this tombstone, find out the details of its discovery and any other information I could learn. I had found scattered references to this particular Pantera tombstone in various books but as far as I could tell no one had really studied it and everyone was simply quoting that original Deissmann article from 1906. Surely there was

The Tiberius Julius Abdes Pantera inscription

much more to learn. Of course I had no evidence that the tombstone could even be located. And I had to wonder about the odds of it surviving two world wars, and whether a museum that Deissmann mentioned in 1906 in Bad Kreuznach could possibly still be around in 2005.

I located a Web site maintained by the town of Bad Kreuznach and my hopes rose when I found that the town boasted a museum of Roman antiquities called the Römerhalle. My heart skipped a beat when I read that among its treasures was a collection of tombstones of Roman soldiers discovered at nearby Bingerbrück. Surely Tiberius Julius Abdes Pantera would be among them.

I contacted the curator of the museum and was pleased to learn that not only was the tombstone of Tiberius Julius Abdes Pantera safe and on display, but the entire collection of nine other gravestones of Roman soldiers discovered in the same location had been preserved. They had been uncovered quite by accident during the construction of the railway station at Bingerbrück between 1859 and 1861. They had been collected first by the local historical society, then put on display in 1933 in the old city museum, and were now in the newly constructed Römerhalle. Fortunately Bad Kreuznach was not bombed during World War II. The curator also told me that she had a thick file of archives she would open for my examination detailing the original discovery, including funerary urns and coins. Shortly thereafter, prompted by my queries, she reported another discovery previously unknown to anyone at the museum. Hidden away among dozens of old canvases in a back storeroom was a copy of an original oil painting done in 1860 that showed the discovery of the Roman cemetery in lifelike detail. I decided to travel to Germany to examine these materials firsthand.

There is something incredibly exciting about an ancient tomb or an ossuary or a tomb inscription from the time of Jesus and I have certainly encountered my share in Israel. But I had never imagined my research on the historical Jesus would take me to Germany, of all places. Was it remotely possible that I would soon be standing before what might be an authentic relic of the family of Jesus? Admittedly it sounded speculative and even far-fetched, but stranger things have turned up unexpectedly in the world of archaeology. And whether *this* Pantera had anything to do with the tradition that Jesus was the "son of Pantera" or not, he was surely worth investigating.

These questions were on my mind in the summer of 2005 as I flew to Frankfurt, Germany, and took an early morning train to the little town of Bad Kreuznach just an hour to the southwest on the Nahe River. Bad Kreuznach was an important outpost in Roman times and the surrounding countryside is thick with ancient Roman ruins.[15] It is easy to overlook how important this German frontier was to the Romans in the time of Jesus. It was the Vietnam or Iraq of its day. Countless Roman soldiers were transferred to remote outposts in Germany and thousands died and were buried there. But what does this have to do with the father of Jesus?

At the Römerhalle museum I had ample time to photograph, measure, and closely examine these gravestones, and particularly that of Tiberius Julius Abdes Pantera. I also began reading through the original reports of their discovery from 1859. Slowly I began to piece together the evidence and a rather amazing picture started to emerge. I became convinced that the possible association of this particular Roman soldier with the traditions related to Jesus' father should not be dismissed out of hand just because it sounds offensive to piety and faith. All the relevant facts should be set forth and carefully considered.

I learned that three gravestones, including that of Pantera, were initially discovered on the 19th and 20th of October 1859, about three hun-

James Tabor examining the Pantera gravestone in Germany

dred yards from the Nahe River. Pantera's full name is given formally in
the inscription as: Tiberius Julius Abdes Pantera. Pantera was his surname. The names Tiberius Julius are cognomen or acquired names. They
indicate that Pantera was not a native-born Roman but a former slave
who became a freedman and received the rights of Roman citizenship
from Tiberius Caesar for his service in the army. Initial enlistments were
for twenty-five years but Pantera made a career out of the military, serving for forty years until his death at age sixty-two. Since the emperor
Tiberius came to rule in A.D. 14, we can assume Pantera's death at age
sixty-two was some years after that, likely from natural causes, since he
had enlisted in the army when he was just twenty-two.

The name Abdes is Pantera's given name or praenomen. It is most interesting. It is a Latinized version of an Aramaic name 'ebed meaning "servant
of God," indicating that Pantera was of Semitic or even Jewish background, whether native born, a convert, or from a family sympathetic to Judaism. He may have been Jewish. The name Pantera is Greek, even though
it appears here in a Latin inscription. In 1891 the French archaeologist
Charles Clermont-Ganneau made a surprising discovery. In a 1st-century
Jewish tomb on the Nablus road, just north of the Old City of Jerusalem,
was an ossuary with the name Pentheros in Greek, as well as that of a certain
Josepos or Joseph, the son of this Pantera. We know from the burials that
they were Jewish, which gives us definitive evidence that the name Pantera
was used in the time of Jesus by Jews as well as Romans.[16]

Abdes Pantera was from Sidon, a coastal town of Syria-Palestine, just
north of Tyre, which is less than forty miles from Sepphoris. We know
that this particular cohort of archers had come to Dalmatia (Croatia) in
the year A.D. 6 from Palestine and was moved to the Rhine/Nahe river
area in A.D. 9. It should not surprise us that Pantera died and was buried
in Germany, as were so many thousands of other Roman soldiers who
fought in the terrible frontier wars around the time of Jesus. Augustus
even transferred Varus, the legate of Syria, to command the Roman legions just north of this very area of Germany. The Romans retained permanent outposts in Germany, and the Bingerbrück cemetery provides us
with evidence that veterans lived out their lives on the frontier. The other
nine tombstones appear to date from around the same period—mid to
late 1st century A.D., based on the coin evidence found at the cemetery,

the style of the gravestones, and the content of their inscriptions. The 1860 painting of the discovery of the Bingerbrück cemetery clearly shows that funerary urns holding the ashes and bones of the deceased were also uncovered. The oldest documents indicate that most of these urns were destroyed in the excavation process but one was retained. Its whereabouts is presently unknown though there are some clues. I could not help but wonder if fate might have somehow preserved the remains of Tiberius Julius Abdes Pantera. Perhaps time will tell.

So what might we conclude regarding Abdes Pantera? Is it remotely plausible that among all the thousands of tomb inscriptions of the period this might be the tombstone of Jesus' father—and in Germany of all places? The chances seem infinitesimal but the evidence should not just be dismissed out of hand. Pantera was a Roman soldier, possibly a Jew; he was a native of Syria-Palestine, just north of Galilee; and he was a contemporary of Mary, mother of Jesus. So we have the right name, the right occupation, the right place, and the right time. There is no way to prove a connection with this type of evidence—short of DNA tests of identifiable remains.

It is also important not to assume that being the son of a Roman soldier necessarily implies something negative. John the Baptizer was quite accommodating to Roman soldiers who came out to hear him preach and the earliest description we have indicates that John even baptized Roman soldiers and that they were part of the Messianic Movement sparked by John and his kinsman Jesus (Luke 3:14). Several Roman officers were praised for their spirituality and piety in the New Testament, and some were part of Jesus' earliest following.[17] In fact, Jesus commended a Roman centurion at Capernaum, a city on the Sea of Galilee, as having more faith than anyone he had ever encountered—including his fellow Jews (Luke 7:9). It was also a Roman centurion who declared of Jesus at his death, "Surely this was a son of God" (Mark 15:39).

Some who give historical weight to the "Jesus son of Pantera" tradition have suggested that perhaps a Roman soldier raped Mary. Given the times and turbulent circumstances surrounding Jesus' birth such a possibility exists. As jolting as such an idea initially sounds, some have found in this scenario a compelling expression of acceptance and unconditional love, certainly by Mary as the mother, but also Joseph as the husband willing to adopt the child as his own. An alternative would be that Mary became pregnant through a relationship she had chosen. Since we know nothing of the possible circumstances of Mary's pregnancy, and her relationship to Jesus' father, Roman soldier or not, there is no reason to postulate something ugly or sinister. We do not know any details of the circumstances of Mary's betrothal to Joseph. Was she a willing participant in an arranged marriage to an older man? Had she formed a prior relationship with another man? Was the pregnancy perhaps before her engagement to Joseph? He may well have left the area and never even have learned about the pregnancy. Our Pantera buried in Germany would have been a younger man closer to Mary's age at the time of the birth of Jesus. From a historian's point of view, this question in particular should be left open. Even though Matthew and Luke represent Mary as pregnant *after* her engagement, since neither believes Jesus had a human father, their representation should not be taken as the final word. Mary might well have become pregnant first, and her engagement then subsequently arranged by the family and accepted by Joseph with knowledge of the situation. My point is that we simply do not know—so we should not pass judgments and make negative assumptions as soon as the phrase "Roman soldier" is put before us. Jesus' enemies would have made the worst of things and freely used the labels "fornication" and "whore." There is no reason to endorse their assumptions. When it comes to family scandal, unwed pregnancies, and broken engagements, the street gossip of a rural Galilean village is the last place one wants to turn for any objectivity.

There is one other piece of this puzzle that may be significant. It is one of the most curious stories in Mark, our earliest gospel. Remember, Mark is the one who called Jesus "the son of Mary" and never mentions Joseph or Jesus' birth at all. Mark abruptly reports a mysterious side trip of Jesus when he is operating around the Sea of Galilee:

> And from there he arose, and went away into the borders of Tyre and Sidon. And he entered into a house, and *would have no man know it*; and he could not be hid (Mark 7:24)

As he returned we are also told that he went through Sidon back to the Sea of Galilee, not the most direct route (Mark 7:31). No one has ever really explained this. Luke has no idea what to do with this story so he simply drops it. Matthew includes it but carefully deletes the part about Jesus entering a specific house where he is known and he *removes* the details regarding the return route through Sidon (Matthew 15:21, 29). Perhaps the information was irrelevant to him, or perhaps he wanted to avoid having his readers raise the obvious question—why would Jesus abruptly leave the territory of Herod Antipas in Galilee and travel to Syria to the coastal areas of Tyre and Sidon? And whose house is this that he knows and secretly enters? Remember, these are not Jewish cities. It is also noteworthy that Jesus regularly praises the cities of Tyre and Sidon as being potentially more open to his message than the cities of the Galilee where he mostly preached (Luke 10:14). Tyre and Sidon are *not* remote areas from Galilee and we are told that crowds of people from both Tyre and Sidon came to the northern side of the Sea of Galilee to hear Jesus preach (Luke 6:17). Just as there is a positive treatment of Roman soldiers in the gospels, there is a remarkably favorable view of these two Gentile coastal cities. Is it possible or even likely that there is a connection? It seems that the abrupt nature of the story, strangely passed on to Mark, hints at something more.

I am convinced that our best evidence indicates that the Joseph who married the pregnant Mary was not the father of Jesus. Jesus' father remains unknown but possibly was named Pantera, and if so, was quite possibly a Roman soldier. The gravestone in Germany, whether that of Jesus' father or not, like the ossuaries and the tombs in Jerusalem we have studied, reminds us that these names associated with Jesus' family are grounded in the material evidence that archaeology continues to uncover. These were real human beings who lived and died in a past that is becoming increasingly accessible to us.

If Jesus was not the son of Joseph, but Mary was married to him and bore other children after Jesus, one would assume that Joseph would be the father of the rest of the family—but as is often the case when it comes to a family, particularly a royal family, things are never quite so simple.

4

CHILDREN OF
A DIFFERENT FATHER

THAT Jesus had four brothers and at least two sisters is a "given" in Mark, our earliest gospel record. He names the brothers rather matter-of-factly: James, Joses, Judas, and Simon. Mark mentions the sisters without naming them, but early Christian tradition says there were two—a Mary and a Salome (Mark 6:3). Matthew, who followed Mark as his source, includes the same list, though he spells "Joses," a nickname akin to the English "Josy," in its full form "Joseph." He also lists Simon before Judas (Matthew 13:55). Luke, in contrast, drops the list of names entirely. He is an unabashed advocate of the apostle Paul and inaugurates a long process of marginalizing the brothers of Jesus to the obscurity that we find them today. More often than not, when I teach or lecture about the brothers of Jesus, and the important position of James, the eldest, whom Jesus left in charge of his followers, a hand shoots up in the room. The comment is always the same: "I never knew that Jesus even had any brothers."

There are a number of factors behind this gap in our knowledge of early Christianity. The later Christian dogma that Mary was a perpetual virgin, that she never had children other than Jesus and never had sexual relations with *any* man, lies at the heart of the issue. No one in the early church even imagined such an idea, since the family of Jesus played such a visible and pivotal role in his life and that of his early followers. It all has to do with Mary being totally removed from her 1st-century Jewish culture and context in the interest of an emerging view of the time that human sexuality was degraded and unholy at worst, and a necessary evil to somehow be struggled against at best. The material world, and thus anything to do with the body, was seen as lower and of less value than the heavenly spiritual world. Scholars refer to this view, quite common in Greco-Roman culture, as *ascetic dualism*. Humans were trapped in two worlds—the material and the spiritual, with two modes of being—that of the body and the spirit (*dualism*). Those who denied the body and lived a celibate life, placing emphasis on the higher spiritual things "above," were viewed as holy and free from the taint of the lower material world (*asceticism*). Generally this outlook has not found a comfortable home within Judaism because of the emphasis in the Bible upon the goodness of God's material creation (Genesis 1). But there are exceptions. Philo of Alexandria, the 1st-century B.C. Jewish philosopher, honors Plato, the great advocate of ascetic dualism, next to Moses himself. Philo's influence, not to mention Plato's, was enormous on both Jewish and Christian thinkers. The apostle Paul, as we will see, built his theology around an essentially dualistic view of the cosmos in which the earthly was denigrated in favor of the heavenly. He advocated celibacy as a higher spiritual way, though he did not absolutely forbid sex. According to Paul, marriage was an antidote for the spiritually weak who might be tempted toward sexual immorality.[2] It is easy to see how these tendencies to equate the spiritual life with the nonsexual life were transferred to Mary and her family.

Once one insists that "the blessed Virgin Mary" was "ever-virgin," with no sexual experience whatsoever, then the brothers and sisters have to be explained away. I say this with no disrespect for those who hold such views of Mary. Yet it is important to understand when, how, and why these ideas developed. Good history never needs to be the enemy of devoted faith. The conflict arises when later forms of ascetic piety and assumptions about "holiness" are imposed on a culture for dogmatic or political reasons. What is lost is the historical reality of who Mary *truly* was as a Jewish married woman of her time. What we lose is Mary herself! The teaching of the "perpetual virginity" is simply not found in the New Testament and it is not part of the earliest Christian creeds. The first official mention of the idea does not come until A.D. 374, from the Christian theologian Epiphanius.[3] Most of our early Christian writings before the later 4th century A.D. took for granted that the brothers and sisters of Jesus were the natural-born children of Joseph and Mary.[4]

By the late 4th century A.D. the church began to handle the problem of Mary's sexual life with two alternative explanations. One is that *brothers* does not mean literally "brothers"—born of the same mother—but is a general term referring to "cousins." This became the standard explanation in the West advocated by Roman Catholics.[5] In the East, the Greek-speaking Christians favored a different view—the brothers were *sons of Joseph*, but by a previous marriage, and thus had no blood ties to Jesus or his mother.[6] Clearly the problem with the Eastern view for Western theologians was the emerging Western tendency, born of asceticism, to make Joseph a lifelong virgin as well. That way the Holy Family, Jesus included of course, could be fully and properly "holy." Over the centuries it became more and more difficult for Christians, particularly in the West, to imagine Mary or Joseph as sexual human beings, or for that matter even living a "bodily" life at all. Once they become "saints" in heaven, emphasizing such a potentially degrading earthly past became problematic.

If we restore Mary's Jewish name—Miriam or Maria, the most common Jewish female name of the day—and put her back in her 1st-century Jewish village of Nazareth, as a normally married Jewish woman, these theologically motivated concerns seem to vanish. We are free to recover a believable history much more fascinating and rich than any theological dogma. The texts of our New Testament records begin to come alive for us. As one of my university professors used to say about historical investigation: "When you get closer to the truth, everything begins to fit."

So who were the brothers and sisters of Jesus? The most obvious answer is that they were children of Mary and Joseph born subsequently in the marriage. Mary became pregnant while engaged, father unknown; Joseph married her anyway, adopted Jesus as his own; and the couple assumed a normal married life, producing four sons and two daughters. Such might well be the case, but there is a problem here that we must not overlook. Once again, it has to do with understanding the lost *Jewish* cultural and religious context of the times.

There is good reason to suppose that Joseph died early, whether because he was substantially older than Mary or for some other unknown cause. After the birth stories he seems to disappear.[7] Jesus is called "son of Joseph" or referred to as "the carpenter's son" a few times, but Joseph himself never appears in any narratives and nothing further is related about him. Jesus moved "his mother and brothers" to Capernaum at one point—no mention of Joseph (John 2:12). His "mother and brothers" came seeking him in one story—again, no mention of Joseph (Mark 3:31). Even at the crucifixion of Jesus, Mary is mentioned, and possibly one of his sisters, but Joseph is again strangely absent. After Jesus' death his followers were gathered in Jerusalem and "Mary, the mother of Jesus with his brothers" were part of the group—but no Joseph (Acts 1:14). The silence seems to indicate that something has happened to Joseph.

If Joseph died early and Jesus and his brothers and sisters grew up "fatherless" this surely would have had an important psychological and sociological impact on the family. But if Joseph died *childless* there are further consequences for traditional theological dogmas about Mary. According to the Torah, or Law of Moses, the oldest surviving unmarried brother was obligated to marry his deceased brother's widow and bear a child in his name so that his dead brother's "name" or lineage would not perish. This is called a "Levirate marriage" or *yibbum* in Hebrew, and it is required in the Torah (Deuteronomy 25:5–10).[8] It is one of the commandments of God given to Israel, and pious Jews took it seriously. It comes up in a discussion in the Gospels where Jesus is asked about a contrived case in which a woman is widowed no less than seven times and each time successively marries a brother of her first husband (Mark 12:19–22).

Suddenly the issue of who was the father of Jesus takes on a new dimension. If Joseph was not Jesus' father, and Joseph died without children, was Mary the widow required to marry Joseph's brother? And do we know anything about Joseph's brother? Amazingly we do. Though seldom recognized, he is mentioned in the New Testament.

We want to follow the evidence wherever it might lead, but the implications that Mary was the mother of *seven* children through *three* different men does sound outrageous today. But what if such a practice was not only normal but in fact also required and honorable within the Jewish culture of the time? Such was certainly the case. To honor a man who died without an heir and thus assure his posterity was one of the most sacred and holy things a family could do. Remember the four women Matthew mentions in his genealogy? Two of the four, Tamar and Ruth, were widows involved in Levirate marriages. Perhaps Matthew knows more than he is explicitly telling us. It would be a mistake to judge any evidence concerning Mary and the fathers of her children by our theological and cultural standards. What we must do is look at the evidence—in this case a set of complex, but revealing, textual clues left unintentionally within the New Testament itself.

THE MYSTERY OF THE "OTHER MARY"

All four of our gospels note that women from Galilee who followed Jesus were present at his crucifixion and attended to his burial. Mark lists the names of three of these women:

1. Mary Magdalene
2. *Mary the mother of James the younger and of Joses*
3. Salome (Mark 15:40)

Matthew, who used Mark as his source, has the same list with slight changes:

1. Mary Magdalene
2. *Mary the mother of James and Joseph*
3. The mother of the sons of Zebedee (Matthew 27:56)

Mary Magdalene was the well-known companion of Jesus and about whom we will say more in subsequent chapters. Salome, mentioned only by Mark, is very possibly Jesus' sister, or perhaps, according to Matthew, the mother of the two fishermen James and John, who were part of the Twelve (Luke 5:10). In Luke's account he drops the names and simply says that "women" were present, just as he did earlier with the names of the brothers of Jesus (Luke 23:49, 55). As we will see, Luke is not keen to emphasize the family of Jesus.

Note that we have two women named Mary who were present. Later, about the burial of Jesus, Matthew tells us again that Mary Magdalene was there, as well as "the other Mary" (Matthew 27:61). When the women returned to the tomb early Sunday morning to find it empty, again Matthew tells us they were "Mary Magdalene and *the other Mary*" (Matthew 28:1). So the obvious question is this: just who is this mysterious "other Mary"?

Mark identifies her specifically two more times—once at the burial as "Mary the mother of Joses," and then at the empty tomb as "Mary the mother of James" (Mark 15:47; 16:1). He also notes again that Salome was present.

So we know this *second* Mary was the mother of a "James and Joses." But is there any way to identify her further? We do know "another Mary" who has two sons named "James and Joses"—none other than *Mary the mother of Jesus*. These are the very names, even including the nickname "Joses" (that Matthew consistently edits) of her first two sons born after Jesus (Mark 6:3). Is it possible or even probable that this mysterious "other Mary" is Mary the mother of Jesus? It surely should not surprise us that Jesus' own mother would be witness to his death, and participate in the Jewish family burial practices. And if so, why does Mark not openly identify her as such?

Beyond this primary record of Mark, largely followed with some editing by Luke and Matthew, we do have one other independent account as to the identity of these women—namely the gospel of John. Notice carefully his list of the three women at the cross:

1. *Jesus' mother, Mary*
2. His mother's sister, *Mary the wife of Clophas*
3. *Mary* Magdalene (John 19:25)

Notice, we still have three women, but Salome has dropped out and *all three are now named Mary*! No matter how common the name Mary was at the time, surely three Marys should give us pause. Something seems to be going on here. John knows something that either he, or those who later edited his gospel, chose to veil.

The inclusion of Mary Magdalene does not surprise us, since she is in all the lists. But John tells us explicitly that Mary mother of Jesus was present. That would allow us to safely identify Mark's "Mary the mother of James and Joses" as Jesus' mother Mary. But then who is the "new" third Mary—the wife of Clophas? And who is Clophas? This Mary is identified as the "sister" of Mary mother of Jesus—but what is the likelihood that two sisters in the same family would have the same name?

Let's begin with Clophas, since we do know something about him. As I will explain in detail later, when Jesus died he left his brother James in charge of his followers. James was murdered in A.D. 62 and our earliest records tell us that an aged man known as "Simon son of Clophas" succeeded him. We are further told that this Clophas was the brother of Joseph, the husband of Mary.[9] If such were the case it is entirely possible that our mysterious Mary, wife of Clophas, mother of "James and Joses," was a sister-in-law of Mary, married to her husband Joseph's brother. That is the solution the church has settled on over the centuries. But notice, if such were the case, what we have is more than a bit strange:

COMPARISON OF THE "TWO" MARYS

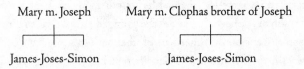

Mary m. Joseph   Mary m. Clophas brother of Joseph

James-Joses-Simon   James-Joses-Simon

Is it really likely that these two women, both named Mary, whether sisters or sisters-in-law, married to brothers and had three sons with the same names and born in the same order: James, Joses, and Simon?

What seems more plausible is that Mark's "Mary mother of James and Joses" was the same Mary as the mother of Jesus and that the gospel of John (or its later editors) has created a *third* Mary, wife of Clophas, who

in fact was the *same* woman—in order to disguise the fact that Jesus'
mother Mary, after the death of Joseph, married his brother Clophas. A
decrypted version of John would read

> Standing by the cross of Jesus were his mother Mary wife of Clophas
> and Mary Magdalene.

This would agree perfectly with Mark and not create the absurdity of
sisters-in-law of the same name having identically named children, including the nickname "Joses," in the same order of birth. According to this
reconstruction our three women at the cross most likely were:

1. Mary Magdalene
2. Mary, the widow of Joseph who married Clophas, Joseph's brother
3. Salome, either the sister of Jesus or the mother of the sons of
   Zebedee

There is one additional point about Clophas that supports this interpretation. His name comes from the Hebrew root *chalaph* and means to
"change" or to "replace." It is an ancestor of the English term "caliphate," referring to a dynastic succession of rulers. So this is likely not his given
name, but a type of nickname. He is the one who *replaced* his brother
Joseph, who died childless. Clophas is mentioned elsewhere by the Greek
form of the same name—*Alphaeus.* His firstborn son was regularly known
as "James son of Alphaeus" or "James the younger" to distinguish him from
James son of Zebedee the fisherman, brother of the apostle John.[10]

Given this information, a rather different but historically consistent
picture begins to emerge. Jesus was born of an unknown father, but was
not the son of Joseph. Joseph died without children, so according to Jewish law "Clophas" or "Alphaeus" became his "replacer," and married his
widow, Mary, mother of Jesus. His firstborn son, James, the brother who
succeeded Jesus, legally became known as the "son of Joseph" after his deceased brother in order to carry on his name. This would mean that Jesus
had four half-brothers and at least two half-sisters, all born of his mother
Mary but from a different father.

This is one plausible reconstruction of the evidence. There are things we can never know with certainty. Clophas is mentioned only once in the entire New Testament (John 19:25).[11] If he and his brother Joseph were much older than Mary it is likely that neither was alive when Jesus was an adult. This is further indicated in the gospel of John when Jesus, the eldest son in the family, just before his death, handed his mother over to the care of a mysterious "beloved disciple" that John prefers not to name (John 19:26). I will show evidence later that this person is most likely James, his brother, the next eldest in the family. But whoever it was, Jesus' giving his mother into the care of another indicates she was a widow. We have to remember that the gospels are primarily *theological* accounts of the Jesus story written a generation or more after his death. When it comes to Jesus' family there is much they do not spell out, and there are things they appear to deliberately suppress. We have seen that Mark preserves material that is edited or removed by Matthew and Luke. John knows more than he is willing to say explicitly. The reasons for these tendencies will become clearer as we trace our story through to the end. It is truly a tangled tale of political intrigue and religious power plays with stakes destined to shape the future of the world's largest religion.

What we can say with some degree of certainty is the following: Joseph was not the father of Jesus, and Mary's pregnancy by an unnamed man was "illegitimate" by societal norms. Jesus had four half-brothers and two half-sisters, all children of Mary but from a different father— whether Joseph or his brother Clophas. Jesus by age thirty functions as head of the household and forges a vital role for his brothers, who succeed him in establishing a Messianic Dynasty destined to change the world. This extended family of Jesus is the foundation of the mostly forgotten and marginalized Jesus dynasty and it is long overdue for resurrection. By restoring the various historical possibilities related to the family, we are prepared to gain a truer understanding of Jesus and how he might have understood what he believed was his God-ordained mission as Messiah and King of a restored nation of Israel. We now turn to Jesus' own life and the so-called "lost years."

Part Two

GROWING UP
JEWISH IN GALILEE

5

THE LOST YEARS

I T is impossible to write a full biography of Jesus' life. According to the most plausible reconstruction of the chronology, Jesus died at age thirty-three.[1] We are missing any historical record of the first *thirty* years of his life. If such were the case with any other figure in history, surely no one would attempt the task. How then could it be that more books have been written about Jesus than any other character in human history? Clearly in the case of Jesus there is an unprecedented desire to peer through the veil and somehow dispel the mystery. His influence has been so profound, and the intrigue surrounding what we do know of his story so riveting, that we simply cannot relegate him to a shadowy past. For millions the endlessly fascinating question remains open—what can we really know about Jesus of Nazareth?

Many have the mistaken impression that our New Testament gospels offer us four fairly complete biographies of his life. The facts are otherwise. Mark begins his story with Jesus at age thirty. By chapter eight, more than halfway through his sixteen chapters, he has already come to the final weeks of Jesus' life. Matthew and Luke add birth stories and they include more of the teachings of Jesus but basically they follow Mark's lead—devoting over half their accounts to Jesus' final journey to

Jerusalem, where he is crucified. John begins with Jesus at thirty and he likewise devotes half his book to his final days in Jerusalem.

Scholars appropriately refer to the first thirty years of Jesus' life as the "lost years." We do have other writings that have survived outside the New Testament, often called "Infancy Gospels," as well as floating bits of tradition that offer us a few childhood stories. But they are late and legendary (2nd to 4th century A.D.) serving more to entertain and mythologize than to inform a critical reader.

For example, in the *Infancy Gospel of Thomas*, which is not the same as the more authentic *Gospel of Thomas* I have already cited, we read that when Jesus was five years old he formed twelve sparrows out of mud on the Sabbath. His father Joseph reprimanded him for "playing" in this fashion on the holy day of rest and Jesus clapped his hands and his clay birds were instantly transformed to life and flew away—astounding everyone who heard the tale. On another occasion, when Jesus was walking through the crowded streets of his village, another child bumped against his shoulder and Jesus declared in exasperation—"You shall go no further." The offending child instantly fell dead. Once when a child fell off a roof and died, Jesus was accused of pushing him so he leaped down and promptly raised him from the dead. As he grew up he worked with Joseph as a carpenter and if a piece of wood was accidentally cut too short he would just stretch it to proper size with a pull of his hand.

The notion that Jesus traveled to Egypt as a young man in order to learn magical powers is a theme common in later Jewish polemics against the Christians. In fact this legend is mentioned by the Greek philosopher Celsus, who related the story of the Roman soldier Pantera as Jesus' biological father.[2] There are legends that Jesus went to India as a child to study with Hindu teachers, amazing them with his precocious knowledge.[3] Perhaps the most fantastic are the tales of Jesus traveling as a boy with Joseph of Arimathea to Great Britain. According to these legends, Joseph, said to be an uncle of Mary, was a tin merchant and made regular trading trips to Cornwall. The town of Glastonbury in southwest England on the former island of Avalon, where King Arthur was buried, still celebrates this tradition today and has even become a popular pilgrimage center.[4]

Historians give such legendary material little credibility. We have to face the fact that thirty years of Jesus' life are simply missing and attempts to fill them in with legends and fables do nothing to advance our quest for the historical Jesus. Surprisingly, however, there is much we can responsibly determine about these "lost years." In such a case we are left to something akin to detective work. By skillfully combining the archaeological evidence with what we know from contemporary historical records and guided by some tantalizing hints in the gospels themselves, we can begin to fill in some of the blanks.

TWO YOUNG DOVES

We know that Jesus and his family grew up poor. Luke gives a shocking indication of just how poor. According to Jewish law, as it was commanded in the Torah or Law of Moses, every firstborn male child was ritually accepted into the Jewish community through an ancient ceremony called "Redemption of the Son" (*pidyon ha-ben*). God had declared, "every firstborn among the Israelites, man as well as beast, is mine" (Numbers 8:17). Rather than sacrifice the child to the deity, as was practiced in some ancient cultures, the parents paid the priests five silver shekels as part of a ceremony that "freed" the child from death. This ceremony was carried out thirty days following the birth of the child. On the fortieth day there was another obligation for the mother of any male child, firstborn or not. The child was brought to the Temple sanctuary and the mother was required to give a lamb as a burnt offering and a dove for a sin offering to the officiating priests. In cases of dire poverty the Torah stipulated further, "If she cannot afford a sheep she shall take two doves or two pigeons, one for the burnt offering and the other for the sin offering" (Leviticus 12:8). It is Luke who tells us that Mary and Joseph, as observant Jews, took Jesus up to the Jerusalem Temple to fulfill these ritual obligations. There she offered sacrifice "according to what is stated in the Law of the Lord—a pair of doves or two young pigeons" (Luke 2:24). There is no mention of a sheep. They evidently could not afford even such a modest gift.

In contrast Matthew tells quite a different story. He has Mary and

Joseph living in a house in Bethlehem, visited by Magi from the East, who lavished the newborn child with expensive gifts, and paid him homage as "King of the Jews." Mary and Joseph have the means to travel to Egypt, where they stay for a time, fleeing the wrath of Herod the Great, who has murdered every child in Judea under the age of two. Only after Herod's death do they travel back to Galilee and settle in a town called Nazareth. Matthew does not even appear to realize that the couple is *from* Nazareth in the first place. We have extraordinarily good historical records for the reign of Herod the Great. It is inconceivable that such a "slaughter of the infants" would go unrecorded by the Jewish historian Josephus or other contemporary Roman historians. Matthew's account is clearly theological, written to justify later views of Jesus' exalted status. But he is surely right about one point—Herod did fear the birth of a child who could potentially grow up and become a claimant to the royal throne of David as a legitimate "King of the Jews."

Luke's story, stripped of its overtly theological elements, rings true. Mary was a teenager pregnant out of wedlock with an illegitimate child. The birth had taken place in a cavelike stable attached to a guesthouse where animals were sheltered and fed. The newborn infant was swaddled and placed in a feeding trough. Joseph, her fiancé, was with her and apparently eight days after the birth, at the circumcision, the child was given the legal name "Yeshua bar Yosef," or Jesus son of Joseph, but the marriage was not consummated until their return to Nazareth. There is no indication that the couple had friends or resources of any kind. According to Jewish law they were obligated to stay in the Bethlehem-Jerusalem area for a period of forty days in order to fulfill the Jewish rituals involved with the birth of a firstborn male child. It is possible the cavelike stable was their dwelling during that entire period. To purchase a sheep for the final offering was a relatively modest expense and surely if they could have afforded it they would have.

The offering of the two doves tells us something vitally important about the beginnings of the Jesus dynasty. Roman Emperor Augustus had officially given the coveted title "King of the Jews" to Herod the Great. He was the wealthiest and most influential client king in the eastern Mediterranean Empire. His lavish building programs, both inside and outside the country, were unparalleled even in Rome. When Mary and Joseph made their way to the Temple they would have seen the splendorous palace of Herod along the western wall of the city with its impressive towers, the foundations of which are still visible today. Herod had begun a remodeling of the Temple itself in 20 B.C. with the intention of making it a wonder of the ancient world. This is quite a study in contrasts. Jesus was born poor and virtually homeless, despite the royal Davidic bloodline he inherited from his mother. And yet it was this very dynastic bloodline that Herod and his sons so desperately coveted and feared despite their extraordinary wealth and political power.

WAS JESUS A CARPENTER?

A good trivia question would be "What was Jesus' vocation?" Everyone knows he was a carpenter, or at least the son of a carpenter. One would assume there are dozens of verses in the New Testament gospels affirming this well-known fact. This widespread idea is based on a single phrase in a single verse in Mark in which the townsfolk at Nazareth ask of Jesus—"Is this not the carpenter?" (Mark 6:3). Matthew changes it to "Is this not the son of the carpenter?" (Matthew 13:55). The traditional English translation "carpenter," which goes back as early as William Tyndale's 1526 edition of the New Testament, is misleading.

The Greek word *tekton* is a more generic term referring to a "builder." It can include one who works with wood, but in its 1st-century Galilean context it more likely refers to a stoneworker. The 2nd-century *Protoevangelium of James* refers to Joseph as a "builder of buildings."[5] Houses and buildings were built of stone. Wood was used sparingly, mostly for roof beams and doors, since wood was a scarce building material in the rocky terrain of Palestine. Jesus often drew upon images of stone building to illustrate his teachings. In one of his well-known stories he speaks of the wise man who in building a house digs a deep foundation and lays the solid stone foundation of the building upon bedrock (Luke 6:48). He appears to have been exposed to the building trades, and stonework of some type was most likely his trade.

The quaint image of Jesus working happily alongside his father in the family "carpenter shop" is familiar from centuries of reverential paintings. It is a far cry from the harsh grinding social reality that we know was part of day-to-day life in Galilee, where the rich got richer and the growing masses of poor were evident. A *tekton* in this context was something akin to a day laborer. There were no unions or "blue collar" wages. To be a *tekton* meant first and foremost that one had no land and took work as one could find it with no guarantees or security. These itinerant peasants were left to eke out a subsistence existence on two or three sesterces a day—barely enough to sustain a slave.[6] But the life of a "free" day laborer was surely harder than that of an urban slave, whose basic needs of food and shelter were provided. In Roman culture the artisan trades were regarded as akin to slave labor. They were viewed as the toilsome, backbreaking work of the lower classes. Sophocles, the Greek poet, emphatically objected to someone who wrote that his father was a *tekton*, as if that would demean his social class. He wrote that perhaps his father had such workers as slaves, but he himself was surely not of such a trade.[7]

This embarrassment regarding Jesus' social status might well be reflected in Mark's reference by the townsfolk where he grew up—as if to say, "Is this not that day laborer we all know well—you know, that illegitimate son of Mary?" Matthew reacts to this with a bit of subtle editing: "Is not this the son of the *tekton*? Is not his mother called Mary?" For Matthew to be a "son" of a *tekton* carries less of a stigma. In Matthew's portrayal, Jesus is "King" from his birth despite his father's occupation. Mark knows a more original tradition. Once again we see how Matthew consistently edits Mark, his main source, in a way that reflects later theological views of Jesus' exalted status.

A FATHERLESS FATHER

I have already noted that Joseph, husband of Mary, mysteriously disappears from the scene in all our records. Tradition holds that he was considerably older than Mary and mostly likely died when Jesus was a teenager. It is possible that he was the father of the four boys and two girls whom Mary had over the years following the birth of her firstborn son Jesus. It is also possible that he died childless and his brother

Clophas was the father of these six children. If such were the case, and Clophas was also much older than Mary, he too might have died when the children were growing up. We simply have no way to know the details in this regard.

What does seem clear in all our records, as I have noted already, is that when Jesus begins his career as a preacher and healer at age thirty we consistently find "his mother and his brothers" mentioned but never a father. He took his "mother and his brothers" to Capernaum not long after his baptism (John 2:12). Later his "mother and his brothers" came looking for him when he was out on the road (Mark 3:32). When he returned home to Nazareth at one point, as we have seen, the townsfolk spoke of his mother Mary, his brothers and sisters, but again, no mention of a father (Mark 6:3). Just before Jesus' death he turned over the care of his mother to a mysterious "beloved disciple," whom I identify as James, the next oldest brother (John 19:26–27). After he is killed "Mary the mother of Jesus and his brothers" gathered behind closed doors with the rest of his followers, hiding for their lives (Acts 1:14).

What we can safely assume given this silence is that Jesus himself takes on the role of a "fatherless father" to these six younger children. Just how early this responsibility fell to him we cannot say. But if we want to guess what occupied Jesus during his twenties, before he makes his public debut, we can best picture him acting as father and caretaker to his mother and younger siblings.

This was surely no easy burden. The family had no inherited land or wealth. Celsus, the 2nd-century A.D. Roman writer, passes on a tradition that Mary earned money as a spinner. Whether this is accurate or not we have no way of knowing, but it would have surely fallen to Jesus as the eldest son of this fatherless Jewish family to act as the primary bread-winner. To support oneself as an artisan peasant in a small village in Roman-occupied Galilee was burden enough, but to support a large family on daily wages was a nigh impossible task. Jesus later tells a story about such day laborers, hired out to work in the vineyard of a landowner for a denarius (four sesterces) a day. The workers assembled at dawn in the marketplace of a village and were hired on the spot to labor until dusk. They were paid the agreed amount in the evening. Jesus specifically mentions the "burden of the day and the scorching heat" (Matthew

20:12). He seems intimately familiar with the lot of the working poor, and one gets the impression he is speaking more from experience than detached observation.

Herod Antipas, son of Herod the Great, using such peasant labor, began to rebuild Sepphoris as his gleaming capital city following its savage destruction in 4 B.C. as punishment for those who participated in the revolts that followed the death of his father, Herod the Great. It was a Jewish city but over the next decades was thoroughly reshaped in fashionable Roman style to become the "ornament of all Galilee." The building trades were surely booming. Sepphoris soon became the economic hub of the dozens of peasant villages that crowded the Bet Netofa valley of lower Galilee—including Nazareth. In fact, Galilee was one of the most densely populated regions of the entire Roman empire, crisscrossed by major roads and characterized by a booming economy. Jesus spent his "lost years" growing up just outside this urban Roman capital of Galilee that lay just over the low hills that ringed the small village of Nazareth. The village itself was clustered around a natural spring at the base of those hills, today called the "Well of Mary."

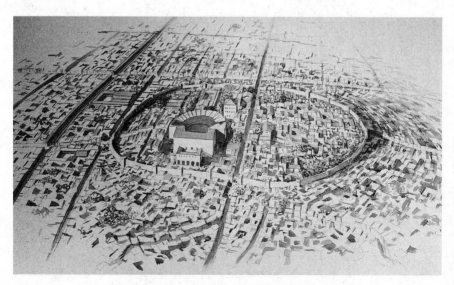

Drawing of Sepphoris as rebuilt by Herod Antipas

Excavations at Sepphoris with Nazareth in the background

It is surely reasonable to suppose that Joseph would have been drawn to the massive building projects in Sepphoris, where he would be able to ply his skills as a stoneworker, and that Jesus would have learned the same trade as he grew into manhood. Inspired by this thought some of us decided one early afternoon to try walking from our dig site at Sepphoris to Nazareth. It took us about an hour and a half at a moderate pace in the heat of the day. We do not know the precise chronology of Sepphoris' rebuilding but one can assume such a massive project might have well taken ten or fifteen years. If Jesus was born in 5 B.C., which seems likely, he would have been old enough to work with Joseph during the boom years. And there is every reason to suppose that building projects in the city continued after that. We don't know when Joseph died but we can imagine that Jesus might well have labored as a stoneworker in Sepphoris into his twenties—particularly if he had the responsibility of caring for his family.

The second season I excavated at Sepphoris our team got down about two meters below the present surface of the ground and began to uncover a stone wall and floor that we were able to date to the early 1st century

A.D. The main draw for my students to dig at Sepphoris was its close proximity to Nazareth and the possibility that Jesus labored there in the building trades during his late teens and twenties. Upon being told that the stones we had uncovered belonged to that period, one of my students asked, half in jest, "Dr. Tabor, do you think it is possible that Jesus might have laid these very stones?" Everyone had a good laugh at the unlikelihood of such a possibility, given the vast area that the ancient city occupied. And yet there was no doubt that uncovering layers of remains from the time of Jesus and trying to imagine the arduous life of a poor Galilean day laborer had given us a new appreciation for the "lost years" of Jesus. One could not help but wonder what thoughts might have been in the mind of one destined to declare himself "King of the Jews" as he toiled at cutting and laying stones in place in Herod's magnificent capital city. And that brings us to the question—what do we know about Jesus' attitudes toward the Roman military occupation of his country and the powerful dynasty of Herod the Great and his family? Was he a militant, a pacifist, or did he consider such worldly matters a thing of indifference? To what degree did he begin to see his bid to be King of Israel a realistic threat to the powers of Rome?

6

A KINGDOM OF
THIS WORLD

T H E Romans occupied the country the Jews called "the Land of Israel" in 63 B.C. The great general Pompey, onetime ally of Julius Caesar, led his armies into the eastern Mediterranean, conquering Asia Minor, Syria, and Palestine. He took Jerusalem after a three-month siege, slaughtering twelve thousand Jews.[1] He took advantage of the Sabbath day, attacking ferociously when he knew the observant Jews would be less inclined to fight. He and his staff dared to enter the inner sanctum of the Jewish Temple—the "Holy of Holies," a small curtained chamber that housed the Ark of the Covenant in ancient times. According to the Torah only the high priest was allowed to enter this room and only once a year on the Day of Atonement (Yom Kippur). In an ironic twist of history Josephus says that Pompey's violation of the Temple fell on the "day of the fast," or Yom Kippur. Perhaps more than any other, this single act epitomized Roman arrogance and power. How could it be that the God of Israel, whom the Jews daily worshipped as "Master of the World," was unable to protect his own sanctuary on the most holy day of the Jewish year? Political and military power is one thing, but religious humiliation quite another. The Jewish prophetic vision of a Messiah King who would rule the Land of Israel and eventually all the nations of the world never looked more hopeless.

Pompey's conquest of the East brought incalculable wealth to Rome in the form of war booty and new taxes. Syria was annexed and made a Roman province, and its governor divided Palestine into several self-governing districts with local rulers under Roman military control. The most ambitious of these client rulers was Antipater, father of Herod the Great. It was a time of instability and civil war in Rome. Over the next two decades Julius Caesar defeated Pompey, who had become his enemy, but was later assassinated by Brutus and Cassius, whom Mark Antony then vanquished. Caesar's nephew Octavian, who was to become known as Augustus, the first of the Roman emperors, subsequently overpowered his rivals Antony and Cleopatra in 31 B.C. Augustus desperately needed a stable eastern border and he realized the one man who could do the job was Herod.

THE MAN WHO WOULD BE KING

Herod proved to be more ruthless than his father. We know him as "Herod the Great" because he was the first of a dynasty of his descendants who ruled in Roman Palestine down to A.D. 100. He might just as well be called Herod the Horrible in view of the cruelty and oppression that characterized his long reign.

Herod was determined to be King of the Jews and sole ruler of the land of Israel. In 40 B.C. he had traveled to Rome and managed to convince Antony and Octavian, who were still allies at the time, to declare him "King of Judea." They recognized that Herod was the only one capable of solidifying rule in Palestine and standing with them against the Parthians, who had invaded from the east. At his coronation Herod offered sacrifice to Jupiter on Capitoline Hill, flanked by Octavian and Antony. He returned to Palestine and began to subdue Galilee in the north, moved south into Samaria, and finally, with Roman legionary support, laid siege to Jerusalem. He ruthlessly slaughtered all who opposed him, and in the summer of 37 B.C. Herod finally consolidated his rule and officially occupied his bloodied throne as "King of the Jews." Herod's mother was Jewish but his father Antipater was a foreigner from Idumea to the east. Herod married Mariamne, who was a descendant of the family of priests known as the Hashmoneans or Maccabees. Although her family could not claim Davidic descent they did rule the country during a tiny window of independence from around 165 B.C. until the Romans arrived in 63 B.C. They formed a royal dynasty and put the title "king" on their coins. There was a certain mystique attached to this priestly family that had successfully expelled the Syrians from the Land of Israel a hundred years earlier. Herod the "half Jew" thought that he might achieve a bit more legitimacy for the title he coveted with the beautiful Mariamne by his side.

In 31 B.C. there was a devastating earthquake in Judea that left thirty thousand dead. Those who despised Herod and all he represented saw it as the beginning of God's judgment upon the Jews for accommodating themselves to Roman rule. Octavian defeated Antony the same year, and one of his first acts as the new Emperor Augustus was to confirm Herod's title "King of the Jews." He placed a crown on his head in a formal ceremony at Rhodes, where Herod had sailed to meet and congratulate him.

One of Herod's first acts was to execute forty-five of the seventy members of the Jewish Sanhedrin, the council in charge of Jewish legal affairs.

Ruins of Herod's desert fortress Masada

Early in his reign he enlarged and fortified the various desert fortresses that the Hashmoneans had founded, including Masada, the Alexandrium, Machaerus, and Hyrcania. He supplied them with arms, food, and water as potential places of refuge for his family in a time of crisis. What he most feared was a native revolt that might gain the popular support of those people who were looking for a legitimate ruler from the house of David.

Herod the Great is remembered for his cruel lust for power and his massive building programs. In Samaria he built Sebaste as a defensive citadel, complete with a temple to Emperor Augustus. Despite his Jewish pretensions, and the requirement that he accommodate himself somewhat to Jewish religious sensibilities, Herod was Roman at heart. In an effort to foster the Greek culture that the Romans had adopted he even built a theater and amphitheater in Jerusalem, not to mention his own extravagant palace in the upper part of the city. Herod did not limit his largesse to his own territory. He funded public building projects in cities all over the eastern Empire. Herod's sons, Antipas and Archelaus, grew up and were educated in Rome under the direction of the emperor himself. There was no more powerful family in the eastern Mediterranean.

Drawing of Caesarea and its harbor

In 22 B.C. Herod began construction of the new port city of Caesarea, named after Emperor Augustus. It was a vast and lavish twelve-year project that included a beautiful artificial harbor, a theater overlooking the Mediterranean Sea, a large hippodrome amphitheater, and his own royal palace. A massive temple dedicated to the goddess Roma and the honor of Augustus the emperor overlooked the harbor. It was his window on the Roman world and he was proud to entertain visitors from

Herod's Jerusalem with the Temple Mount complex

Rome and the provinces in a style as opulent as anything they could experience elsewhere in the Empire.

Herod's greatest project, begun around the same time, in 20 B.C., involved a wholesale remodeling of the Temple in Jerusalem and an extensive expansion of its courts. According to Josephus he employed ten thousand workers to carry out the work. He never lived to see it finished but spared no expense to ensure that its extravagant beauty, accented with marble, gold, tapestries, and Corinthian columns, would rival any temple in the Roman world. But more important, Herod wanted to be

Massive foundation stones still in place at the Temple Mount

remembered as a second "King Solomon," the son of David, who according to the Bible had constructed the first Temple in the 10th century B.C.
in a style that became the envy of the region.

Tourists still marvel at the beauty and magnificence of the stones out-

lining the border of what was the Temple Mount, a huge platform enclo-
sure that was enlarged to 144,000 square meters. They were cut with precision from local limestone and set into place without mortar. Since the
1967 Israeli-Arab Six Day War, archaeologists have exposed the entire
southern and western walls of this immense compound. The lower
courses of stones, long covered with soil and debris, remain in place to
this day. The largest stone yet uncovered is twelve meters long by three
meters high, and weighs hundreds of tons.

But where did all the money come from? How was Herod the Great
able to finance all these projects? Land and agriculture were the only significant basis of the Palestinian economy. Herod's wealth was essentially
drawn from peasant labor, extracted by taxes and inflated by an economic
shift from family farms to larger estates. There was also a "market tax"
levied on all that was bought and sold in trade and commerce. It was a
pattern echoed throughout the Empire as the urban rich amassed wealth
and the countryside increasingly fell into poverty.

Herod had nine wives and several dozen children. Jealousies, domestic
quarrels, and fits of murder characterized his reign. In 7 B.C. he had his
two older sons strangled and three hundred of their supporters murdered
because he feared plots against him. The sons were royal heirs to the
throne, children of his beloved Mariamne. Sometime later he had Mariamne executed on charges of committing adultery with his sister's husband. Just five days before he died he ordered another son, Antipater,
killed. There was a Greek quip circulating in Rome in Herod's time to
the effect that one might do better to be Herod's pig (*hus*) than his son
(*huios*). In a final act of madness he had hundreds of leading officials and
their families imprisoned in the hippodrome with orders that they be
killed at his death so that every family in Jerusalem would have something to mourn when he passed.[2] These orders were never carried out but
they show the degree of Herod's insane depravity at the end.

Herod drank heavily and developed numerous illnesses—according to
Josephus these included intestinal pains and tumors, asthma, genital "gan-
grene," and "worms."[3] Toward the end he could not even stand upright
and stayed at his palace near the Dead Sea at Jericho. In Jerusalem a disturbance broke out and two very popular rabbi-preachers there named

Judas and Matthias incited their followers to tear down the Golden Eagle that Herod had set up over the Temple Gate as a symbol of Roman rule. They were arrested with forty of their followers and brought to Jericho, where Herod had them burned alive following a mock trial at which he presided from a bed.[4]

Just before his death he traveled to the hot springs of Callirrhoe, on the Jordanian shore of the Dead Sea, in an attempt to get some relief. Those springs are still there today with hot water bubbling up into well-worn rock pools. A few years ago I took my students to the exact spot and some of us went into the waters. In the cliffs above our heads we could see the ruins of Machaerus, the fortress where Herod's son Antipas beheaded John the Baptizer. Somehow both stories seemed to move out of the text and take on a new life for us, as if time had suspended itself in a desert that changes little in two thousand years.

When Herod died in March of 4 B.C. Jesus was a six-month-old infant living in Galilee. Herod's will divided his kingdom among three of his sons. Herod Antipas became ruler of Galilee and Perea, the region just across the Jordan. His older full brother Archelaus was made "ethnarch" of Judea, a term meaning "ruler of the nation." Philip, a third son, by a different wife, was given territories northeast of the Sea of Galilee. The Emperor Augustus ratified the will and all three sons were in Rome for the occasion. Augustus favored Archelaus and promised him that he would be made king if he proved himself worthy. Archelaus gave his father an elaborate funeral and his body was laid to rest in a secret chamber inside the Herodium, a large palace fortress six miles south of Jerusalem that Herod had had constructed to serve as his mausoleum. So far the tomb itself has not been found though the fortress has been excavated.

There were riots in Jerusalem at this time, and Passover was near. Archelaus reacted with force and his armies massacred over three thousand people. Soon the whole country was up in arms; that is when Varus and his legions marched into Galilee from Syria, destroyed Sepphoris, and marched on Jerusalem, burning towns and villages on the way and crucifying those who were resisting Roman rule shortly after the birth of Jesus. In Galilee a man named Judas, son of Ezekias, had sparked the uprising, breaking into the royal armory at Sepphoris and seizing the arms.

Josephus says that this Judas aspired to be honored as a king. In the south one Simon, a slave of Herod, gathered a group of followers, had himself proclaimed king, and burned and plundered the royal palace in Jericho. The Romans caught up with him and he was beheaded. A shepherd named Athronges, supported by four brothers, proclaimed himself king and raised up a large armed band, ravaging the countryside for months. According to Josephus all three of these leaders wore the diadem signifying their claims to royal honors as king.[5] In Jewish tradition a king is a "messiah," or anointed one, so it is not inaccurate to understand these leaders as aspiring messiahs of one type or another.

Archelaus turned out to be more arrogant and cruel than his father. He became so unpopular with the local populace of Judea that Augustus removed him from power in A.D. 6 and banished him to Gaul. Rome annexed Judea with its capital Jerusalem and placed the district under direct Roman military rule, administered by a procurator or governor. Augustus sent the high-ranking senator Quirinius to take charge of things in Syria. He was accompanied by a Roman equestrian named Coponius, who was to take over as procurator in Judea. Coponius was given specific authority to inflict capital punishment as needed. Quirinius was to take account of Archelaus' enormous estate and to conduct a census of the populace for taxation purposes.

Judea was far from pacified. A fiery figure known as Judas the Galilean incited a full-scale revolt, taking advantage of the change in administration. He urged his fellow countrymen to refuse to pay the Roman taxes that would result from the annexation. Judas preached that God was the only master and that they should throw off the yoke of Roman rule. According to Josephus, Judas was the founder of the party of the Jews that took the name Zealot. Whether Judas was of Davidic lineage or thought of himself as a messiah or king we simply do not know. Josephus does not report his fate but Luke, our gospel writer, says in the 2nd volume of his Acts of the Apostles that "Judas perished and his followers were scattered" (Acts 5:37). Presumably they went back to Galilee, where they had sympathetic supporters who would hide them.

This revolt of Judas the Galilean was more significant than earlier attempts following the death of Herod because it had a larger political and religious goal. As bad as Herod the Great had been he was at least nominally "Jewish," and thus a native king, and when he died his territory was passed to his sons. Augustus intended to annex Judea and put it directly under Roman administration and taxation. Judas was not merely seeking personal power but he was the inaugurator of a movement—the Zealots—who had as their agenda the independence of the Jewish state. Their agenda was not only political but religious as well. The Zealots maintained that one could not separate the two. Israel was God's chosen people living in the Promised Land and governed by the Law of Moses or Torah. For Romans to be in charge of the Land of Israel was a travesty and affront to God.

Judas does seem to fit a certain "dynastic" pattern in that his sons, James and Simon, followed in his footsteps and were tried and crucified by the Roman procurator about a decade after the death of Jesus.[6]

The names are interesting—a Judas with sons named James and Simon. They are common names among Jews of the time but particularly popular in Galilee among families that identified with efforts to declare Jewish independence from foreign rule. These names came from the Maccabean family that had successfully thrown out the Greeks in the 2nd century B.C. It was likely no random choice that Mary, mother of Jesus, used three of these very names—James, Simon, and Judas—for her own sons, or that Simon gets the nickname "the Zealot." Jesus was ten years old at the time of Judas' revolt and one can only assume that the local Galilean populace avidly followed the news about it. It seems likely that Mary chose these names as a way of honoring and showing solidarity with the cause that Judas the Galilean espoused—the cause for which three of her five sons were to die brutal deaths, Jesus and Simon by crucifixion and James by stoning.

THE MAN TO WHOM JESUS
REFUSED TO SPEAK

Herod Antipas, ruler of Galilee, was only sixteen years old when he came to power at his father's death. This is the Herod who had John the Baptizer executed and before whom Jesus appeared the morning of his crucifixion. Like his father, his lifelong desire was to be King of the Jews. While still in Rome he had appealed to the Emperor Augustus to make him the primary heir over his brothers and give him the title of "King." He was the most ambitious of the three and to be given Galilee rather than Judea with its capital Jerusalem was a disappointment to him.

Herod the Great had neglected Galilee and concentrated his vast building projects in Jerusalem, at Caesarea on the coast, and in Samaria. Galilee was mainly populated by a network of hundreds of small towns and hilltop villages, such as Nazareth, Cana, and Nain, all mentioned in our New Testament gospels. The basis of the economy was agricultural, with a thriving fishing industry on the Sea of Galilee. The Galileans were considered backward by Roman standards and they were known for a fierce spirit of independence. Herod Antipas had grown up in Rome as the proverbial "pampered prince" and quite possibly had never even visited Galilee before he began to rule.

Herod Antipas' first order of business was to create his magnificent capital city at Sepphoris. His dream was to build a modern Roman urban center, complete with forum, markets, theater, public buildings, armory, and of course his own palace at the center of rural Galilee, which had never seen the likes of such splendor. It would function as the governmental, marketing, and military center of his kingdom. He had his eye on two things—trade and taxes. According to Josephus he was able to extract the value equivalent to two hundred talents of gold (nine tons) annually from his subjects.[7] And this was at the beginning of his long forty-two-year reign. Historians estimate that Herod extracted as much as one-third of the produce of his territory. It is no wonder that the New Testament gospels mention tax collecting and tax collectors so frequently and with such invective.

In A.D. 14 the Roman emperor Augustus died and was succeeded by his adopted son Tiberius. Jesus would have been twenty years old. Herod Antipas saw his chance to consolidate and increase his power. He began to mint his own coins with a palm branch stamped on one side and a Roman laurel-wreath crown on the other. Around A.D. 19 he began the construction of a new Roman-style capital city on the western shores of

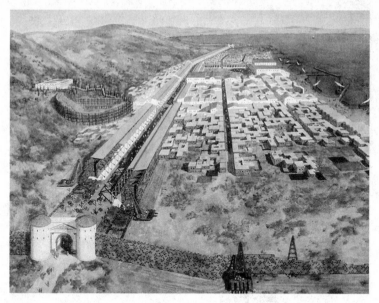

Ancient Tiberias in the time of Jesus

the Sea of Galilee, declaring the year of its founding as the beginning of a new era. Appropriately he named it Tiberias in honor of the new emperor. He was following in his father's footsteps. By placing his capital in the midst of the heavy commerce around the Sea of Galilee, and forging closer links with his eastern territory of Perea, he hoped to advance his prestige and influence.

Tiberias is a thriving Jewish city in Israel today, but portions of the ancient capital have only just recently been excavated. What is emerging is truly astonishing. A monumental gate has been uncovered at the southern edge of the city. The remains of a theater, every bit as impressive as the ones at Caesarea and Sepphoris, have also been discovered. Remnants of streets and markets are being revealed. We know there was a large palace nestled in the hillside to the west, overlooking the lovely Sea of Galilee. The city was so dominant in the area that it became common to refer to the Sea of Galilee as the "Sea of Tiberias."[8] In fact Herod Antipas wanted his new capital on the sea to be a "mini" Caesarea. What both Sepphoris and the new Tiberias lacked, due to Jewish sensibilities to which Antipas gave weight, were temples or shrines to Roman gods or to the emperor. After all, Herod Antipas had messianic aspirations—he wanted to be King of the Jews.

Like his father, Herod Antipas wanted to marry a Maccabean princess in an attempt to increase his favor with the people by having some type of "royal" connection. His mother, Malthace, was a Samaritan. With Judea now under Roman military rule and his half-brother Philip decidedly weaker in territory and aspirations, he decided to act. Philip's wife, Herodias, was of the royal Hashmonean line. Herod boldly proposed marriage to her in the palace at Caesarea as he was starting on a journey to Rome to visit Emperor Tiberius. Herodias immediately accepted, recognizing her chance to be free of Herod's weaker son and ally herself with Antipas. Upon his return from Rome they were married. We don't know the exact year this took place but this adulterous relationship must have been the talk of all Galilee. The marriage was destined to play a critical role in the careers of both John the Baptizer and his kinsman Jesus.

The economic impact of Herod's move to Tiberias must have been considerable. The Sea of Galilee was already a thriving hub of trade and commerce. The coastal town of Magdala, just to the north, home of Mary Magdalene ("Mary of Magdala"), exported its famous "salt-fish" throughout the Roman world. Further north was the town of Capernaum, which Jesus later made his operational headquarters.

Jesus watched Sepphoris rise to its splendor in his teenage years and witnessed the founding of the great city of Tiberias into his twenties. He grew up in the shadow of one city and set up his headquarters a few miles north of the other. Neither city is mentioned in our New Testament gospels—not a single story was passed on about anything Jesus ever did in either. As far as the New Testament records are concerned these cities did not exist. What are we to make of this silence?

As we shall see, Jesus held Herod Antipas and all he stood for in utter contempt. He sarcastically spoke of those who dress in fine soft robes and live in luxury in royal palaces. He once referred to Herod directly as "that fox" and when Herod questioned him the very morning he was condemned to crucifixion he refused even to open his mouth in reply. It was Herod who had brutally murdered his kinsman and teacher John the

Baptizer, and Jesus had witnessed firsthand how Herod's aspirations for wealth and power had unjustly oppressed the lives of his countrymen.

I don't think there is much doubt that Jesus walked the streets and marketplaces of both Sepphoris and Tiberias many times. He was thoroughly exposed to the urban Roman culture that Herod imported into Galilee. He surely saw it all. By the time he was thirty years old he had begun to formulate a plan that he believed would lead to the complete overthrow of all that Rome and its Jewish sympathizers and supporters represented, including the corrupt religious establishment that ran the Temple in Jerusalem. What he envisioned he found written in the sacred texts of the Hebrew Prophets. The time had arrived—the kingdoms of the world were about to become the Kingdom of God and of his Messiahs.

7

THE RELIGION OF
JESUS THE JEW

JESUS was a Jew, not a Christian. This single historical fact opens the door to understanding Jesus as he really was in his own time and place; it's a door that many have never thought to enter. Jesus was circumcised, observed Passover, read the Bible in Hebrew, and kept Saturday as the Sabbath day. Two thousand years of relatively hostile separation and alienation between Judaism and Christianity has tended to obscure the fact that Jesus grew up in a religious and cultural world that has been almost wholly lost to the subsequent developments of Christianity.

To understand Jesus in his own time and place we have to understand his deep commitment to the ancestral faith of his fathers. He saw himself as doing nothing other than fulfilling the words of Moses and the Prophets, and the messianic hope that guided his life, and led him to his death, was the central core of his innermost being.

In one sense this book is about the religion of Jesus the Jew—that is, what he believed, how he lived, his vision of God's will in the world, and what led to his execution by the Romans. But in this chapter I want to try to shed light on what we can know about Jesus growing up as a Jew in 1st-century Galilee.

So the question arises—just how Jewish was Jesus, and given the varieties of Judaism in his time, what kind of Jew was he? One tendency among scholars of the last century, now largely discarded, was the attempt to strip him and his message of its Jewish contexts. The idea was that Jesus, though born a Jew, realized the deficiencies of his obsolete ancestral faith and moved beyond it into a type of "universalism." Jesus, according to this view, proclaimed the Fatherhood of God and the brotherhood of humankind with a set of universal ethics that superseded the legalistic ways of Judaism. Judaism was seen as a fossilized precursor of the final revelation that Jesus brought to the world. We now understand that such views have no historical basis and in fact are subtle manifestations of Christian anti-Semitism. Yet they have become deeply etched into our Western cultural consciousness.

To be a Jew in 1st-century Roman-occupied Palestine had as much to do with national and ethnic identity as with abstract religious beliefs. To put it another way, for many Jews it was impossible to separate the social and political realities of military occupation and economic oppression from Jewish piety and faith. The Jewish belief that the people of Israel had been chosen by God to become a "model nation" that would exemplify justice and righteousness to the entire world was fundamental. The Hebrew Prophets had predicted that in the last days all nations would go up to Jerusalem to learn about the one true Creator God, irresistibly drawn by Israel's moral example of peace and justice. Not all Jews accepted such an idealistic vision but enough did that John the Baptizer, Jesus, and his brother James were able to spark a movement that threatened the highest levels of the political and religious establishment.

Jesus' family, like all Galilean Jews, would have made the pilgrimage trek south to Jerusalem as required by the Torah three times a year, every year, in the spring at Passover, in the early summer for the feast of Pentecost, and in the fall for the feast of Tabernacles. At Passover, in particular, Josephus claims that as many as two and a half *million* Jews, from Palestine and all over the world, gathered in Jerusalem.[1] It was there that Jesus regularly encountered the most poignant symbols of Roman power fused with what he considered the epitome of Jewish religious corruption. Herodian Jerusalem with its palaces, theater, hippodrome, luxurious mansions, and magnificent Temple might be viewed as a wonder of the world by many, but to Jesus and thousands of others it was a "den of thieves" soon to come under God's judgment. It is no accident that Jesus at age thirty-three deliberately chose Jerusalem at Passover as the setting for his most dramatic confrontation with what he called the "powers of darkness." We have to imagine that his perceptions are deeply rooted in his experiences growing up. Sepphoris and Jerusalem—the two chief representations of Roman oppression and religious corruption—were absolutely fundamental to how he viewed his calling and his destiny.

GROWING UP JEWISH IN NAZARETH VILLAGE

Jesus grew up poor in a rural Jewish town in Galilee. The region was dotted with hundreds of such towns and villages populated by extended clans and family groups who farmed the adjacent land. Archaeology has shown that the houses were modest, made of fieldstones packed with mud and straw. The floors were beaten dirt, windows were few, the roofs were thatched reeds laid over wooden beams and covered with mud to form a flat rooftop area that was utilized year-round for sleeping, eating, and domestic chores. Houses often had underground chambers used for storage. Furniture was sparse and pottery was local and practical, almost wholly undecorated and unadorned. Absent were mosaics, imported ceramics, fine glassware, gold and silver coins, cosmetics, jewelry, and bronze vessels—all common in the urban areas of Sepphoris and Jerusalem. The larger houses might have a courtyard and several rooms and extended families living together; these houses often expanded into a haphazard network of shared structures. Livestock lived in enclosures attached to the houses or in dugout areas and caves, and small gardens were cultivated wherever space allowed. Staples were olives, bread, and lentils. Eggs, milk, cheese, salted fish, meat, fruits and vegetables were welcome additions. Skeletal remains show evidence of dietary deficiencies, and death from disease before age forty was not uncommon.

One can get a sense of things as they were in that time by visiting the Nazareth Village archaeology project in the modern city of Nazareth. It is much like a Colonial Williamsburg of Jewish village life in the time of

Jesus. Archaeologists and historians are in the process of meticulously re-constructing a replica of 1st-century Nazareth built entirely with meth-ods and materials used during that time. They are also attempting to reproduce the ancient methods of farming, raising livestock, and domes-tic crafts as authentically as possible. Visiting Nazareth, one cannot help but be impressed with the expertise that has gone into the effort. But much is missing—the noise, the stench, the crowding, the grime and grit of daily peasant life, the feel of living under military occupation, and of course Herod's virtual army of ever watchful inspectors, agents, and tax collectors.

All the archaeological evidence from rural Galilee points to a typical peasant life—but it was a *Jewish* peasant life. Stone vessels, required for purposes of ritual purity, are typically found, as well as plastered pools or *mikvahs* used for ritual immersion. The bones that turn up are from goats, sheep, chickens, and some cattle, but no pigs. Tombs were outside the living area, expanded from natural caves or cut into the bedrock. As described in the Introduction, the corpse was laid out in a shaft or *loculus*

The village of Nazareth in the time of Jesus

to decompose and after a year the bones were gathered and placed in an ossuary or separate niche. The Roman preference for cremation was shunned, probably because of belief in resurrection of the dead.

The center of civic and religious life in a Jewish village was the synagogue. At least two 1st-century synagogues have been found—one at Gamla on the east side of the Sea of Galilee, the other at the desert fortress of Masada, and so we have some idea of what they looked like. Gatherings were held on the Sabbath day when the normal work activities of the whole town came to an abrupt halt from Friday at sunset until dusk on Saturday. Precious handwritten copies of the Torah, or Jewish Law, and the books of the Prophets were read aloud and discussed. Aramaic was the spoken language but judging from the Dead Sea Scrolls the sacred books were written in ancient Hebrew. Luke relates that Jesus at age thirty returned to his hometown Nazareth, entered the synagogue "as was his custom," and stood up to read aloud from the scroll of Isaiah (Luke 4:16). He then sat down and began to address those who had gathered, offering his interpretation of the text he had read. One assumes there were prayers, chants, and ceremonies tied to special occasions but

James Tabor in front of a Dead Sea Scrolls cave

the central activity appears to have been the reading and discussion of the Scriptures.

Among the Dead Sea Scrolls was a complete copy of the book of Isaiah that scholars have dated to 100 B.C.; thus we know precisely what a biblical scroll looked like in Jesus' time. It had been hidden for two thousand years sealed in a clay jar in a cave near the settlement of Qumran. The Isaiah scroll has fifty-four columns of Hebrew text. It is twenty-four feet long and made of seventeen panels of goatskin, ten inches high, sewn together. It was rolled from right to left and one would need to put it on a table or podium in order to hold it steady for unrolling or reading. The Great Isaiah Scroll, as it is called, is arguably the single most amazing discovery in the history of biblical archaeology. When it was found, everyone, including the scholars, found it hard to believe that it could be that old. Prior to the Dead Sea Scrolls the oldest copies of books of the Hebrew Bible dated to the 9th century A.D.

How much Jesus spoke and how much he listened in these adult gatherings growing up we have no way of knowing, but from a young age he must have begun to absorb the variety of ideas and conflicting opinions

The Dead Sea Scroll copy of Isaiah open to chapter 40

that were expressed. Judging from the oral Jewish tradition that eventually was written down in the Mishnah, as well as from the texts of the Dead Sea Scrolls and evidence in the gospels, the range of topics was endless.[2] What activities were forbidden and allowed on the Sabbath? Should one pay taxes? How was the Jewish calendar to be determined—by the cycles of the moon or the sun or both? To whom should tithes be paid? Were none, some, or all of the dead to be raised at the end of the age? For what cause could one divorce his wife? How was ritual impurity transmitted and what was required for purification? When and how were the various messiah figures to appear? Was marriage to a niece allowed? What dealings might one have with non-Jews? Was it permitted to charge interest on loans? Was the kingdom of God to manifest itself in a literal way on earth or only after death in the heavenly world? Would the scattered or "lost tribes" of Israel return to the Land in the days of the messiahs? And then there were the stories, the endless stories of Abraham, Isaac, Jacob, Joseph, Moses, King David, and all the prophets that were told and retold from Scripture and legend to entertain, admonish, and educate.

Judging from our sources there was no systematic treatment of these and a hundred other subjects related to the core beliefs of Judaism. What characterized Jewish life, even peasant Jewish life, was this endless ongoing discussion and debate of the meaning and implication of the stories, commandments, and teachings of the Torah and the Prophets. One can assume a level of literacy and intellectual engagement that might not normally exist among the lower classes and the poor. Jews were a people of "the Book," and as the Romans were to learn, that made them different from any other people over whom they ruled.

Judaism can be summed up under four rubrics: God, Torah, Land, and Chosen People. As a Jew, Jesus would have affirmed his belief in the one Creator God Yahweh above all other gods or spiritual entities; the divine revelation of the Torah as a blueprint for social, moral, and religious life; the holiness of the Land of Israel as a perpetual birthright to the nation; and the notion that the people of Israel, descendants of Abraham, Isaac, and Jacob, had been chosen by God to enlighten all nations. Their historic mission was to draw humanity to the one God and his Torah revelation. As a Jew, Jesus was circumcised at the Jewish Temple in Jerusalem at eight days old, he observed the Sabbath as a weekly day of rest, he avoided eating certain forbidden animals or consuming blood, he celebrated the required pilgrim festivals, and he practiced ritual purity as commanded in the Torah. As a Jewish male Jesus wore the fringed tassels (*tzitzit*) on his outer garment, which indicates his strict observance of the *mitzvoth* or commandments of the Torah or Jewish Law.[3] In that sense he is not "liberal" with regard to Jewish observances in any modern sense of the term. What he did not accept, as we shall see, were certain oral traditions and interpretations that some rabbinic teachers had added to the biblical commandments.

There is a sense in which Judaism is both exclusive and universal. These "marks" of being Jewish can be seen as social "separators," and they were well known in Roman society. We find Roman writers who attack the Jews and hold them in contempt, but also those who admire them and even adopt some of their ways.[4] There is substantial evidence that significant numbers of non-Jews were attracted to Judaism and even attended synagogues throughout the Roman world. To do this it was not required that one formally convert and become Jewish, although that could be done. Gentiles who turned from "idols" to the "true and living God" and observed the prohibitions against stealing, murder, and sexual immorality were considered "righteous Gentiles" or "Godfearers." Various Jewish groups differed radically in attitudes toward non-Jews ranging from exclusion and separation to welcoming accommodation.

I think it is safe to assume that the tiny village of Nazareth had few if any Gentile residents though in nearby Sepphoris one might daily rub shoulders with non-Jews. Jesus appears to have been accommodating toward outsiders, and one might assume this had come from his experience growing up. He was neither provincial nor separatist in his attitudes. He seemed to detest the Roman establishment and its Jewish collaborators while at the same time welcoming *individuals* whom he judged to be spiritually worthy. If his biological father was Roman, or became Roman, that might further explain his openness.

If in fact Nazareth was a village that got its name because of its concentration of clans or families that could claim ancestry from the royal lineage of King David, one has to wonder what this might imply about Jesus growing up there. When he returned home as an adult, having achieved some reputation through his activities of preaching and healing, the townsfolk on the whole seem to have scoffed at the idea that Jesus had some special prophetic role. His famous quip "prophets are not without honor except in their hometown, and among their own kin, and in their own house" might well indicate a certain social isolation he experienced even growing up. His honorable Davidic pedigree through his mother was likely disparaged by the locals who knew the stories of his illegitimate birth, not to mention his lack of economic status as a *tekton*. Even in his "own house" it seems that Jesus might well have drawn a skeptical reaction as he came to believe that he was chosen by God and destined for the throne of Israel. Davidic lineage was one thing but inaugurating a specific program of implementation quite another. It was every bit as foolish as it was dangerous.

Beyond these general observations regarding village life in a town such as Nazareth, is there anything more we might be able to say in trying to address the question of what kind of Jew Jesus was? Was he a "card-carrying" member of any of the Jewish groups of his day?

PIGEONHOLING JESUS

Josephus, our contemporary 1st-century Jewish witness, tells us that there were three main sects or "philosophies" of Judaism: Pharisees, Sadducees, and Essenes.[5] At one point he explains there was a "fourth philosophy" founded by Judas the Galilean, followed by the so-called Zealots, but he says in their religious views they were much like the Pharisees. He writes that he belongs to the Pharisees though in his younger years he might have spent time with the Essenes.

Josephus wrote for a sophisticated Roman audience and intends to present his fellow countrymen in the best possible light. When the great Jewish Revolt against the Romans broke out in A.D. 66, Josephus, who was only about thirty years old, served as the military leader of the Jewish forces in Galilee. He soon realized the hopelessness of the struggle and surrendered to the Romans. The Roman general Vespasian and his son

Titus, who were conducting the campaign in Palestine, befriended him. Vespasian became emperor in A.D. 69. Josephus ended up living in Rome, became a Roman citizen, received an imperial pension, and wrote his memoirs in a former palace of Vespasian. By then Jerusalem lay in ruins and Jewish forces had been utterly devastated. Josephus wanted to rehabilitate the reputation of his people. He presented the Jews as an ancient nation with honorable traditions and laws. He blamed the revolt on misguided fanaticism and fratricidal jealousies among a minority of the people. When he described the four religious sects of Judaism he purposely called them "philosophies." Josephus's "sects" of Judaism are very much kin to the philosophical "schools" of the Greek world, whether Platonic, Stoic, Pythagorean, or Epicurean. The impression Josephus wanted to give was that the Jewish people, far from being a backward or rebellious element of Roman society, were an ancient race with venerable traditions and respectable schools of religious thought. He even described the beliefs of the three main schools in such a way that his educated readers would equate the Sadducees with the Epicureans, the Pharisees with the Stoics, and the Essenes with the Platonists or perhaps the Pythagoreans. Given his apologetic purposes we have to use what he says with great care.

He briefly characterized the Pharisees and Sadducees in a few lines, mainly contrasting their views on "fate" and the "afterlife." He said that the Pharisees emphasized that God was in control of all things and that they believed in life after death and the eternal judgment of departed souls. The Sadducees, on the other hand, denied an "afterlife" and put their emphasis on life in this world. They did not believe that God controls everything but believed that humans freely choose either good or evil and are rewarded accordingly. Josephus claimed that the Pharisees were much more popular with the people and were integrated into local communities, while the Sadducees were elite and aristocratic.

Josephus's basic description fits with what we know from the New Testament and from later Jewish sources. The Sadducees were mostly drawn from the priestly classes. The high priest, endorsed by Roman political appointment, was chosen from their ranks. Accordingly they exercised the main control of the Jerusalem Temple that was the primary focal point of Judaism worldwide, and they held sway over the Sanhedrin, a type of Jewish "council" or "senate" that the Romans allowed a certain limited rule. The Sadducean interpretation of the Jewish Law tended to be stricter and more rigid than that of the Pharisees and their concentration on "this world" rather than a "world to come" contributed to their skepticism about subjects related to the heavenly world, whether angels, demons, resurrection of the dead, or events associated with the end of the age. The Pharisees, on the other hand, freely indulged in speculations about such matters. Their interpretation of the Jewish Law was more liberal and accommodating to change. Although there was a more rigidly conservative wing of the Pharisees led by the 1st-century Rabbi Shammai, his rival Rabbi Hillel seemed to have the greater influence. It is common to think of Jesus as the bitter enemy of *all* Pharisees when in fact many of his views on Jewish Law reflect the more accommodating positions of Rabbi Hillel. Hillel and Jesus both emphasized "love of neighbor" as primary and quoted the "Golden Rule" as a thumbnail summary of the Torah and Prophets. But in the end it was a coalition of Sadducean priests and their supporters among the Pharisees who delivered Jesus to the Roman governor Pontius Pilate.

In contrast to his brief sketch of Pharisees and Sadducees, Josephus devoted many pages to an elaborate and detailed description of the Essenes, with whom he was evidently sympathetic. However, it appears that he purposely left out anything regarding their radical apocalyptic expectations, which would certainly not be admired by the Romans after the Jewish Revolt. As we have previously seen, the Essenes who wrote the Dead Sea Scrolls expected the end of the world and were awaiting the coming of Two Messiahs—a priestly figure and a Davidic King. They were intensely anti-Roman and detested the Jewish religious establishment in Jerusalem, whether Pharisee or Sadducee, as hopelessly compromised and corrupt. The Essenes called themselves the people of the "New Covenant," believing they were representatives of a newly purified Israel at the end of the age. They practiced communal living, initiation rites involving immersion or baptism, and sacred meals. Curiously, the Essenes are never mentioned in the New Testament, whereas the Pharisees and Sadducees regularly appear in opposition to Jesus. Jesus shared some important beliefs and practices with the Essenes but judging from the Dead Sea Scrolls he would have been roundly condemned and despised by their core leadership for his open attitude toward Gentiles and women, and his stance on Sabbath observance and ritual purity, which was considerably less strict than theirs. But what we should not assume is that all those who were Essenes, or even those more loosely affiliated with their ways of thinking, would have shared their rigid interpretations of the Jewish Law.

Judaism in 1st-century Roman Palestine was incredibly diverse. The problem with Josephus's categories is that one might get the impression that most Jews were somehow formally affiliated with one of these main groups. It is easy for us to think of them as akin to modern religious denominations like Baptist or Catholic or Reform Judaism. We know such is not the case. Estimates of the Jewish population of Palestine vary widely among the experts but they range from one to three million. Josephus tells that there were only 6,000 Pharisees and 3,000 Essenes. Philo, another 1st-century Jewish writer, puts the Essenes at 4,000. They represent broad categories of religious thought or philosophy that only a handful of the elite or learned might take on as formal labels. And each group, as would be expected, had a complex history and a range of views from liberal to conservative. Even though many have attempted to place Jesus in one or the other of these "schools" of Judaism such categorization is questionable. Jesus would have grown up familiar with each of these schools. It is unlikely that many Sadducees lived in Nazareth but it is probable that both Pharisees and Essenes were around. Josephus says the Essenes settled in every town and that the Pharisees were the most influential with the local populations. The gospels seem to indicate that Pharisees who lived locally in Galilee were widely dispersed and Jesus encounters them frequently.

The movement Jesus eventually forged had attractions for those who identified with any of these philosophies of Judaism. Jesus' younger brother was known as Simon the Zealot. He became part of the inner Council of Twelve Apostles. And in the end the Romans crucified Jesus for sedition—his claim to be the rightful King of the Jews. As such he joins a cast of Zealot types from Judas the Galilean to Bar Kochba, a final "messiah" the Romans crushed in A.D. 135. Jesus had his share of sympathizers even among the Pharisees. In fact, two members of that council were influential enough with Pontius Pilate, the Roman governor of Judea, that Jesus' corpse was released into their care for burial. Eventually, under the thirty-three-year dynastic reign of Jesus' brother James, large numbers of Pharisees identified with the movement that John the Baptizer and Jesus had inaugurated.[6] As surprising as it sounds to modern ears there were in fact Nazarene or "Christian Pharisees"—and lots of them. We also learn from Luke that "large numbers" of Sadducean priests in Jerusalem became part of the movement even though Jesus seems to have the least in common with the Sadducees (Acts 6:7). And James the brother of Jesus begins to exercise certain priestly messianic functions with their permission and support. Even though the Essenes had a much more rigid interpretation of the Torah than Jesus, there were surely some who must have identified with the apocalyptic excitement that John the Baptizer and Jesus began to ignite all over the country.

In broad terms, Jesus is best identified with what might be described as the Messianic Movement of 1st-century Palestine. It was intensely apocalyptic, and though sharing certain ideas with the Essenes, it had a much broader appeal to rank-and-file Jews of all persuasions, united in their hope for God's deliverance. When we grasp the history, core values, and mythological world of this movement we will be able to place Jesus properly within the incredible diversity of 1st-century Palestinian Judaism. There were Jews who were largely at home in their political and social world, accepting the status quo, even if dictated by Rome, and making the best of it. But there were others, whether Pharisees, Sadducees, or Essenes, or those of no affiliation at all, who expected a radical change based on the messianic predictions of the Hebrew Prophets. What matters are not so much the labels but a certain vision of reality—a faith that God would intervene to fulfill those messianic predictions. Jesus did not originate this movement; in fact it began to take shape two hundred years before he was even born. But it was Jesus, his kinsman John the Baptizer, and his brother James who gave it the definitive shape that changed the course of history. At some point before age thirty Jesus began to formulate his plan. There were doubtless stages along the way. But in the fall of the year A.D. 26 Jesus was ready to go public, and the Jesus dynasty began to emerge.

Part Three

A GREAT
REVIVAL AND A
GATHERING STORM

8

HEARING THE VOICE

SOMETIME in the spring or early summer of the year A.D. 26, John the Baptizer responded to the "Voice." He had just turned thirty years old.[1] He was a priest, a descendant of Aaron the brother of Moses of the tribe of Levi. According to the Torah the priests were to serve in the Temple from age thirty to age fifty (Numbers 4:3). There was no more honorable calling for an Israelite. John turned his back on it all and as far as we know, unlike his father Zechariah, he never served a day in Temple service. Instead, at age thirty, he retreated to the Judean desert east of Jerusalem, into the area where the Jordan River flows into the Dead Sea. It is twelve hundred feet below sea level, the lowest spot on earth.

John was captivated by a text from the prophet Isaiah: a voice cries out, "*Prepare the way* of Yahweh in the desert" (Isaiah 40:3). This he associated with another text, the last words of the last Hebrew prophet, Malachi, who wrote, "I am sending my messenger to *prepare the way* before me" (Malachi 3:1). At some point in his life John began to understand his own role as that messenger, that is, the one who would respond to the "voice" and literally go out into the Judean desert to *prepare the Way*. Indeed, one of the Hebrew words that Isaiah used for "desert" was *Aravah*— a geographical term still used in Israel today for the area by the Dead Sea

Ancient Roman road in the Judean desert toward the Dead Sea

in the Jordan River Valley. This was to be the staging ground for the Apocalypse, and John purposely stationed himself in that specific area to inaugurate what he believed was his God-sent role and task.

Christians later read this as preparing the way for Christ but the texts say nothing about a Messiah. John, like other Jews of his day, understood it as a call to prepare *the people* of Israel, turning them from their sins and toward the righteous way of God. The early followers of John and Jesus referred to themselves as the "people of the Way" even before terms like "Nazarene" or "Christian" were used.[2]

John proclaimed to the crowds that came to hear him that "the ax was even *now* at the root of the tree," implying the imminence of God's apocalyptic judgment on all unrighteousness from the highest to the lowest levels of society. He preached that people should repent of their sins and be "baptized" or immersed in water for the remission of their sins. By such a response they would become "people of the Way."

Josephus has a short but significant treatment of "John surnamed the Baptizer."[3] He writes that John urged the people to lead righteous lives and practice justice toward their fellow men and devotion to God, signifying such by immersion or baptism in water. He says the crowds were "overjoyed" at John's appearance, and that his effect on the populace was such that the massive crowds he attracted began looking to him for guidance and were ready to do anything he said.

John was not the first to hear this Voice and respond in this way. A hundred years earlier, the Jews we know by the name Essene, read that same verse in Isaiah and literally *moved* to live in the Judean desert out by the Dead Sea in a little settlement called Qumran, where they wrote the Dead Sea Scrolls. In their founding document, called the *Community Rule*, they record that they had "separated from the habitation of unjust men" and had gone into the desert to prepare there the Way of Him, as it is written "Prepare in the wilderness the Way." They further declared, "This is the time for the preparation of the Way in the wilderness."[4] They too referred to themselves as the "people of the Way."

In A.D. 26, when John began his public preaching, this Qumran settlement was still thriving. It might well be that John had spent time with them. John and the Essenes had many things in common. But there was a

Aerial view of the excavated ruins of the Qumran settlement

fundamental difference between their movement and the one John sought to inaugurate. They saw themselves as a segregated group that would achieve righteousness by their strict separation from society. In contrast, rather than separate from society, John addressed the entire nation of Israel with a clarion call to repent and an apocalyptic warning of God's impending judgment. He began to see himself in the role of the ancient prophet Elijah, who had rebuked even the king and queen of Israel—Ahab and Jezebel—to their faces.

Herod Antipas became quite alarmed at the revolutionary potential that John represented. It is difficult to overestimate the dramatic impact John created by his preaching. Initially he based himself in the south, in the Judean wilderness, along the Jordan just north of the Dead Sea. Mark tells us that the whole country of Judea and all the people of Jerusalem flocked out to the desert to hear his preaching. Josephus tells us he was popular, bold, and eloquent. This is what so many had been waiting for. John's message was a radical one, similar to others who had sought to inspire a revolt among the Jewish population, but there was something different about him, something that went beyond the political. John had the appearance and style of an ancient biblical Prophet. The populace was electrified at the possibility—had God at long last sent a true messenger who would inaugurate the New Age of the Kingdom of Israel?

As the summer passed and fall arrived, John moved north along the Jordan and finally stationed himself just south of the Sea of Galilee at a place called Aenon near the settlement of Salim. We find this important bit of information only in the gospel of John, who often records details of both chronology and geography that become vital missing pieces of our story.[5] It was a strategic location for two reasons. First, this area was associated with Elijah the prophet. Elijah's birthplace, Tishbe, was just a few miles across the Jordan River to the east along the "brook Cherith." This is the famous Wadi Cherith (called Wadi el-Yabis today) where Elijah hid from Ahab and Jezebel and was fed by the ravens. But just as important, the spot John chose lay at the intersection of the Valley of Jezreel and the Jordan River. This was the route the entire country of Galilee used in traveling south to Judea for the upcoming fall holidays—Rosh HaShanah, Yom Kippur, and the feast of Sukkoth or Tabernacles. John literally stood at the crossroads of a national thoroughfare.

Jesus near his thirtieth birthday joined the crowds that were streaming out to hear John. He traveled from Nazareth down to the Jordan, along this very route, to be baptized by John in the Jordan River (Mark 1:9). By such a response he was publicly joining and endorsing the revival movement John had sparked. As he was coming up out of the water he too heard the Voice, also from Isaiah, but a different text about a different figure: "Look! My servant whom I uphold, my chosen one in whom my soul delights!" (Isaiah 42:1). Matthew turned this "voice" into a public announcement from heaven—"*This is* my beloved son in whom I am well pleased," while Mark, preserving an earlier, likely more authentic tradition, knows this as a voice that *Jesus heard*—not one the crowds heard (Matthew 3:17; Mark 1:11). It is significant that the Old Syriac version of Matthew still preserves the original reading: "You are my son my beloved in whom I have been pleased," further attesting to Mark's authenticity.[6] We cannot be certain of the precise nature of this revelation, and whether it is something that came suddenly to Jesus at that moment, or something for which he had prepared himself along the way. What we can say is that from the time of Jesus' baptism he was ready to take his destined place alongside John as a full partner in the baptizing movement. Together they were prepared to face whatever lay ahead in the prophetic roles to which each believed he was called.

THE "LOST YEARS" OF JOHN

John was no stranger to a life of solitude. He was born in A.D. 5 in the little village of Ein Kerem, a few miles west of Jerusalem. Luke offers a one-sentence summary of John's first thirty years: "The child grew and became strong in spirit, and he was in the desert places until the day he appeared publicly to Israel" (Luke 1:80). Luke refers to this area as the "hill country" of Judea. It is rugged, mountainous, and desolate, with scattered villages and a stark terrain. Even driving west of Jerusalem today on the modern roads the hairpin turns can make one dizzy.

As I mentioned in the Introduction, in December 1999, archaeologist Shimon Gibson discovered a cave a few miles west of Ein Kerem at a place called Suba that had primitive drawings of John the Baptizer etched into its walls.[7] It turned out to be an enormous plastered water

The excavated entrance to the Suba cave

reservoir cut out of solid bedrock in the time of Isaiah (8th century B.C.). It is seventy-eight feet long by thirteen feet wide by sixteen feet deep with an entranceway and twelve plastered steps leading inside. It was almost completely filled with soil and rocks when it was discovered. One had to crawl on hands and knees to enter or move around inside. The steps were completely hidden. The drawings near the ceiling on the sides of two of the walls were barely visible, partly covered with the debris.

Gibson invited me to join him in excavating the site in March 2000. It has taken us nearly five years to complete our initial work. We were quite excited at what we might find since we knew this was the desert area in which John had grown up. As far as we could tell, these drawings were likely the oldest artwork ever found related to his life. One showed a figure standing with right hand raised in proclamation, left hand holding a staff, wearing a skin garment. Another showed a bodiless head. A third showed a platter with a sword across it. Finally there were three crosses. Even before excavating we were convinced that early Christian pilgrims had come to this cave to somehow remember and commemorate the life and death of John and Jesus. The drawings seemed to suggest a narration of the story. Nothing like this had ever been found anywhere in the world—and it was right in the area where John grew up.

We began to excavate the front third of the cave, layer by layer, and to our utter surprise we found we were not digging through haphazardly washed-in debris and fill but carefully built up archaeological layers, one after another. It was like a layered cake, taking one back in time through the Islamic, Crusader, Byzantine, and Roman periods. What we discovered was that the front of this cave had gone out of use as a water facility sometime in the early Roman period (1st century A.D.). Floors had built up over the centuries. People were coming into the front of the cave on dry ground, but then using the back, which sloped down and still filled with water from a shaft in the ceiling, presumably for ritual immersion. The layers from the Roman period were the deepest, as much as two meters, while the later layers were relatively shallow. This indicated that the main activity in the cave responsible for the building up of these

The John the Baptizer drawing carved on the wall of the Suba cave

floors had taken place during the 1st and 2nd centuries A.D.

I will never forget the excitement the day we reached the early Roman layers—the period of John and Jesus. We found thousands of fragments of small handheld water vessels that had accumulated on the floors. They had been purposely broken. I realize this sounds odd, and often at a site one finds whole or partially whole vessels. It was possible to tell by the kind of breaks in these jugs, and the way in which they were shattered, that such an accumulation could not have resulted from normal breakage.

We also found a carved rock with a perfectly shaped depression for a right foot with a little trough and basin above it—clearly for pouring some liquid to anoint the foot. No one had been living in this cave. There was no evidence of cooking areas, olive pits, bones, or pottery of a domestic type. People were coming here, carrying out ceremonies involving the pouring water, the anointing of feet, and immersion in the pool toward the back. And this was happening, based on the dating of the pottery, in the early years of the 1st century A.D. The drawings were made later—

probably 5th century A.D. By that time Christians were making pilgrimage to the cave to remember John. By the time of the Crusades the cave was forgotten and the undifferentiated debris began to accumulate.

The question that intrigued us was, What was going on in the early 1st century A.D.? Had we perhaps stumbled onto the "Cave of John the Baptizer"? He grew up in this area and wandered the desolate hills around us at precisely the time that matched our evidence. And all the evidence

Reconstructed scene of the anointing ritual at the Suba cave

pointed to rites and ceremonies involving water purification. Water is scarce in the area, mainly confined to natural springs. There are no rivers or lakes and this was clearly the largest water reservoir in the entire area. Had our Suba cave served as a ritual center for groups of Jews, such as the Essenes, who practiced rites of initiation and spiritual purification involving immersion in water?

Since the discovery of this amazing site I have naturally wondered whether John the Baptizer himself might have come to this cave. Clearly, short of an inscription, which we did not find, that can never be proven. However, it is far from unlikely and may even be probable. As we've seen, John grew up in this very area. He lived a solitary and reclusive life in the "desolate places." John ended up inaugurating his public call to the nation of Israel to "repent and be immersed" in the Jordan River. But it makes sense to think that during his first thirty years of life, living in this very area, he would have had disciples and practiced ceremonies involving water purification. It is unlikely that his whole life's work started with no background or context whatsoever. Josephus says the Essenes practiced immersion in water on a daily basis. They also immersed candidates in water as an initiation ceremony into their group. Their communal stepped pools are one of the most obvious features of their settlement at Qumran. I am convinced that the Suba cave is our earliest archaeological evidence related to John the Baptizer—and very possibly to Jesus himself, as we shall see.[8]

There is no indication that John married or pursued a trade. He was a *Nazirite*—a "separated one" who let his hair and beard grow long, never drank wine, and wore a rough camel's hair garment with a leather belt. This lifestyle was based on instructions in the Torah involving a special vow of separation from society (Numbers 6). The term Nazirite is often confused with a similar word—*Nazarene*. They are different in Hebrew even though they seem close in English. The former refers to this vow of separation that one could undergo for spiritual purposes. The latter refers to the town of Nazareth, and means the town of the "branch," a term, as we have seen, that refers to the royal line of King David. The Jesus movement was early on referred to as the "Nazarenes," which roughly translates as "the Messianists" or the people of the "Branch." The term came from Isaiah 11, where the Davidic Messiah is referred to as a "branch" of David's lineage springing forth.

The Greek New Testament gospels say that John's diet consisted of "locusts and wild honey" but an ancient Hebrew version of Matthew insists that "locusts" is a mistake in Greek for a related Hebrew word that means a cake of some type, made from a desert plant, similar to the "manna" that the ancient Israelites ate in the desert in the days of Moses.[9] Jesus describes John as "neither eating nor drinking," or "neither eating bread nor drinking wine." Such phrases indicate the lifestyle of one who is strictly vegetarian, avoids even bread since it has to be processed from grain, and shuns all alcohol.[10] The idea is that one would eat only what grows naturally.[11] It was a way of avoiding all refinements of civilization. Given John's appearance, diet, and ascetic solitary life, one could not imagine a more countercultural figure. John's cultural opposite was Herod Antipas, who eventually had him arrested and beheaded. Jesus had contrasted John's lifestyle with those clothed in soft robes who live luxuriously in kings' palaces (Luke 7:25). The reference to Herod and his ilk is unmistakable.

NONE GREATER THAN JOHN

As the head of a large family, Jesus pursued a less isolated life, but since he and John were related through their mothers, and only six months apart in age, it is fair to assume that they knew each other growing up. The two families would have been in Jerusalem together several times a year for the major Jewish festivals, and it is entirely possible that Jesus had visited John in Judea, or John had visited Jesus growing up in Galilee. Jesus and John were no strangers. Indeed, there is some evidence that they began to formulate a plan together—a dramatic and bold strategy that they believed would bring the downfall of Roman rule in Palestine and lead to the worldwide inauguration of the Kingdom of God.

When it comes to understanding John the Baptizer and Jesus, as they understood each other, and as they would have been viewed in their contemporary Jewish society, the New Testament gospels are both our best source and our greatest obstacle. By the time the gospels of Mark, Matthew, Luke, and John were written (A.D. 70–100) there was an overt attempt by the Christians to downplay and marginalize John the Baptizer while extravagantly exalting the singular role of Jesus. There was no room for Two Messiahs. And for the same reason, James, the brother of Jesus who succeeded him, was largely written out of the history. Christians began to see Jesus as the one Lord and Christ with the combined roles of Prophet, Priest, and King. John was viewed positively, but only as a forerunner, who introduced Jesus to the world and then quickly faded from the scene.

The great embarrassment that the Christians faced was that it was well known that John had baptized Jesus—not the other way around! Jesus had come to John and *joined his movement*—which in the context of ancient Judaism meant that Jesus was a disciple of John and John was the rabbi or teacher of Jesus. For later Christians, who had exalted Jesus, this idea was inconceivable. We can document in the four New Testament gospels a progressive tendency to deal with this stubborn historical fact and its implications by playing down the importance of John without denying his role as a precursor of Jesus.

In Mark, our earliest account, Jesus comes to the Jordan to be baptized by John but John tells the people that one is coming more mighty than he, whose sandals he is not worthy to stoop down and untie (Mark 1:7). In Matthew, John tries to prevent Jesus from being baptized, insisting that instead Jesus should be baptizing him (Matthew 3:13). Luke mentions that Herod had John shut up in prison, then in the next verse writes "Now when all the people were baptized and when Jesus was baptized . . ." as if to imply that maybe John himself did not even baptize Jesus—*since he was already locked up* (Luke 3:19–21). Finally, in the gospel of John, the last account, John the Baptizer does not even baptize Jesus—it might be implied but it is not stated. Instead John sees Jesus and declares, "Behold the Lamb of God who takes away the sins of the world" (John 1:29). John later tells his disciples, speaking of Jesus, that "he must increase and I must decrease" (John 3:30). Although these accounts are heavily influenced by later Christian theology, they provide a basic witness to the fact that Jesus was baptized by John. Fortunately, other sources have survived that allow us to reach back through these layers of dogma and recover a lost perspective. It is truly an exciting endeavor.

Over one hundred and fifty years ago scholars in Germany identified the lost gospel Q.[12] Their discovery is an amazing bit of textual sleuthing. This "gospel" is called Q from the German word *Quelle* or "source." It was not found in a cave or buried in the ground but imbedded in the New Testament gospels of Matthew and Luke. It had been there all along, hidden away for centuries, but no one had noticed it. Mark wrote first and Matthew and Luke used Mark as their basic narrative source. But they both used another source too, a document we call Q that we no longer have. By extracting from Matthew and Luke the material that they both have in common, but that is not in Mark, we are able to reconstruct this lost source.[13] It turns out to be an early collection of the sayings and deeds of Jesus that even predates Mark. It has allowed us to go behind the gospels as they now stand, and peer through to an earlier time.

As one might expect, the Q source has a lot of material about John the Baptizer. Jesus asks the crowds concerning John, "What did you go out into the wilderness to see?" He rhetorically answers: "A prophet? Yes I tell you *more than* a prophet" (Luke 7:26). He then makes the startling statement: "I tell you among those born of women none is greater than John" (Luke 7:28). Since Jesus is clearly one "born of a woman," it is clear in the Q source that Jesus is declaring John to be greater than he. This statement was such a problem for later Christians that the qualifying phrase was added: "Yet the least in the kingdom is greater than he," referring to John—but this addition is clearly an interpolation. As the saying goes, it "protests too much." This is now confirmed by the publication of a Hebrew version of Matthew that offers a version of this Q saying that is untouched by the Greek copyists and editors.[14] There Jesus' astounding testimony to John's greatness stands unedited and unqualified: "Among those born of women there is none greater than John." Since Matthew was originally written in Hebrew it is possible that this important manuscript might be closer in certain ways to the original text. In this text of Hebrew Matthew, Jesus also says of John, "For all the prophets and the Law spoke *concerning* him" (Matthew 11:13). This appears in Greek translation as: "All the prophets and the Law spoke *until* him." It is a slight change but one with an enormous difference. Christians later viewed Jesus as the one of whom all the Scriptures spoke—not John. But the phrasing of Hebrew Matthew appears to be more original, that is, *all* the prophets spoke of the coming of John, which is quite a testimony to his status. Finally, in this Hebrew text of Matthew, Jesus says that John has been sent to "save the world" whereas our Greek Matthew has "restore all things" (Matthew 17:11). Later Christians would be bothered by any words of Jesus that might imply John was the "savior" rather than Jesus.

The reconstructed Q source also preserves for us a short but significant sample of John's preaching, where he tells the people, "He who has two coats, let him share with him who has none; and he who has food, let him do likewise" (Luke 3:11). Such a saying has become so characteristically associated with Jesus' teaching that few seem to notice that it originates with John. In the Q source Jesus' followers once asked him to "teach us to pray *as John taught* his disciples" and Jesus repeats to them the prayer that he had learned *from* his teacher John:

> *Father, let your name be holy,*
> *Let your kingdom come!*
> *Give us bread of the morrow*
> *And forgive us our sins*
> *As we forgive those who sin against us,*
> *And bring us not to the hour of trial.* (Luke 11:1–4)

Christians of course know by heart "The Lord's Prayer," in an expanded version that Matthew gives. But this one from Luke's Q source is the shorter, more original version that likely came to Jesus from his teacher John.

The message of Jesus so well known to Christians in the Sermon on the Mount shows evidence of being part of a message that John and Jesus both shared and preached. Jesus and John become full partners in the work to which they believed they were jointly called, but Jesus' deference to John is unmistakable in our sources once the veil of Christian theology is removed. According to Jesus, John is "more than a prophet," there is "none greater born among woman," and he is the one "of whom all the Torah and prophets spoke," who has come to "save the world." It is no accident that the following year of A.D. 27 is largely blank in our records. That was the year of the joint work of the Two Messiahs—now lost to Christian history and memory.

9

A CRUCIAL
MISSING YEAR

JOHN baptized Jesus in the fall of A.D. 26. In the gospels of Mark, Matthew, and Luke, the following year, A.D. 27, is entirely missing. This is hardly an accident. That John baptized Jesus at all was a problem for later Christians since it could be seen to put Jesus in a secondary role to John his teacher, of whom he speaks in such exalted language. Jesus' baptism was an undeniable historical fact that could not be removed from the record. But what then followed was even more of a problem.

Mark records that after Jesus' baptism he withdrew for forty days into the desert, where he was "tempted by Satan" (Mark 1:12–13). Matthew and Luke add that he was fasting during this time and supply details about his temptations. Mark then says, in the very next verse: "Now *after John was arrested* Jesus came to Galilee proclaiming the good news of the Kingdom of God" (Mark 1:14). Mark leaves the impression that hardly any time had passed—Jesus is baptized, he retreats to the desert for forty days, John is arrested, and Jesus begins his public work. With a stroke of his pen he has removed John from the scene, only to be mentioned again when his death is reported. He can now give his full attention to Jesus—front and center stage, leaving John behind as a mere precursor to the main act. Matthew and Luke follow his lead. Whether it was all they

The Jordan River near Salim where Jesus was baptized

knew or all they chose to tell, we can't really say. But we know this was hardly the whole story. What is missing here are scenes no Jesus movie ever includes and no Christian sermons ever mention. It is the gospel of John that provides us with clues.

JESUS THE BAPTIZER

John is our latest New Testament gospel and it contains a more exalted view of Jesus than Mark, Matthew, or Luke give. John's Jesus is the glorified preexistent Son of God sent from heaven as Savior of humankind. John gives no birth story, no temptation, no agony in the Garden of Gethsemane, no cry at the end asking why God has forsaken him. Jesus is victorious throughout, hardly human, and seems to barely "touch earth" before he is speaking of his return to heaven to be with his Father. As we have seen, the gospel of John does not even report the baptism of Jesus by John the Baptizer. Instead, the moment Jesus arrives at the Jordan River, John the Baptizer cries out—"Behold the Lamb of God who takes away the sins of the world," declaring Jesus to be the Son of God (John 1:29, 33). The gospel of John is the gospel of Christian theology *par excellence.* In fact John's gospel plays down the importance of John the Baptizer in the interest of exalting Jesus more than any of our other three New Testament gospels. So it is even more surprising that we would turn to John's gospel, of all places, to find this missing historical information. But such is the case. In the course of making his point of how much more important Jesus was than John the Baptizer, the writer tells us just enough to allow a plausible historical reconstruction of a period that would otherwise be totally lost to us.

Despite its exalting of Jesus, the gospel of John is built upon a narrative framework, with attention to details of geography and chronology that Mark, Matthew, and Luke lack. A hundred years ago it was fashionable to dismiss John's gospel entirely when it came to providing us with anything related to the "quest for the historical Jesus." Now that has changed. Many scholars believe that John provides us with important missing pieces of the story.[1] Indeed, it is possible that underpinning John's gospel is the testimony of an unnamed "disciple" who was credibly an eyewitness to the events of Jesus' life, and that this accounts for some of the missing details. That is in fact the claim made at the end of the book (John 21:24). If we do have imbedded in John such eyewitness testimony we are truly fortunate.

Luke claims to have consulted with eyewitnesses in writing his two-volume work, the gospel of Luke and Acts of the Apostles, but he himself witnessed nothing of the life of Jesus firsthand (Luke 1:2). He uses Mark and Q as his main sources, and he has gathered some of his own material. Even though the gospel of Matthew bears the name of the apostle Matthew, one of the Twelve, the work itself never makes such a claim. The association with Matthew's name is a later tradition. The fact is that we don't know who wrote Matthew but we are reasonably sure that the author was not an eyewitness and that his work is an edited version of Mark and the Q source with a bit of his own material. Mark is our earliest gospel but again, its association with Mark, who was said to be a companion of Paul and later Peter, is also a late tradition. We have no idea who wrote "Mark." And the same goes for the gospel of John. All these names are based on later Christian tradition, and although our New Testament gospels contain historical material, the theological editing is a factor that the discerning reader must constantly keep in mind.

If one leaves aside John's theological view of Jesus as "God in the flesh," and concentrates on his narrative details, a neglected picture begins to emerge. When Jesus first encountered John the Baptizer at the Jordan River, the gospel of John informs us, *four* individuals who end up being part of Jesus' inner Council of Twelve—namely Simon Peter, his brother Andrew, Philip, and Nathanael—were *already* disciples of John the Baptizer (John 1:35–49). We are subsequently told:

> After these things Jesus and his disciples went into the country of Judea and there he remained with them and *baptized*. And John was also baptizing in Aenon near Salim because there were pools of water there, and people kept coming and were baptized. John of course *had not yet been thrown into prison.* (John 3:22–24)

Notice it is Jesus who is baptizing here; John is still operating freely as well, and this is a full year before Mark picks up his story after John is arrested by Herod Antipas and thrown into prison. I don't think there has ever been a book, a movie, or a play that has presented Jesus the Baptizer. Yet here we have it.

This was nothing less than a joint baptizing campaign by John and Jesus, with John staying in the north, at the strategic crossroads of the territories of Galilee, Perea, and the Decapolis, and Jesus going south into the countryside of Judea. But there is much more.

Before inaugurating this campaign in the south, Jesus traveled back home to Galilee to participate in a wedding at the little village of Cana, just north of Sepphoris. Since his mother appears to have been in charge of the social arrangements we can assume one of his brothers, perhaps James the next eldest, was getting married, possibly to a girl from that village. Later John's gospel mentions in passing that Nathanael is from that very village of Cana (John 21:2). Jesus then took his entire household— his mother and his brothers—from Nazareth to the city of Capernaum, north of Tiberias on the northwest shore of the Sea of Galilee (John

21:2). It was the spring of A.D. 27 and the festival of Passover was approaching. The Capernaum connection is important here. Jesus definitely had something strategic in mind.

John's gospel says that the fishermen brothers Peter (Simon Peter) and Andrew, as well as Philip, were from Bethsaida, another village on the Sea of Galilee just to the east. They had gone down to join John the Baptizer near Salim on the Jordan River sometime before Jesus' baptism in the fall of A.D. 26. The year A.D. 26–27, stretching from fall to fall, was a Sabbatical year. According to the Torah, once every seven years all agricultural activity ceased and the land was allowed to "rest." The beginning of the Sabbatical year provided a crucial opportunity for their unfolding plan. Thousands of the peasants and villagers whose normal life was tied to the agricultural cycles of the seasons were largely free from their normal work. It was the right time to spark a movement among the masses.

The three of them had now joined up with Jesus. There was another family, Zebedee, his wife Salome, and their sons, James and John, who lived at Capernaum. Peter and Andrew knew them and had worked with them in the fishing business. We don't know if Mary Magdalene was part of the group at this time but she was from the fishing center of Magdala, just down the road south of Capernaum. At this point Jesus had assembled at least ten male disciples—Peter, Andrew, James, John, Nathanael, Philip, and likely his brothers James, Joseph, Simon, and Judas—who had come with him from Nazareth with his mother and sisters. Long before Mark picks up the story, Jesus already has the makings of his "Twelve" apostles in place.

All this we can glean from the gospel of John. None of it is mentioned in Mark, Matthew, and Luke. What Jesus was doing in the spring of A.D. 27 in Capernaum was consolidating a core band of followers for the upcoming campaign in Judea in the south. Rather than assuming some rift or break between Jesus and John the Baptizer, with Jesus "taking away" some of John's followers, what is more likely was that this was an orchestrated group plan. Jesus had become a full partner with John the Baptizer and their plan was to arouse the entire country and shake the establishment, both political and religious, during the coming summer and fall months of A.D. 27. The timing of this campaign was significant on more than just a strategic level.

THE TIME IS FULFILLED

The year A.D. 26–27 was not just one more Sabbatical year. There was an intense interest among pious Jews, who shared an apocalyptic vision of the future, to calculate what was called the "time of the end." The New Testament is full of this type of language. John the Baptizer told the crowds that the ax of judgment was "now at the root of the trees" (Luke 3:9). Jesus spoke of knowing how to "interpret the times" (Luke 12:56). He referred to his own generation as the terminal one that will live to see the Apocalypse (Mark 13:30). He told his disciples that some of them would not die until they saw the "kingdom of God come with power" (Mark 9:1). He promised his Council of Twelve that they would sit next to him like princes "on twelve thrones, ruling over the twelve tribes of Israel" (Luke 22:30). Paul wrote in the 50s A.D. that "the appointed time has grown very short" (1 Corinthians 7:29). Peter wrote that "the end of all things is at hand" (1 Peter 4:7). James declared, "The Judge is standing at the door" (James 5:9).

We now know, particularly with the discovery of the Dead Sea Scrolls, that such language was tied to actual chronological schemes and calculations as to just when the end would come. When Jesus declared that the "time is fulfilled" and "the kingdom of God is at hand," he was not generalizing, but specifically referring to events unfolding according to a prophetic timetable.

There were various schemes but the one that drew the most attention was Daniel's "Seventy Weeks" prophecy. The book of Daniel contains several prophetic visions regarding the "time of the end" but one in particular provides a calculated countdown of years. According to this prophecy, from the time of a certain decree to "restore and rebuild" Jerusalem following the 6th-century destruction by the Babylonians there would pass a period of "seventy weeks of years." Every Sabbatical year marked one "week" or seven years. The total period then, of 70 times 7 equaled 490 years. This period as a whole was referred to as the "appointed time of the end." Remember, the Qumran community that wrote the Dead Sea Scrolls had declared, "This is the time for preparing the Way in the desert." They were basing their calculations on this prophecy in Daniel. Josephus wrote that the major impetus inspiring the Jewish Revolt against Roman rule was an "oracle" found in the "sacred scriptures" to the effect that "at that time one from their own country would become ruler of the world."[2] He was clearly referring to the "Seventy Weeks" prophecy of the book of Daniel, and the ruler to whom he refers is none other than the Jewish Messiah or King. The Essenes who wrote the Dead Sea Scrolls correlated this period of 490 years with a period of ten final Jubilees, each lasting forty-nine years.[3] Each Jubilee was then divided into "weeks" of seven years each. When the time of the tenth Jubilee arrived there would be just forty-nine years until the end. That final Jubilee would mark the terminal generation that "would not pass until all things were fulfilled."

We don't know the precise chronological scheme that John the Baptizer and Jesus might have endorsed. Their ways of counting years were different from our own and they certainly did not have our Gregorian calendar. However, it is worth noting that if one begins with the year 457 B.C., when Ezra returned to Jerusalem and began to restore things after the Babylonian captivity, and one counts forward sixty-nine of these prophetic "weeks" (483 years), one comes to the year A.D. 26–27—with one "week" of years to go to reach the magic number 490. It might well be that John the Baptizer and Jesus had something akin to this type of calculation in mind. Perhaps they believed that the Sabbatical year A.D. 26–27 had ushered in a final seven-year period before the Apocalypse. Whatever their scheme, there is no doubt that they had become convinced that the time was at hand, and with God on their side they were poised to usher in the prophesied events of the last days. Because of Daniel's critical prophecy an apocalyptic storm was brewing in 1st-century Roman Palestine. There was never a time before quite like it, and there has never been one since. But timing alone is not enough. The other component of the equation, absolutely essential to the mix, was the appearance of Two Messiahs.

THE TWO OLIVE BRANCHES

Christians and Jews have come to focus on the appearance of a single Messiah. Such was decidedly not the case in the time of Jesus as we have already seen in the Dead Sea Scrolls. In text after text we read about not one but *two* Messiahs who are to usher in the Kingdom of God. One is to be a kingly figure of the royal line of David, but at his side will be a priestly figure, also a Messiah, of the lineage of Aaron from the tribe of Levi.

Zechariah, the 6th-century B.C. Hebrew prophet, foretold a man called "the Branch" who would bear royal honor and sit on his throne, but Zechariah adds, "There shall be a priest by his throne with peaceful understanding between the two of them" (Zechariah 6:13). Here is a clear picture of the Davidic King and his counselor, the anointed Priest. Zechariah refers in another vision to "two sons of fresh oil" (i.e., "anointed ones" or "messiahs") who "stand before the Lord of the whole earth." He likens them in his vision to two "olive branches" that stand before the Menorah, the seven-branched oil lamp that symbolized God's spirit and presence.

This ideal vision of Two Messiahs became a model for many Jewish groups that were oriented toward apocalyptic thinking in the 2nd to 1st centuries B.C. The Testament of the Twelve Patriarchs, dating from the 2nd century B.C., puts things succinctly: "For the Lord will raise up from Levi someone as high priest and from Judah someone as king."[4] Throughout this influential work there is an emphasis that salvation for Israel will come jointly from the tribe of Levi and from the tribe of Judah, the tribe of King David. The Priest Messiah receives more attention than the King Messiah and in many ways he stands superior to the Davidic figure. In fact, the patriarch Judah himself declares, "For to me the Lord gave the kingship and to him the priesthood, and he set the kingship under the priesthood."[5] The book of Jubilees, coming from about the same period, pronounces a perpetual blessing upon Levi as the progenitor of the priest, and Judah as the father of the "prince" who will rule over Israel and the nations.[6] It seems, based on these texts, that the notion of Two Messiahs was the ideal structure of Jewish leadership. It is for this reason that in the 2nd and 1st centuries B.C. the Maccabeans or Hashmoneans, who could claim only the Levitical priestly bloodline, were never really able to effectively establish themselves in the eyes of the populace as "kings," despite massive political and military power. Ingrained in the Jewish imagination was the ideal future in which both a Priest and a King would rule together.

John the Baptizer identified himself as the "messenger" who was to prepare the Way based on a prophecy from the book of Malachi. The version we read in our modern Bibles today is as follows:

> Behold I am sending my messenger to prepare the way before me,
> and the Lord whom you seek will suddenly come to his temple.
> The messenger of the covenant in whom you delight—indeed, *he*
> is coming says Yahweh of hosts, but who can endure the day of *his*
> coming, and who can stand when *he* appears? (Malachi 3:1–2)

This translation is based on the standard Hebrew text (Masoretic), the oldest copy of which dates to the 9th century A.D. We now have a version of this very passage from Malachi found among the Dead Sea Scrolls. This scroll dates to the 1st century B.C., so it is a thousand years older than our standard Hebrew text. Notice carefully the differences in the pronouns:

> Therefore behold I send my messenger, and *he* shall prepare the
> way before me. And *they* will suddenly come to his temple, the
> Lord whom you seek *and* the messenger of the covenant, whom
> you desire; behold he himself comes, says Yahweh of hosts, but
> who can endure *them* when *they* come?[7]

This ancient version of Malachi has two figures that are to come jointly—a messenger of the covenant who prepares the Way, but also one called "the Lord whom you seek." The word translated "Lord" (*'adon*) is not the Hebrew name for God, Yahweh, but a word that means a "master" or ruler of some type. It may well be that Jesus and John the Baptizer were familiar with this version of Malachi with the plural pronouns, and identified themselves accordingly. This was certainly the understanding of the Essenes who wrote the Dead Sea Scrolls.

In one of the oldest founding documents of the Dead Sea Scrolls, the *Community Rule*, the Essenes were expecting the coming of a prophet they called the Teacher, but also the "Messiahs of Aaron and Israel." They imagined a future in which the Priest Messiah would preside over a "messianic banquet," with the King Messiah of Israel, whom they call the "Prince of the congregation," or the "Branch of David," as his companion. There are many references in the Dead Sea Scrolls to their fervent expectation that these Two Messiahs would appear. As important as the "Branch of David" was to be, they nonetheless had the most extravagant hopes for the coming priest. In a text called the *Testament of Levi* we read the following:

> He will atone for the sons of his generation and he will be sent to all the sons of his people. His word is like a word of heaven and his teaching is according to the will of God. His eternal sun will shine, and his fire will blaze in all the corners of the earth. Then darkness will disappear from the earth and deep darkness from the dry land.[8]

This amazing text seems to match the high view in which Jesus held his teacher John the Baptizer—at least according to the Q source. It is the very opposite of the theological overlay that our New Testament gospels in their final edited forms project in their effort to make Jesus greater than John. It certainly supports the historical probability that Jesus did view John as his teacher as well as the priestly Messiah of Aaron of whom the prophets had spoken. For those reasons Jesus would have deferred to John's leadership and direction, a point completely lost in our gospels other than in the Q source.

The Dead Sea Scrolls community waited a long time for the fulfillment of these central expectations. They had retreated to the Judean desert sometime in the 2nd century B.C. in response to the prophetic Voice they heard through the prophecies of Isaiah, Daniel, and Malachi. They became convinced, as we have seen, that "this was the time" of the preparation of "the Way." Sometime in the 1st century B.C. an influential figure arose among them who had great spiritual and interpretive gifts. They refer to him in the Scrolls as the "Teacher of Righteousness." We don't know his name but many events of his life, and even some of his writings, are preserved in the Scrolls. The community saw him as a type of "Prophet like Moses" who had called them into a "new covenant." They viewed themselves as a remnant group of faithful Israelites who had turned from their sins and separated themselves from the ungodly society around them. They considered the religious establishment of their day, whether Pharisee or Sadducee, to be hopelessly corrupt and compromised. They lived by the strictest interpretation of the laws of the Torah and firmly believed they were living in the "last days." They believed that their Teacher had given them the definitive inspired interpretation of all the secrets of their prophetic writings.

When their Teacher was killed, probably sometime in the mid-1st century B.C., they were convinced the final countdown had begun and that the Two Messiahs would soon appear. There are some texts that speak of a final period of "forty years" following the death of their Teacher. The forty years passed but there is no record in any of the Dead Sea Scrolls that the Two Messiahs ever appeared. It was as if all their hopes and expectations were stopped in time and put on hold. A small group of their community still lived at the settlement we know as Qumran in the 1st century A.D., and if they are indeed the people we know as the Essenes, they were scattered in communities all through the land of Palestine. They did not die out despite the failure of their original expectations. It is likely that they were partly responsible for keeping alive the hope of the coming of the Two Messiahs.

Given these deeply rooted hopes and expectations among these messianic Jews one can scarcely imagine the excitement and fervor that John the Baptizer and Jesus would have stirred as they prepared their next moves in the spring of A.D. 27. John as a priest from the tribe of Levi and Jesus as a descendant of David from the tribe of Judah must have stirred the hopes of thousands who had come to expect the arrival of the Two Messiahs as a sure sign of the end. Even Herod Antipas soon felt the sting of John the Baptizer's blistering message of repentance. Christians are prone to imagine a "meek and lowly" Jesus who seldom raised his voice but the evidence will show that he learned well from his teacher and that like John the Baptizer, Jesus' radical message divided households and villages and shook the religious and political establishment.

JESUS IN JUDEA

Based on the indications we get from the gospel of John, the baptizing campaign of Jesus and his disciples in the countryside of Judea must have lasted through the summer and fall and into the winter of A.D. 27.[9] The campaign was enormously successful, with Jesus making and baptizing even more disciples than John the Baptizer, who was working in the north. Even though the gospel of John seems pleased to report such success as a way of implying Jesus is greater than John, there is no reason to assume some type of rivalry. The southern campaign evidently went very well. That Jesus was baptizing at all was clearly a problem for later Christians. He is not administering a "Christian baptism" in the name of the "Father, Son, and Holy Spirit." A later editor of John even added a parenthetical qualification:"although it was not Jesus himself who baptized but his disciples" (John 4:2). That type of interpolation is like a red flag telling us that someone is very uncomfortable here, even though the text plainly says that Jesus was baptizing and making disciples!

The historical facts are plain: Jesus joined the movement of John the Baptizer and was baptized by John with a "baptism of repentance for the remission of sins." He then linked up with John in a strategic move to reach the whole country at once. Jesus was preaching and practicing that same baptism—the baptism of John. They were allies and there is no reason to think that either their message or their mode of operation differed.

It appears certain that Jesus' mother, brothers, and sisters responded to the baptism of John, as well as all those working with him as "disciples," including Peter and Andrew, the fishermen James and John, Philip, Nathanael, and all the rest. We have no record of any of the disciples or apostles of Jesus ever getting rebaptized once they became"Christians." In other words their allegiance to Jesus as the Davidic Messiah in no way involved a religious stance different from what they had experienced with John the Baptizer. The shocking truth is that none of the apostles or disciples of Jesus ever had a proper"Christian baptism" as it came to be defined in Christian dogma—that is "in the name of the Father, the Son, and the Holy Spirit." They were baptized by John and that was it. According to the Q source, our most authentic early Christian document, those who rejected John's baptism had "rejected God's purpose" (Luke 7:29–30). The last week of Jesus' life he in fact raised this very issue with his religious opponents, challenging them to say publicly that John was a false prophet since they had rejected his baptism. They did not dare do so, knowing that the populace as a whole revered John and considered him a great Prophet. Later, after Jesus' death, when a replacement on the Council of Twelve was chosen for Judas Iscariot, who had betrayed Jesus and committed suicide, it was specified that only candidates who had been with Jesus and the group "beginning from the baptism of John" would be considered for this important office (Acts 1:22). Christians later tended to separate the two movements—that of John the Baptizer and Jesus, as if one was "Jewish" and the other "Christian." In the lifetime of Jesus, and among his immediate followers, there was one unified movement and one baptism.

By the end of A.D. 27, from the standpoint of this Messianic Movement there were only two kinds of Jews in Palestine—those who had positively responded to the preaching of John and Jesus and had been baptized, and those who had not. There was no middle ground. The "wheat" had been separated from the "chaff." The ax was poised over the root of the tree.

We are told that Jesus carried out his baptism campaign in the "Judean countryside." This implies it was outside the city of Jerusalem, probably to the west in what was called the "hill country" of Judea. To the east was the arid Judean desert. To the north was the alien territory of Samaria. So just where is it likely that Jesus carried out his mass baptizing efforts?

As we have seen, one of the questions we have wrestled with since 2001, when we began to remove the vast quantity of 1st-century A.D. pottery from the Suba cave, is how did it get there—and why? The evidence in the cave points to an extraordinarily high level of activity in this cave in the early 1st century A.D.—far more than any normal water gathering activities from the local area can account for. Shimon Gibson and I had postulated that large crowds of people were coming to this cave, that water was poured ritually over the head from small jugs as part of an immersion ceremony, and the jugs were then broken to prevent subsequent

use for common purposes. We had explained this unusual activity as possibly associated with John the Baptizer's early activities.

I returned to Suba recently, while writing this book. A new thought
occurred to me. I had asked myself, Who do we know that was baptizing
large crowds of people in the Judean countryside? I began to ask myself
why one should assume it was John when we have a reliable tradition that
Jesus himself preached and baptized in the Judean countryside and baptized large crowds of people? I recalled that Mary his mother had fled to
this very area when pregnant with Jesus to live with John's parents, Elizabeth and Zechariah. One might assume that during the years when Jesus
was growing up his mother and her family would have visited Elizabeth,
since they traveled to Judea several times a year for the Jewish festivals.
Jesus surely had a relationship with John before age thirty when he encountered him for baptism at the Jordan River in Galilee. John had spent
his years of solitude wandering these very hills and valleys. It is no wild
stretch of the imagination to think both John and Jesus would have been
familiar with such an impressive water reservoir in the area that dated

The hill country of Judea near Suba where Jesus baptized multitudes

back to the time of Isaiah the Prophet. One has to assume that all the local population knew of its existence.

I remember sitting outside the cave late one afternoon at sunset trying to imagine what could have occurred. Was it possible that Peter, James, John, and the other apostles, and maybe even Jesus' mother and brothers, had stood on this very ground and entered this very cave? Had Jesus perhaps preached to large crowds that gathered in the wide flat valley that was right in front of me? Had he and his entourage lived and camped in this lovely area, making use of some of the natural caves we had discovered all around? And if not here, then where? There are no rivers or pools or significant springs in the area that compare in size with this one. Just outside the cave is a wide valley that would have accommodated the large crowds that might have gathered. Our Suba cave might well have been a central staging ground for Jesus' preaching and baptism campaign in late A.D. 27. That afternoon I found it easy to imagine Jesus and his followers at the Suba cave.

Jesus' baptism campaign, as successful as it was, ground to an abrupt halt sometime in early A.D. 28. Shocking news had come from Galilee in the north. Herod Antipas had arrested John the Baptizer. According to the gospel of John, Jesus then heard that some of the Pharisees in Jerusalem, who opposed John, were alarmed at Jesus' success with the crowds and so were making threatening moves against his own operation (John 4:1–3). It was time to go underground.

10

USHERING IN THE KINGDOM

I<small>T</small> was a shocking and terrible blow to the Messianic Movement. Its founder and leader, John the Baptizer, had been thrown into prison by Herod Antipas, ruler of Galilee and Perea. According to the gospel of Mark, John the Baptizer had publicly denounced Herod for taking the beautiful Herodias, his brother Philip's wife, who was a willing partner to the adulterous affair. Josephus does not specifically mention this incident but he says that Herod was alarmed at John's extraordinary influence over the people and feared he would raise a "rebellion." John had strategically stationed himself at the border of Herod's territory in eastern Galilee so he could escape if necessary across the Jordan River into the region called Decapolis, outside his jurisdiction. Herod's troops were able to catch him unawares and he was taken to the eastern side of the Dead Sea to one of Herod's desert fortresses called Machaerus. Herod's idea was to put him in the most remote area of his kingdom so that there would be less chance of a popular uprising.

In the south Jesus knew his own baptizing days were numbered. A new Roman procurator named Pontius Pilate, directly appointed by the emperor, Tiberius, had taken over military rule of the province of Judea in A.D. 26. He had immediately established himself as a brutal taskmaster with no concern for Jewish religious sensibilities. He had brought Roman military standards with their busts of Caesar into the holy city of Jerusalem. Shortly thereafter he had taken money from the sacred Temple treasury to pay for costs of finishing an aqueduct into Jerusalem. The Jewish crowds were in an uproar and both incidents provoked riots to which Pilate responded with force, killing large numbers of Jews.[1] The one thing the Romans insisted on in Judea was stability, and the last thing they wanted was a Jewish prophet of Davidic ancestry drawing large crowds and talking about the coming Kingdom of God.

Jesus had to somehow get safely back to Galilee where he could lie low for a bit until he and his followers determined what they would do next. He knew he could not travel back through Jerusalem, and down to Jericho, taking the main highway along the Jordan River north, right past the spot were John had been arrested. He decided to go directly north, through the rugged mountainous territory of Samaria. Pious Jews normally avoided this area, since they considered the Samaritans inferior in religion and culture and the region in general as "pagan." Herod the Great had built his capital there at Sebaste and crowned the citadel of the city with a temple to Emperor Augustus. Jesus did not return to his hometown of Nazareth, perhaps fearing Herod might be looking for him as well. Instead he went to the little town of Cana, north of Sepphoris, where the wedding had taken place the previous year. If it was one of his brothers who had married a girl from Cana perhaps the bride's family provided Jesus and his band of followers with temporary safe haven. It was likely there as the spring of A.D. 28 approached that Jesus came up with his plan.

THE MAKING OF A MESSIAH

How and when Jesus developed his own self-understanding of his role and mission in what he believed was God's plan to usher in the Kingdom of God we cannot be sure. He surely knew growing up that he and his brothers were male heirs of the royal line of King David and he would have been well aware of the significant messianic implications of this heritage. The Hebrew Scriptures were full of promises that God in the "last days" would raise up a King of the line of David who would be instrumental in throwing off foreign rule and establishing an independent Kingdom of Israel, thus inaugurating the New Age of peace and justice for the entire world. Jeremiah's prophecy put things most succinctly:

> The days are surely coming, says Yahweh, when I will raise up *for David a righteous Branch and he shall reign as king* and deal wisely, and shall execute justice and righteousness in the land. In his days Judah will be saved and Israel will dwell safely. (Jeremiah 23:5–6)

Isaiah used much the same language: "Of the increase of his government and of peace there will be no end, upon the throne of David and upon his kingdom to establish it and uphold it with justice and righteousness forever more" (Isaiah 9:7). Micah had predicted that this one "would be great to the ends of the earth" (Micah 5:4). Amos had promised that God would "raise up the tent of David that had fallen" and rebuild his house as in the days of old (Amos 9:11). This Messiah, the "Branch of David," was to fill the earth with the knowledge of Yahweh as the waters cover the sea, and cause the wolf to dwell with the lamb and the lion to eat straw like the ox (Isaiah 11:6–9). The complete portrait of this new King of the Jews was captured well in a popular 1st-century B.C. text known as the *Psalms of Solomon*:

> *Behold O Lord and raise up to them their King, the son of David,*
> *At the time in which you see, O God,*
> *That he may rule over Israel your servant.*
> *And gird him with strength that he may shatter unrighteous rulers,*
> *And that he may purge Jerusalem*
> *From nations that trample her to destruction.*
> *Wisely, righteously he shall thrust out sinners from the inheritance . . .*
> *He shall destroy the godless nations with the word of his mouth.*
> *At his rebuke nations shall flee before him . . .*
> *And he shall gather together a holy people,*
> *Whom he shall lead in righteousness.*
> *And he shall judge the tribes of the people,*
> *Who have been sanctified by the Lord his God.*[2]

His is a "six-point" program: ruling over Israel on the throne of David; purging Jerusalem and the land of Israel of foreign rulers; establishing a rule of righteousness; separating the sinners from the people of Israel; extending his rule to all the godless nations of the world; and gathering together all the scattered tribes of Israel.

This is the ambitiously extravagant agenda required of any candidate of the lineage of David who might feel messianic stirrings toward such a calling. To the Romans such notions must have seemed totally delusional, and practically minded Jews could always interpret the language of their Prophets in a less literal way, or ignore it altogether. But thousands of Jews believed that this ideal Davidic King would appear on the scene and with God's supernatural powers accomplish these things. All our evidence indicates that Jesus was such a Jew.

The Kingdom of God in these texts is not a sentiment or ethereal concept. The language is concrete and particular. The word "kingdom," in both Hebrew and Greek, means "government" or "rule" just as one might speak of Herod's "kingdom" or of Roman "rule." The prayer John and Jesus taught defined the *kingdom of God* as the "will of God done *on earth*" as it already was being done in heaven. This was not a kingdom "in" heaven, but the idea of the rule *of* heaven breaking into human history and manifesting itself on earth. It was understood in a literal way, nothing less than a revolution, a complete overthrow of the political, social, and economic status quo.

As we saw in the previous chapter, timing was everything. Daniel had had a dream-vision in which four great "beasts" arose from the sea and ruled over the earth. He was told that each represented a successive "world kingdom" that would arise. In Jesus' day these were understood to be Babylon, Persia, Greece, and Rome.[3] Daniel was further told that "in the days of these kings," speaking of the rulers of this fourth kingdom, "the God of heaven would set up a kingdom that would never be destroyed," breaking in pieces all the other kingdoms of the world (Daniel 2:44). Once Rome moved into the eastern Mediterranean, occupying Palestine, as Alexander the Great, Cyrus, and Nebuchadnezzar had done in centuries past, the days of the "fourth kingdom" had arrived. That coupled with Daniel's final countdown period of 490 years or ten Jubilee

cycles had convinced those in 1st-century Roman Palestine who took the
Hebrew Prophets seriously that they were living in the "last days" or the
"end of the age." It is extremely important to point out that they did not
expect the "end of the world"; that phrase never occurs. It is always the
end of the "age," or the period of time in which Gentile kingdoms hold
sway prior to the arrival of the New Age—the Kingdom of God. In the
Dead Sea Scrolls it is called the "final age of wickedness."

Jesus shared this understanding of time and history. His message
following John's arrest, as he began preaching, was, "The time is fulfilled,
the Kingdom of God is at hand." He may have grown up with such an
apocalyptic outlook but it surely intensified as he became an adult and
began to consider what he believed was his own destiny and his calling.
He was the right person at the right time—but there was another vital
component.

I am convinced that Jesus most likely began to read certain passages
of the Hebrew Scriptures and apply them directly to himself.[4] As I see
things, this factor is absolutely vital for understanding his developing
sense of messianic self-identity. There are various texts of Scripture that
set forth the general agenda of the Davidic King as I have noted above.
But there are other messianic texts, particularly in the latter half of the
book of Isaiah and in the Psalms, that have a much more personal quality—some of them are even written in the first person. For example,
Isaiah 61 begins, "The spirit of the Lord Yahweh is upon *me* because
Yahweh has *anointed me*; he has sent *me* to bring good news to the oppressed, to bind up the brokenhearted, to proclaim liberty to the captives,
and release the prisoners; to proclaim *the year* of Yahweh's favor, and the
day of vengeance of our God." If one who is convinced of a personal messianic destiny reads such a text, and "hears" one's own voice, a powerful
dynamic begins to work. The text serves to confirm and reinforce one's
identity while the identity finds specific expression and direction through
the text.

In some of these texts God speaks to the chosen figure directly. Often
the language moves back and forth from God addressing the individual
to the individual responding. Notice carefully the switch in pronouns in
this single passage:

I, even I have spoken and called him, I have brought him and he
will prosper in *his* way [God speaking].

Draw near to *me* and hear this! From the beginning *I* have not
spoken in secret, from the time it came to be *I* have been there,
and *now the Lord Yahweh has sent me* and his spirit [individual re-
sponding].[5]

There are passages where an actual "conversation" takes place between the
chosen figure and God, with God offering both direction and correction
related to the divine mission. Isaiah 49 is one of the best examples of this.
The chosen one declares, "Yahweh called me before I was born, while I
was in my mother's womb he named me" (Isaiah 49:1). At a later point,
when the chosen one becomes discouraged, God chastises him: "Is it too
light a thing that you should be my servant to raise up the tribes of Jacob
and to restore the survivors of Israel; I will give you as a light to the nations, that my salvation may reach to the end of the earth" (Isaiah 49:6).
Some of these passages exhibit an amazing degree of intimacy and personal emotion: "The Lord Yahweh has given *me* the tongue of a teacher
that I may know how to sustain the weary with a word. Morning by
morning he wakens, he wakens my ear to listen as those who are taught"
(Isaiah 50:4).

Dozens of the Psalms function in the same way, particularly those that
appear to be messianic in content. Psalm 40 is quite amazing in this regard. It claims to be written by David, but surely a descendant of David
could easily find in it his own voice: "Sacrifice and offering you do not desire, but you have given me an open ear . . . Then I said, 'Here I am; *in the
scroll of the book it is written of me.* I delight to do your will O my God, your
Law is within my heart" (verses 6–8). Here we have an explicit statement
that the one spoken of is also *written of* in the scrolls of Scripture.
And the notion of the "open ear" nicely connects to the passage above
from Isaiah 50.

If Jesus did begin to appropriate and to find his voice in such texts of
Scripture he was not the first to do so. In the Dead Sea Scrolls there is a
most remarkable text called the *Thanksgiving Hymns,* parts of which

scholars believe were written by the Teacher of Righteousness himself. The Teacher, leader of the Dead Sea Scrolls community, definitely saw himself in such a chosen role and regularly applied some of these very texts to his own life and times. This fascinating text, which in places takes on the tone of an autobiography, gives us a glimpse into the Teacher's inner consciousness and how he formed his own messianic self-identity as Prophet to his community. With that model, it is easier to imagine one such as Jesus, given his Davidic lineage along with his times and circumstances, undergoing a very similar process.

I believe that at some point in Jesus' life, perhaps even before he joined up with John at his baptism and began to go public with his mission, Jesus found his own voice in texts of Scripture such as these. They not only gave him inner assurance and strength of conviction but they also provided a type of road map to what would happen. There is a fine line between believing that prophecy predicts a certain unfolding sequence of events and seeking, to some degree, to orchestrate those events because they are predicted in prophecy. Scholars and historians have engaged in a protracted chicken-or-egg debate over whether Jesus was driven by texts of Scripture or whether texts of Scripture were imposed on his life after the fact in an effort to show that he fulfilled Scripture. In all but a few cases I think that it is much more likely that he was driven by the Scriptures.[6]

Even though we have much less material about John the Baptizer, in the texts we do have he is regularly asked: Are you the Messiah? Are you Elijah? Are you the Prophet? Each of these designations reflects a certain reading of texts of the Hebrew Bible dealing with the predicted arrival of key figures and their expected roles in ushering in the Kingdom. When John answers it is significant that he answers *textually*—not from a personal vision or revelation that he might have claimed. He quotes Isaiah 40 and Malachi 3 and says he is the Messenger spoken of in those texts. When Jesus is baptized the "Voice" he hears is an echo of a *text* from Isaiah. Later, when he openly identifies himself to the townspeople of Nazareth he does it *textually*, by reading Isaiah 61 with its first-person voice and concluding—"This day this scripture is fulfilled in your ears" (Luke 4:21). It seems likely to me that both Jesus and John formed their own self-identities and the vision of their joint mission as Priest and King from specific texts drawn from the Hebrew Bible as well as traditions of interpretation popular among the apocalyptically oriented Jews of their time. The Dead Sea Scrolls are our best window onto how one envisions the future through the text.

THE KINGDOM OF GOD IS AT HAND

The arrest of John the Baptizer by Herod Antipas must have been a terrible shock and surprise to everyone—including Jesus. He retreated to the Galilee to consider his next move. And that is where Mark picks up the story:

> Now after John was arrested, Jesus came to Galilee, proclaiming the good news of the kingdom of God and saying, "The time is fulfilled, and the kingdom of God is at hand, repent and believe in the good news." (Mark 1:14)

Simon Peter, his brother Andrew, and the "sons of Zebedee," James and John, had returned to Capernaum to continue with their fishing business while they waited to hear what Jesus had in mind next. Peter had set up their operation in a house and moved his family there. Jesus left the little village of Cana, where he and his family had likely been keeping a low profile, and headed for Capernaum to let his disciples know his decision to go on the road again. It was a daring move, and one that he knew could very well get him arrested as well.

When he told them, "Let's leave the nets and go fish for people," they did not blindly drop everything in some mesmerized state of devotion to his irresistible bidding as is so often portrayed. These disciples had worked with him and lived with him for months the previous year in Judea when they were baptizing huge crowds of people. The same likely goes for Levi or Matthew, who had gone to work at the toll station in Capernaum. This occupation does not imply he is a pro-Roman collaborator, but merely that he had found work in the complex financial network that the fishing industry had produced in that area. Jesus set up a head-

Capernaum with Peter's house in center

quarters for the movement in Peter's house and quickly the word spread among his followers who had been with him from the beginning that something big was afoot. Everyone gathered at Capernaum.

From the headquarters in Capernaum Jesus and his entourage began to travel all around the towns and villages of Galilee, preaching to all who would hear. They would periodically return to Capernaum to regroup, and then go out again. We don't know how many disciples were following Jesus at this time, but one should imagine a cadre of adherents, perhaps several dozens, including many women who traveled along with the group and provided logistical support (Luke 8:1–3). They moved from village to village, dealing with the huge crowds that flocked to them by day and camped out at night.

The message was a simple one: "Turn from your sins, for the Kingdom of God is near—the judgment is at hand." In each place Jesus would lay his hands on those who were sick or physically impaired and cast out evil spirits or demons. Sickness was thought to result from demons "binding" people, so his activities of healing and exorcism were connected.[7] Jesus was a political revolutionary who expected nothing less than the violent overthrow of the kingdoms of the world, but he did not think it would come about by collecting arms and gathering rebel bands of troops as some of his contemporaries had attempted. The first step was to defeat Satan and his powers. As he saw things, in order for the Kingdom of God to come not only would Herod, Pontius Pilate, and the Roman legions have to be deposed, but first and foremost Satan himself, who was seen as the behind-the-scenes "ruler of the age." Jesus directly linked his power to cast out demons to "binding Satan" and destroying his kingdom. In a passage from the Q source, he makes a decisive pronouncement: "If I by the finger of God cast out demons then the Kingdom of God has come to you" (Luke 11:20). The one was a sure sign of the other.

The preaching campaigns went on into the early months of A.D. 29. The effect was enormous. Huge crowds gathered to hear him preach and to witness the reported healings and exorcisms. According to Mark, people streamed into Galilee from Judea and Jerusalem, from the east side of the Jordan, and even from Tyre and Sidon to the north. John had stirred things considerably in Galilee but he was not a healer or an exorcist, and now he seemed powerless in prison at Machaerus. These new activities of Jesus, and the resulting power he was beginning to sense in his person, energized the Messianic Movement and propelled it to center stage. Not everyone, of course, was pleased with what was happening. There were groups of opposing Pharisees from the area, whose power base was threatened. They likely feared that both their influence and their economic base might be challenged by widespread support among the populace for a charismatic preacher of the Kingdom of God. Agents of Herod, whom the New Testament refers to as "Herodians," began to conspire to have him stopped (Mark 3:6). Jesus was well aware of the danger but decided to push things to the limit. He made a momentous decision, rife with political as well as spiritual implications.

A STRATEGIC PLAN

As future King of Israel, Jesus moved to set up a provisional "government" made up of an inner cabinet or Council of Twelve. From among his followers he chose twelve men that he designated as "delegates," or envoys.

That is the meaning of the Greek word translated "apostle." His ultimate intention was that when his government was fully operational each of them would sit on a "throne," one over each of the twelve tribes of Israel (Luke 22:30). Christianity might later look on the choosing of the "Twelve Apostles" as a step in spiritual organization—and it was surely that. The Dead Sea Scrolls community had been structured around an inner Council of Twelve and it is entirely possible that this model had influenced Jesus.[8] But one should not overlook the revolutionary implications of Jesus' actions.

One of the Davidic Messiah's main tasks was to assemble the tribes of Israel, including the so-called Lost Tribes that had gone into exile during the 8th-century B.C. Assyrian invasion of Israel. According to Josephus only two of the tribes of Israel were subject to Roman rule—Judah and Benjamin, with some mixture of Levi—while the bulk of the other ten tribes had migrated northwest and were concentrated up around the area of the Black Sea.[9] The term "Jew" refers to someone of the tribe of "Judah" but it had come to be used loosely for anyone of Israelite descent. Jesus' vision of the future, as we shall see, involved extending a call to Israelites scattered all over the world to return to the Land. This is what all the Prophets had predicted would happen in the "last days." In fact Jeremiah even said that the "new Exodus" of Israelites from all the lands of their "dispersion" or scattering, would rival in size the original Exodus from Egypt in the time of Moses (Jeremiah 16:14–15).

A close examination of the composition of this Council of Twelve is most revealing. Each time they are listed, in Matthew, Mark, and Luke, they are consistently grouped into three tiers of four names each:

1. Simon Peter, Andrew, James, and John
2. Philip, Bartholomew,[10] Matthew,[11] and Thomas
3. James, Jude,[12] Simon, and Judas Iscariot.

The first eight are well known, but the final four are mysteriously intriguing. They are always listed last in all of our sources.[13] We would expect Judas Iscariot to be placed at the very bottom of the list, since he is the betrayer of Jesus, but who are the other three—James, Jude, and Simon? In contrast to the others, nothing is ever related about them in any of the New Testament gospels. This strange silence is surely purposeful and the ordering of the lists is intentional. What we have here is a classic example of the "last" being the "first."

By the time of our New Testament gospels, the vital role these three were to play, and even the existence of the Jesus dynasty, was in the process of being painted out of the picture, but their names as part of the Twelve could not be excised. James, Jude, and Simon are clearly the brothers of Jesus. In fact Jude is called "Judas of James" in Luke 6:16, an expression probably meaning "brother," and he calls himself "brother of James" in his one-page letter at the end of the New Testament, a document that came close to being excluded from the canon. James is called the "son of Alphaeus" (Luke 6:15), and, as we have seen, "Alphaeus" is another form of the name "Clophas," the brother of Joseph and likely second husband of Mary. Simon "son of Clophas" is the one who takes over leadership of the Jesus movement after James is killed—so he too is a brother. I am convinced that these are the three brothers of Jesus.

So what about the brother named Joseph? There is no Joseph listed here as part of the Twelve. Is it likely that Jesus chose three of his brothers and left one out? Joseph was the next oldest after James. There is something very curious going on here. The one called Matthew is described as "Levi son of Alphaeus" in Mark 2:14. So we have *another* son of our mysterious "Alphaeus" or Clophas. That makes him the brother of James, Jude, and Simon. But why would he be called Matthew or Levi rather than Joseph? It is entirely possible that he was known by both names. One was "his" and the other was given to him in honor of Joseph, the deceased husband of Mary and brother of Clophas. This combination of names was quite common in the period, especially among those connected to a priestly lineage, as was Mary, Jesus' mother. Remember in her line alone are listed half a dozen "Matthews." In fact it is the *most* common name in Jesus' lineage from his mother's side. Jesus' great-grandfather was named Matthew, and his great-great-grandfather was Levi. It is worth noting that the 1st-century Jewish historian we know as "Josephus" was named "Joseph" and he had a father and brother named Matthew and a grandfather named Joseph. His family was of that same "priestly" lineage, descended from the Maccabeans or Hashmoneans. It is entirely possible that Mary's line had ties to this very family, which gave her a measure of "priestly" royalty, as well as her direct Davidic descent. Remember, the Talpiot tomb had the names Joseph, Mary, Jude, and Jesus—but also a Matthew. It is not an alien name for a family such as Mary's, which favored revolutionary names.

This is perhaps the best-kept secret in the entire New Testament. *Jesus' own brothers were among the so-called Twelve Apostles.* This means they were the muted participants in all those many references to the "Twelve." They were with Jesus at the "last Supper" and when he died he turned his movement over to his brother James, the eldest, and put his mother into James's care. James is none other than the mysterious "beloved disciple" of the gospel of John.

It seems that the one thing people think they know about the brothers of Jesus is that they did not believe in him. This spurious opinion is based on a *single* phrase in John 7:5 that many scholars consider to be a late interpolation. Modern translations even put it in parentheses. Once we realize that the brothers are part of the Twelve, and that James is the "beloved disciple," then many things begin to make new sense. There are two passages in Mark that some have taken as downplaying the importance of Jesus' family, but they have been misread based on the false assumption that the brothers did not believe in Jesus.[14] It is amazing what firm opinions have been built upon such shaky foundations.

Sometime in the spring of A.D. 29, before Passover, Jesus divided the Twelve into six two-man groups. This was a strategic move and his intentions were as grandiose as they were dangerous. Their mission was to fan out over the whole country. They were to travel unaccompanied, to carry nothing with them—no money, no provisions, no luggage or even a change of clothes, taking only a staff, a pair of sandals, and a tunic. He instructed them: "Go nowhere among the Gentiles and enter no town of the Samaritans, but go rather to the lost sheep of the house of Israel" (Matthew 10:5–6). They would approach each town or village and declare: "Repent, for the kingdom of God has drawn near," and would then lay hands on the sick and exorcise demons. They were not to linger, staying only one night in each place, with whatever household took them in.

What Jesus initiated was nothing less than a spiritual offensive that was to usher in the arrival of the Kingdom of God. Based on Isaiah 61:1–2, which he understood to be speaking of his own role as Yahweh's anointed one or Messiah, he had proclaimed "the acceptable year of Yahweh." That critical time period, from spring A.D. 28 to spring A.D. 29, was almost up—God's judgment was ready to manifest itself. He boldly told the Twelve, "You will not have gone through all the towns of Israel before the Son of Man arrives." This arrival of the "Son of Man," which Christians later took as a reference to the Second Coming of Jesus, was coded language from the book of Daniel. It does not refer to Jesus' arriving, since he was standing with them when he said it, predicting the effect of their vital mission. Daniel had had a dream about "one like a son of man coming in the clouds of heaven," and it was interpreted symbolically in the book of Daniel to mean that the people of God would take over the kingdoms of the world (Daniel 7:13–14). The term itself, in Aramaic (bar 'enosh), means simply a human being.[15] The expression is even used in this very book to address the prophet Daniel (8:17). The phrase "son of man" in the dream vision of Daniel 7 stood collectively for the faithful people of Israel who would receive rule from their Messiah. In our earliest collection of the sayings, such as those of the Q source, Jesus speaks of the "Son of Man" in the third person. The coming of the "Son of Man" is an event, not a single figure popping out of the clouds. The "sign" of the Son of Man coming would be astronomical—the sun and moon darkened by eclipse and the stars "falling from heaven" (Matthew 24:29). This would mark the decisive overthrow of Satan and his kingdom in the heavens. Earthquakes and other heavenly signs would follow and the whole society would be shaken by these cosmic events. This would then prepare the way for the King Messiah to gather his chosen ones, get John his Priest Messiah co-ruler out of prison, and then with John travel up to Jerusalem to declare the inauguration of the new kingdom.

Jesus appears to expect that the mission of the Twelve would lead right up to these climactic events. His reading of the Prophets told him that the "acceptable year of Yahweh" was about up, and the mission of the Twelve would give all of Israel a chance to either repent or perish. The phrase referred to a one-year probation period when each person stood in the balance. That was to be followed by the "year of vengeance" in which God would overthrow the kingdoms of the world through a succession of cosmic manifestations (Isaiah 61:2).

As seems nearly always the case with apocalyptic predictions, what was most expected did not come and what was least anticipated happened. Herod decided to act and the entire movement reeled back in shock.

Part Four

ENTERING THE
LION'S DEN

II

HEROD STRIKES

Herod Antipas allowed John's disciples to visit him at the desert fortress at Machaerus where he was imprisoned. They kept him apprised of the extraordinary effect Jesus' preaching campaign had stirred throughout the country. He must have been overjoyed to hear that Jesus, in inaugurating his mission, had openly declared himself to be the one "anointed of the Spirit" who was to fulfill the pivotal prophecy of Isaiah 61. This figure was to "preach good news to the oppressed, bind up the brokenhearted, proclaim liberty to the captives, and release to the prisoners," declaring that the "year of Yahweh's favor" had arrived. Luke's version of the Q source preserves a sample of Jesus' message:

> Fortunate are you who are poor, for yours is the kingdom of God.
> Fortunate are you who are hungry now, for you will be filled.
> Fortunate are you who weep now, for you will laugh.
> Fortunate are you when men hate you, for your reward is great.

These positive pronouncements were followed by four parallel denunciations of judgment:

Woe to you who are rich, for you have yours now.
Woe to you who are full now, for you will be hungry.
Woe to you who are laughing now, for you will mourn and weep.
Woe when all men speak well of you, as they did of their ancestors the false prophets.
(Luke 6:20–25)

This revolutionary message, the "good news of the Kingdom of God," predicted the radical apocalyptic reversal of society from top to bottom. Those in power would fall, and those oppressed would be lifted up. The casting out of demons was understood as part of the Messiah's task to "proclaim liberty to the captives," but John the Baptizer, sitting in a literal prison cell at Machaerus, surely anticipated that the Messiah's "release of the prisoners" would bring an end to his own literal incarceration as well. The Prophets after all had predicted that the Two Messiahs, the Davidic King and the Anointed Priest, would rule side by side in Jerusalem.

The Dead Sea community had focused its messianic expectations on this very text of Isaiah 61. A precious fragment from Cave 4 that scholars call the *Messianic Apocalypse* predicted that the Messiah would "heal the sick, raise the dead, and bring good news to the poor."[1] Jesus and John the Baptizer knew either this text from Qumran, or one like it. John sent word to Jesus from prison asking him: "Are you the one or are we to expect another?" He wanted direct confirmation from Jesus that he had indeed inaugurated this messianic program. Jesus replied, not by quoting Isaiah 61 directly, but replying in the very words preserved in this Dead Sea Scroll: Go and tell John what you have seen and heard: the sick are healed, the dead are raised, the poor have good news brought to them (Luke 7:22). It is important to note here that Isaiah 61 does *not* specify that the Messiah will "raise the dead" but Jesus includes that phrase in his reply, as a "sign of the Messiah," knowing that John the Baptizer would be familiar with it, possibly from this very scroll. Both the scroll and Jesus' reply indicate how important the fulfillment of Isaiah 61 was to the Messianic Movement.

But what about the "raising of the dead"? There was an extraordinary report circulating that Jesus had in fact raised a young man from his funeral bier at the little village of Nain, just south of Nazareth (Luke

7:11–15). Shortly after this exchange with John, when Jesus had returned to Capernaum before sending out the Twelve, he had raised a twelve-year-old girl from the dead (Mark 5:42). She was the daughter of the leader of the local synagogue.

Expectations of dramatic and extraordinary things to come could not have been higher. I don't see any indication that Jesus had plans to gather arms and take a band of troops down to Machaerus to force John's release from prison, but he surely expected certain imminent cosmic events to unfold, whether earthquakes or heavenly signs, that would soon result in John's freedom. The powers to heal and cast out demons, so evidently manifested, left no doubt that God was ready to act decisively to overthrow the kingdoms of this world with the Kingdom of God.

THE GREAT DISAPPOINTMENT

Herod Antipas had troubles of his own making in the opening months of A.D. 29. He had moved his capital to the gleaming Greco-Roman style city of Tiberias. He had built this new city in honor of the emperor who had succeeded Augustus at his death in 14 B.C. It was located on the western shore of the Sea of Galilee just eight miles south of Capernaum. Many years earlier he had married a princess named Phasaelis, daughter of King Aretas IV, the king of Nabataea. It was purely a political alliance to strengthen his eastern border territory of Perea, across the Jordan. When he took his brother Philip's wife, Herodias, a Hashmonean princess, he felt obligated to divorce Phasaelis, embarrassing and infuriating King Aretas, who ordered his army to attack Herod's forces in Perea. Herod's army was decimated. His brother Philip had allied his forces with the Arabian king. Emperor Tiberius had to order legions from Syria to come to Herod's aid and defeat Aretas.

Josephus tells us that Herod had arrested John the Baptizer for fear of his popularity leading to a rebellion but according to Mark, Herod had John killed because of his outspoken criticism of his adulterous marriage. At a drunken party at the fortress Machaerus to celebrate his forty-eighth birthday, Herod had been so taken with the erotic dancing of Herodias's daughter Salome that he rashly promised her anything she asked. Prompted by her mother, who detested John the Baptizer for his denunciation of her marriage, she asked that John's head be brought into the banquet on a platter. Her gruesome request was carried out that very evening.

John's disciples were allowed to take his body, and Mark recorded that they buried him in a tomb, but no location is given (Mark 6:29). Josephus wrote that many believed that Herod's army had suffered defeat as just retribution for his murder of John the Baptizer.[2] This comment is surely an indication of how highly John had been regarded by the people.

A few years ago I visited the partially excavated fortress of Machaerus, shaped from a natural plateau that rises 2,300 feet above the Dead Sea. As at Masada, Herod the Great had fortified it to withstand a five-year siege in case he and his family ever had to flee a native uprising. The name Machaerus means "sword." It is ironic that the individual who Herod Antipas most feared might lead a revolt died at this very fortress, beheaded by a sword. I was surprised to see the mosaic floor of the main banquet hall still intact—the very scene of Salome's infamous dance that night. One could walk down to lower levels within the fortress where

Ruins of Herod's palace atop Machaerus where Salome danced

there were many rooms or cells, some of which appeared to be fortified to hold prisoners. I knew I was at least close to the very place where John spent the last few moments of his life.

With John's sudden and shockingly brutal death all the hopes and dreams of the Messianic Movement appeared to be crushed. No one had been thinking about Messiahs suffering and dying at that point. The celebration of success that might have followed the return of the Twelve from their preaching campaign dissolved into despair. The situation was also very dangerous. Herod had heard of the extraordinary effect Jesus' latest activities had created and according to Mark he superstitiously imagined that somehow "John the Baptizer had been raised from the dead" (Mark 6:14). He could think of no other way to explain how the movement he thought he had crushed now seemed to be led by one whose success was every bit as extraordinary as John's had been.

The gospels record that Jesus "withdrew privately to a city called Bethsaida" (Luke 9:10). It was on the north edge of the Sea of Galilee, just over the border of Herod's territory, out of his reach. Peter and Andrew had grown up there, as had Philip. There they could find safe refuge and somehow deal with the grief and shock the entire group felt. Looking back it is easy to imagine Jesus as invincible, knowing everything that was to happen even before it transpired. I think this is unlikely. The death of John surely had to be the most disappointing and shocking event in Jesus' entire life. His beloved kinsman, the man he had declared to be "more than a Prophet," and "greater than anyone born of woman" was dead. How could it possibly be true? What did it all mean? Was not the Kingdom of God at hand?

Keeping a low profile was no easy matter. The excitement Jesus had stirred with the crowds around the Sea of Galilee only increased. Word got out about the whereabouts of Jesus and his band of close followers and thousands flocked to find him. There was a period in which he and his band would regularly get in a boat and try to escape the crush, sailing out of sight to one of the many harbors or docks that dotted the lake, only to be spotted again by townsfolk in another area.

The picture has become a bit easier for us to imagine with the chance discovery in 1986 of the partly preserved hull of an ancient Galilean fish-

ing boat.³ Drought had dropped the level of the lake to such an extent
that the 8-by-26 cedar-and-oak boat was exposed in the mud not far
from the port of Magdala, where Mary Magdalene grew up. It was scientifically dated to the 1st century A.D. From the size of this vessel, it seems
likely that Jesus and his intimate entourage numbered around 15–20 at
this time. All the references we have mention them getting in and out of
"the boat" as if they are using only a single vessel. The Twelve were surely
with him, and likely his mother, his sisters, Mary Magdalene, and perhaps a few other select followers.

Model of a 1st-century Galilean fishing boat based on the ancient hull

GOING UNDERGROUND

Apparently, Jesus did not judge his temporary haven at Bethsaida to be a
secure enough location given the attention from the local populace that
he could not seem to avoid. He and his band of followers made a surprise
move. They headed due north to the villages of Caesarea Philippi, a journey of thirty miles, into the rugged mountainous territory of the Upper
Galilee, but still well outside the border of Herod's territory. There at the
headwaters of the Jordan, at the foot of snowcapped Mount Hermon,
was a place called Banias or Panias, after the god Pan. It is a lush and

lovely area, tropical in appearance, with steep cliffs and natural grottoes from which springs feed the Jordan River.

The Romans saw it as a holy area, a natural sanctuary, and there Herod the Great had built a shrine to the Emperor Augustus whose foundations are still visible today. Statues of various Greco-Roman deities were placed in niches carved into the cliffs all around. Philip, brother of Antipas, had built his capital just to the south and named it Caesarea Philippi. Excavations show that worshippers came from all around the Syro-Phoenician territory to eat and drink and ask the favor of their gods.

Jesus' followers must have been puzzled at his intentions. Why choose this area, of all places? His choice was likely based on several factors. First there was the matter of safety. This was surely the last place anyone would think to look for him. It was considered a pagan cultic area by pious Jews, and it was thoroughly removed from Herod's borders. Jesus had formulated a plan but this was the late fall of A.D. 29 and he did not intend to implement it until Passover the coming spring. It was necessary that the group essentially go underground through the winter months.

Shrine area at headwaters of Jordan near Caesarea Philippi

Second, he wanted a remote and private area, a place of retreat, to begin to teach his followers about the insights he was having as to what lay ahead. He realized his decisions for their future involved actions that would come as a complete shock to them, perhaps even drawing their opposition and objections.

Jesus had discovered an explanation as to why John the Baptizer had been so brutally removed from their midst. If I am right about Jesus turning to the prophetic texts of the Hebrew Bible for guidance, then he might well have looked there for his answer. If God allowed such a thing to happen then it must be part of the divine Plan and one should find evidence of such in the Hebrew Prophets. The two texts that John himself had appropriated and applied to his mission were Isaiah 40 and Malachi 3. He was the "messenger of Yahweh" who was to "prepare the Way in the desert." But there was nothing in either text indicating this Elijah-like figure would be killed. However, in the latter chapters of the Prophet Zechariah's book there was something everyone seemed to have overlooked. Zechariah had laid out a sequential scenario that would lead up to the climactic battle for Jerusalem when Yahweh himself would intervene and establish the Kingdom of God (Zechariah 14). Just prior to the description of this great victory are some chilling words that Jesus might well have begun to ponder:

> "Awake O sword against my shepherd, against the man who is my associate," says Yahweh of hosts. "Strike the shepherd, that the sheep may be scattered; I will turn my hand against the little ones." (Zechariah 13:7)

Who could this be, other than John the Baptizer? He was the one who had begun to "gather the sheep" like a shepherd. When Jesus sent the Twelve out he told them they were to preach to those he called "the lost sheep of the House of Israel." According to Zechariah, Yahweh's shepherd, one of the Two Messiahs who stood next to the Lord of all earth as his "associate," is to be *struck with a sword!* There it was, written for anyone to see. And this "striking of the shepherd" was to come just before the end of the age, so it could not be a reference to some figure of the past.

But there was more. In the previous chapter, Zechariah 12, one from the "house of David" was to be wounded or "pierced" and mourned over by his relatives. But the relatives of this pierced one are specified—they are of the house of David, but specifically through the line of Nathan—Solomon's obscure brother, the second son of Bathsheba, who never sat on the throne. And another group is mentioned—those of the "house of Levi." It was as if Jesus' own name had been written across the page. Was not his mother a descendant of David, but through Nathan, and did she not have this unusual mixture of Levitical blood in her lineage? If the shepherd was to be struck by a sword, then the Davidic Messiah was also to be wounded by piercing. This all had to take place before the Kingdom of God could arrive.

According to one of the Dead Sea Scrolls, the *Damascus Document*, an eerily similar course of events had transpired more than a hundred years earlier. This document mentions the "gathering in" or death of the one they called the "True Teacher," otherwise known as the Teacher of Righteousness. His death came in some unexpected way and the Qumran group turned to the Prophets to try to make sense of his tragic end. They found their explanation in the very same passage from Zechariah that Jesus began to ponder—"Strike the shepherd and the sheep will be scattered."[4]

Jesus began to talk to his followers about John the Baptizer. They knew that the "Elijah" figure had to "come first to restore all things" but they had never dreamed he was to be killed. Jesus told them outright: "I tell you that Elijah has come, and they did to him whatever they pleased, *as it is written about him*" (Mark 9:13). Mark does not elaborate but he alone preserves this precious bit of tradition. Here is an outright statement in the gospel of Mark that Jesus interpreted the *death* of John the Baptizer in the light of what was "written about him." The phrase was a technical one and referred to something being predicted or written in the Hebrew Scriptures. The passage from Zechariah 13 about striking the shepherd with a sword fits what had transpired, so it might well be one of the texts that Jesus had begun to ponder. Christians became accustomed to thinking of Jesus' suffering and death as predicted by the Prophets, but Jesus' statement that John's death had similarly been foretold was fortunately preserved for us in this single line in Mark. Both Matthew and Luke remove it. This is one more example of their tendency to downplay the role of John the Baptizer.

As Jesus began to grapple with the unexpected and tragic loss of his own teacher, John the Baptizer, he might well have begun to believe that he himself would meet a similar fate. Given the Roman attitude toward any who might seek to spark a messianic revolution this possibility was far from remote, but it might have been reinforced in Jesus' thinking by his reading of various prophetic texts. Mark writes that it was first at Caesarea Philippi, when the group had gone into hiding, that Jesus *began* to teach his disciples about his own impending suffering. He confirmed to them that some of them would live to see that the "kingdom of God would come with power" (Mark 9:1). But he also warned them that to follow him they too would have to "take up a cross" (Mark 8:34).

Jesus was well aware of what the Romans regularly did to rebel leaders. Herod might use a sword, but the Roman method, perfected over a two-hundred-year history, was crucifixion. It took as long as three days to die, the agony was unbearable, and the naked victims served as a shameful and terrifying example for the populace to behold. Pontius Pilate was the Roman governor in Judea and it was in Jerusalem that Jesus contemplated taking his stand. Zechariah had spoken of "piercing." Jesus began to openly warn the group of the trials and suffering that lay ahead for them all if they chose to remain with him. Mark says that Peter "rebuked" Jesus for thinking such a thing—that the King Messiah who was to rule all nations and usher in the Kingdom of God could suffer such a shameful fate. And had he not promised his Council of Twelve their own thrones and authority? Jesus answered Peter sharply, rebuking him in return: "Get behind me Satan, you are no longer on the side of God but men" (Mark 8:33). Mark indicates that even though Jesus brings up this subject a number of times the group as a whole would not accept it. It is as if they could not hear what they refused to imagine.

Zechariah was not the only text that Jesus might have considered. Once he began to contemplate the possibility of his own suffering many scriptural texts could have come to mind. Many of the Psalms spoke of the suffering of the righteous. There was even a passage that spoke of one who was destined to rule all nations being surrounded by a gang of evil-doers who "pierce his hands and feet" (Psalm 22:16). The "cornerstone" of God's spiritual Temple was to be "rejected by the builders" (Psalm 118:22). All through the latter chapters of Isaiah there are passages that fit into this same pattern, some of them in that first-person voice that Jesus might well have begun to identify as his own. The "Servant" figure who is to gather the tribes of Israel and become a light to the nations is also "deeply despised, abhorred by the nation" (Isaiah 49:7). He says to God, "I gave my back to those who struck me, my cheeks to those who pulled out the beard. I did not hide my face from insult and spitting" (Isaiah 50:6).

But did Jesus expect that he would die? We have to remember that our New Testament gospels are all written after the fact, so they present events with full knowledge of how they would transpire. According to Mark, who provides us with the core unfolding narrative of this Caesarea Philippi revelation, Jesus tells the disciples every detail of what is to come—including his death and resurrection from the dead on the third day:

> "See we are going up to Jerusalem, and the Son of Man will be handed over to the chief priests and the scribes, and they will con-demn him to death; then they will hand him over to the Gentiles; they will mock him, and spit upon him, and flog him, and kill him; and after three days he will rise again." (Mark 10:33–34)

This is surely history written after the fact to honor a Jesus who was thought to have known all things before they happened. It is unlikely that this is a verbatim prediction from the mouth of Jesus. Most scholars have concluded it is a composition by Mark intended to show Jesus' fore-knowledge of every detail of his future. But that is not to say that *none* of it is historical. Jesus well might have told his disciples, based on his reading of the texts of Scripture I have indicated, of the impending trials ahead.

If Jesus did come to anticipate his suffering at the hands of his ene-mies, I am convinced that he expected that he would be *saved* from death, delivered from the "mouth of the lion" as the Psalmist had predicted (Psalm 22:21). In text after text that deals with the suffering of God's righteous servants they are always rescued from the "gates of death" at the last moment. God does not give his "faithful one" up to Sheol,[5] nor allow him to see the Pit (Psalm 16:10). Psalm 118 is perhaps the most explicit in this regard. God's righteous servant, the "stone rejected by the builders," and "surrounded by Gentiles" cries out: "I shall not die, but I shall live, and recount the deeds of Yah[weh] . . . Yah[weh] did not give me over to death."[6] It is also possible that Jesus drew inspiration from the words and meditations of the Teacher at Qumran who had pioneered the "Way in the desert" in the previous century. The *Thanksgiving Hymns* in particular, parts of which were penned directly by the Teacher, present a paradigm of the "righteous sufferer" whose faithfulness to God was opposed by wicked forces. Hymn 2 reads in part:

> Violent men have sought after my life because I have clung to your Covenant. For they, an assembly of deceit, and a horde of Satan, know not that my stand is maintained by you and that in your mercy *you will save my life* since my steps proceed from you.[7]

There was an exception. After all, God had not always rescued the righteous. Isaiah 53 predicts the suffering of a "righteous servant" who is "cut off from the land of the living," his throat slit open like a lamb being slaughtered, and his blood poured out like an offering for sins. Jesus might have found in this passage an explanation of the fate of his teacher John the Baptizer, who had been slaughtered in such a way. And if Jesus believed that he was sent to "raise the dead" perhaps he anticipated that he, as Messiah, would "release" John from the prison of the bars of death once he completed his own trial of suffering. Together the Two Messiahs would yet fulfill their destined mission. John was his teacher and as Jesus himself said, "The disciple is not above his teacher, but everyone who is perfected shall be *as* his teacher" (Luke 6:40). Jesus saw his sufferings ahead as a "perfecting" that God required of both him and his followers—in order that the Kingdom of God could fully appear. As he told the Twelve the last night of his life—"You who stand by me in my testing I confer on you a Kingdom as my Father has conferred on me . . . and you will sit on thrones judging the twelve tribes of Israel" (Luke 22:28–30). Suffering had to come before exaltation and glory. It was a lesson hard to accept.

Of course we don't know the inner thoughts and struggles of Jesus. What I have tried to do here is imagine what he might have been thinking based on the evidence that we have in our gospels. It is clear that Caesarea Philippi was a turning point. From that time on, as Luke puts it, "Jesus set his face to go to Jerusalem" (Luke 9:51).

THE FINAL CAMPAIGN

We don't know how long the group stayed in the north but eventually they made their way back to the house at Capernaum (Mark 9:33). One indication that not much of what Jesus had taught them about the suffering that lay ahead had been understood is that an argument arose on the trip back as to who would be the greatest when the Kingdom arrived. In fact, two of the Twelve, the fishermen James and John, asked if they could have the two choice places—one at the right hand, and the other at the left, when Jesus was inaugurated as King (Mark 10:37). Jesus replied that only God could decide that and first must come for all of them the "cup" of suffering.

As the word spread that he and his inner entourage were back in Capernaum, a wider group of followers began to gather there, wondering what would transpire next. The evidence suggests that Jesus had a definite and detailed strategy in mind from this point on. He had made a momentous decision. He had decided to push things to the limit, beginning a process that he believed would result in the dramatic and decisive overthrow of Satan and his kingdoms.

From among his wider group of followers he chose *seventy* delegates, dividing them, as he had done the Twelve, into two-person teams. They were to fan out ahead of him into every town and place he intended to go. Their basic commission was to heal the sick, cast out demons, and proclaim in every place, "The Kingdom of God has come near to you"

(Luke 10). Jesus saw this as a final message, a finishing of the work that he and John had begun three years earlier. He told the teams that any town that rejected them was to be marked for destruction in the impending judgment.

We don't know how widely these teams traveled but they must have surely covered the regions in and around the Galilee and possibly they went into Judea as well. We are told they "returned with joy," ecstatic over the powers that they had been able to exercise over the demonic world by using Jesus' name to heal and cast out evil spirits. Jesus told them, "I watched Satan fall from heaven like a flash of lightning" (Luke 10:18). Jesus had had some type of vision or dream in which he saw the impending overthrow of Satan's kingdoms—perhaps at the very time these teams were carrying out their work. For him it was an absolute confirmation that the Kingdom of God would soon be manifest and the whole country would see the "sign of the Son of Man coming in the clouds of heaven."

At this point Jesus had a core following of perhaps one hundred or more, and they began to make their way around the various towns and villages, moving south toward Jerusalem and Judea.[8] According to Luke the crowds gathered not by the hundreds but by the thousands, so much so that they trampled on one another (Luke 12:1). Herod Antipas became quite alarmed at these activities and put out the word to have Jesus arrested. Some of the Pharisees got word of the plan and warned Jesus that he needed to leave Galilee since Herod intended to kill him. Jesus told them "Go and tell that fox for me, 'Listen, I am casting out demons and healing today and tomorrow and *on the third day* I will be finished' " (Luke 13:32). The reference to the "third day" is prophetic. It is a cryptic but direct allusion to the words of the prophet Hosea:

> *Come let us return to Yahweh;*
> *For it is he who has torn, and he will heal us;*
> *He has struck down, and he will bind us up.*
> *After two days he will revive us;*
> *On the third day he will raise us up,*
> *That we may live before him. (Hosea 6:1–2)*

In this text the people of Israel who have been struck down will be re-vived "after two days" and "on the third day" raised up. Hosea is speaking of the condition of Israel in exile and subject to foreign rule, which God had allowed for their sins. In prophetic texts a "day" is often used symbol-ically for a "year."[9] Jesus had begun his "healing" of Israel, in fulfillment of Isaiah 61, in the spring of A.D. 28 and had continued for nearly two years. He planned to finish his work "on the third day," which would be the up-coming spring of A.D. 30. According to Hosea it would be at that point that God would "raise up" Israel from its oppression. Whether the mes-sage ever got to Herod or not, the coded cryptic content would likely have been lost on him. But to Jesus each of these prophetic texts was a piece of the puzzle. Given this reading of the text, and Jesus' own vision of Satan's fall, Hosea's "two days" were about over, and Israel's "raising" was at hand.

Jesus' reference to Israel being raised "on the third day" subsequently was confused with ideas about Jesus himself being raised from the dead "on the third day." But the text of Hosea is clearly talking about the na-tion, not the Messiah. And neither Hosea nor Jesus had literal twenty-four-hour days in mind. Jesus used the phrase as a type of "apocalyptic code" to signify his own understanding of the final period of time leading to Israel's redemption.

Around this time, in the late fall of A.D. 29, Jesus also got word that his enemies in Jerusalem were looking for a way to have him arrested and killed (John 7:1). Presumably these enemies were those leading Jews of the aristocratic class who saw figures like John the Baptizer and Jesus as a threat to their power and control, both of the economics of the Temple and the regulation of religious affairs. Jesus did not be-lieve that the timing was right for him to confront either Herod in Galilee or the authorities in Jerusalem so he decided to move east, across the Jordan River, into a region known as the Decapolis to wait through the winter. The Decapolis was outside the borders of Galilee and Judea and was governed by a loose federation of ten Greco-Roman city-states. It was relatively easy for Jesus and his en-tourage to set up their camp in the mountainous hill country of Gil-ead and find a measure of solitude and safety. We don't know if he took the larger group of over one hundred or just the inner group that he had taken north to Caesarea Philippi. In 1991 through some textual sleuthing I was able to locate and visit this "Jesus hideout" in Jordan where Jesus and his band of loyal followers possibly spent that last winter. It was one of the most exciting discoveries of my life.

12

LAST DAYS IN
JERUSALEM

THE gospel of John provides us with some fascinating details about the last days of Jesus, of which Mark and the other gospels are unaware. One can get the impression, from reading Mark, that after traveling north to Caesarea Philippi, Jesus and his band of followers journeyed south to Jerusalem almost immediately.[1] Apparently this was not the case. Jesus spent the winter months, at least from December of A.D. 29 to the spring of A.D. 30 east of the Jordan in a place I have called the "Jesus hideout." John gives us a clue to the location:

> He went away again *across the Jordan* to the place where John had been baptizing earlier and he remained there. (John 10:40)

John had been baptizing earlier "at Aenon near Salim because waters were abundant there" (John 3:23). This place can be identified today as Tel Salim, eight miles south of Bet Shean, just west of the Jordan River. Even today the rich springs in the area provide water for Israeli fish ponds. Back in 1991 I was studying a map of this area and noticed that directly across the Jordan from Tel Salim is a deep ravine or Wadi today called in Arabic *el-Yabis*. It is on the east bank, part of the Hashemite

Kingdom of Jordan today. I realized that in biblical times this was the famous "brook Cherith" where Elijah had hidden when the infamous King
Ahab and Queen Jezebel were seeking to kill him. It was there that Elijah
was fed by the ravens (1 Kings 17). It made sense to me that Jesus might
choose this location, because of its biblical associations if he was hiding
out from his enemies in Galilee and Judea who wanted to kill him.

But then I noticed something else. Wadi Cherith is just a few miles
south of the Decapolis city of Pella. I knew from my reading that when
Jesus' followers had fled Jerusalem in A.D. 68, just before the Roman siege
in the great Jewish Revolt, they had fled to the region of Pella. James the
brother of Jesus had already been killed and Jesus' brother Simon was
leader of the community of Nazarenes. The book of Revelation gives a
cryptic account of the flight. The community, symbolically referred to as
a "woman," flees from the mouth of the "dragon," a symbol for Satan, "into
the wilderness *to her place* where she is nourished" (Revelation 12:14). Tradition has it that they stayed there for over three years, returning only
after the destruction of Jerusalem in A.D. 70. It dawned on me that their
choice of the Pella region was not a random one. If I am correct about the
"Jesus hideout" then the group would have viewed the Wadi Cherith as a
place of safety, not only because of Elijah being protected and nourished
there, but because some of them had spent time there with Jesus as well.
In fact, it is entirely possible that Simon's choice of this place as a destina-
tion for the flight from Jerusalem had to do with the time he had spent
there with his brother Jesus in the winter of A.D. 29.

Not long after making these connections I decided to visit Wadi
Cherith. I was amazed at what I discovered. As one moves east along the
Wadi it quickly becomes almost inaccessible with waterfalls and rocks,
but after a short distance it opens into an area surrounded by steep cliffs
with many caves—wholly protected from outside access. There were pottery fragments dating to the 1st century Roman period on the floors of
the caves. I tried to imagine Jesus and his small band of followers living
there during those crucial final months of Jesus' life, likely including his
own mother, brothers, and sisters. At the time we could not accomplish
much more than a survey because of tensions from the Gulf War. Perhaps future archaeological work in the area will provide us with a more
definitive link between this location and Jesus' last days—as well as the

Rugged cliffs and caves leading into Wadi el-Yabis

community of Nazarenes who lived there later.

In mid-December of A.D. 29, Jesus made a daring move. We know the date because the gospel of John tells us it was winter, at the time of the Jewish festival of Hanukah.[2] He made a clandestine trip to Jerusalem and was almost killed. He had gone into Herod's Temple and was walking in the area called the Portico of Solomon when some of the Jewish authorities cornered him and demanded that he say plainly whether he was the Messiah or not. It was literally a plot to kill. To make such a claim was to declare oneself King, a political move the Romans would not tolerate even from one who appeared to have no army or any ambitions to spark a revolt. There was zero tolerance for Messiahs. They were not considered to be harmless religious fanatics but potentially seditious enemies of Rome. Jesus' reply, "You do not believe because you do not belong to my sheep," so infuriated his enemies that they picked up stones to stone him. John says they tried to arrest him but he escaped and went back to his hideout across the Jordan.

Jesus had so far never

Drawing of Jesus' hideout in Wadi el-Yabis

publicly said he was Israel's rightful King. Privately up at Caesarea Philippi he had tacitly accepted Simon Peter's assertion "You are the Messiah," when he was telling them about the suffering he anticipated ahead. But he had "sternly ordered them not to tell anyone about him" (Mark 8:30). In the earlier days of his preaching campaigns he would regularly silence any who tried to make him known. Rumors were flying, and the crowds were ready for anyone who would stir things against the Romans and their supporters, but we have no record of Jesus even mentioning his Davidic lineage, much less making an open claim to the throne as King of Israel. Earlier that year, after John's death, one of Jesus' motives for avoiding the crowds was that he knew there was a move to try to take him by force to make him King (John 6:15).

Judging from his actions he was an apocalyptic prophet, an exorcist, and a healer. His message was not about himself but about the arrival of the Kingdom of God. But he *had* explicitly tied the arrival of the Kingdom to his activities: "If I by the finger of God cast out demons, the kingdom of God has come upon you" (Luke 11:20). And he had associated his role with the fulfillment of Isaiah 61, a text that is patently messianic in content. For Jesus, timing was everything. He repeatedly told his followers, "My time has not yet come." He had a specific plan in mind and at the right time he would make his move.

THE DECISIVE CONFRONTATION

In mid March of A.D. 30 the time had arrived. Jesus and his entourage headed south down the Jordan River Valley to Jerusalem. It was a three-day trip and they would have camped out along the way. Passover was near, falling during the first week of April. All of Galilee were on the road, making their way to Jerusalem for Passover. The group around Jesus, however large it was at that time, likely began to swell, both with followers and the curious. There was a sense of great excitement in the air. Everyone wondered what was going to happen next. There was probably a bit of amazement that Jesus planned to openly travel to Jerusalem despite the plots to kill him by Herod and the authorities in Jerusalem.

One of the pilgrim stops mentioned by Josephus just at the foot of the Samaritan mountains is still visible along the way, with caves for shelter by the road and a natural spring. They would have reached it the first night. One should picture a group of mixed ages, men and women, with baggage and gear, and pack animals. Their social makeup was completely diverse. Most were Galileans, though Jesus had his sympathizers in Judea and Jerusalem as well, as we shall see. At the core were the Twelve, including his brothers, then his mother and sisters, Mary Magdalene, and Salome the mother of the fishermen James and John. Luke also names Joanna, married to an official in Herod's household named Chuza; and Susanna—women of means who provided funds for the operation. Luke adds that there were "many other women" in the group (Luke 8:1–3).

Pilgrim way station with caves on the way to Jericho

The second night they reached Jericho, just north of the Dead Sea and fifteen miles east of Jerusalem. The Qumran settlement, the administrative center of the Essenes where the Dead Sea Scrolls were found, was just a few miles to the south. As the group entered Jericho a huge crowd gathered and a blind man began to cry out "Jesus of Nazareth, *son of David*, have mercy on me!" These were revolutionary words. They are equivalent to publicly proclaiming one as the Messiah or King of Israel. Some of Jesus' followers tried to silence the man, knowing Jesus had forbidden such declarations in the past. Jesus stopped and called the man over, and touching his eyes said: "Receive your sight, your faith has made you well." According to the gospels he was instantly healed, joined the band of followers, and the crowd crushing around Jesus became ecstatic with excitement. Jesus at last was ready to permit the open proclamation of his Kingship—come what may.

The group spent Saturday, the Jewish Sabbath day, in Jericho. Sunday was to prove as busy as it would be fateful. It was our March 31 but the 10th of Nisan on the Jewish calendar.[3] Passover began at dusk as the 14th of Nisan ended, which was a Thursday just four days ahead. A final countdown had begun.

One enters Jerusalem traveling up the steep road from Jericho from the east. The Jesus party must have gained quite a bit of attention and lots more people by the time it arrived in the late afternoon at the Mount of Olives. When the group reached the summit at the little village of Bethany on the eastern side, Jesus halted the procession. He sent two of his disciples into the town telling them to find a donkey's colt and bring it to him. Jesus sat on the animal and slowly made his way down the steep path descending the western side of the Mount of Olives, which over-looked Herod's Temple and heart of the city. His followers began to spread garments in front of the animal as it made its way and as the crowds swelled with excitement they cut leafy branches from the trees and did the same, creating a "royal carpet" for the King. Psalm 118 celebrates the procession of one "coming in the name of Yahweh" whose festal procession is celebrated with branches of leafy foliage (Psalm 118:27). Jesus' intention was as obvious as it was deliberate. The prophet Zechariah had written:

> Rejoice greatly, O daughter of Zion; Shout, O daughter of Jerusalem: Behold, your King comes to you; he is just, and having salvation; lowly, and riding upon an ass, even upon a colt the foal of an ass. (Zechariah 9:9)

The time had come. The die was cast. Zechariah's prophetic scenario for the "end of days" was now to unfold. By this provocative act of prophetic "pantomiming" Jesus was openly declaring himself claimant to the throne of Israel. No one who knew the Hebrew Prophets could have

Nineteenth-century photograph showing the approach to the
Mount of Olives from the Judean desert

missed the point. The excitement and buzz about this extraordinary event ignited like sparks in tinder. The crowds began to chant explicit messianic slogans: "Hosanna to the Son of David" and "Blessed is the Kingdom of our father David that is coming." The uproar would have been visible to anyone in the city below. Some Pharisees in the crowd, alarmed at the revolutionary implications of the scene, said to Jesus, "Teacher, rebuke your disciples." Jesus replied: "I tell you, if these were silent, the very stones would cry out" (Luke 19:39–40).

After arriving at the city Jesus melted into the crowd. He had carried out the first stage of his plan. His purpose was not to lead a mob in revolt but to fulfill certain specific biblical prophecies. That he had done. As King he had come to "Zion," or Jerusalem, riding on the foal of a donkey, provoking the rejoicing of the people. The words of the prophet Zechariah had been fulfilled that day.

By the time Jesus entered the city it was late in the day, and Mark says he "looked around at everything" (Mark 11:11). He likely went into the Temple compound through the southern gates, working out in his mind his plan for the following day. He returned to Bethany on the Mount of

Olives by nightfall where he, his Council of Twelve, and the women were staying in the home of two sisters, Mary and Martha, who were support-ers of his movement.

On Monday morning Jesus and a select band of his followers made their way down the slopes of the Mount of Olives once again and entered the Temple. On the south side of the huge Temple compound was an area where the money changers operated and where animals that were ritually acceptable for sacrifice were sold. From a Jewish point of view there was nothing wrong with either of these activities. The popular idea that Jesus objected to "money changing" in the Temple is incorrect. Jews from all over the world brought coinage of all types as offerings to the Temple and it was necessary to have some standard of evaluation and conversion. There was also a need for people to be able to purchase sacri-ficial animals right at the Temple rather than to try to bring them from afar—especially at Passover when hundreds of thousands of pilgrims re-quired one lamb per household. Some have assumed that the money changing had to do with converting coins with "pagan" images and slo-gans to Jewish coinage that was considered religiously acceptable. The very opposite was the case. The *only* coins accepted at the Jerusalem Tem-ple were silver Tyrian shekels and half-shekels, which had the image of

Tyrian silver shekels—required coinage at Herod's Temple

Hercules on one side and an eagle perched on the bow of a ship on the other! The issue was not pagan images but consistency of value. Tyrian shekels were guaranteed to be made of 95 percent pure silver.[4] The Sadducean priests who ran the Temple conveniently argued that the "purity" of one's offering to God superseded any defilement that the images might bring.

At Passover the money-changing operation was vastly expanded since Moses had commanded that each male Jew over the age of twenty donate a half-shekel of silver to the sanctuary once a year (Exodus 30:13). This offering, due by Passover, necessitated special tables to be set up in the Temple three weeks before to handle the huge crowds who would come to Jerusalem for the festival.[5] Josephus estimates that two and a half million Jews from all around the world gathered in Jerusalem at Passover. He based his number on the 225,600 lambs that were sacrificed on the day of Passover itself.[6] Scholars find his numbers likely inflated, but even with that taken into consideration the task of handling the numbers of Passover pilgrims must have been staggering.

The profit from these activities was enormous. The Jerusalem Temple had the most lucrative system of temple commerce in the entire Roman world. As one might expect, there were certain fees and surcharges added to these services. These funds went to support the wealthy class of Sadducean priests who had their lavish homes just west of the Temple compound in the area called the "Jewish Quarter" of the Old City today. These priests in turn worked closely with their Roman sponsors. To understand the economy in Jerusalem, which really was a type of "Temple state," one needs only to "follow the money."

But what about the poor or those who could scarcely afford the trip to Jerusalem, much less the inflated charges for these required sacrifices? Maybe Jesus had been told the story growing up of how his mother Mary and his adopted father Joseph had not even been able to afford a lamb for an offering at his birth. They had managed to purchase two doves. And somehow they had to come up with the five Tyrian silver shekels to fulfill the commandment of "redeeming the firstborn." Jesus' family was typical of thousands of others at the time—large, poor, and yet devoted to fulfilling God's commandments.

Jesus arrived that Monday morning at the very height of the trade season. He had three words on his mind: Zechariah, Isaiah, and Jeremiah. At the very end of Zechariah's sequential scenario of the "end times" he declares, "And there will no longer be traders in the house of Yahweh of hosts on that day" (Zechariah 14:21). Jeremiah had gone into the Temple of his day, the 1st Temple built by King Solomon, and declared in the name of Yahweh: "Has this house, which is called by my name, become a den of robbers in your sight?" (Jeremiah 7:11). And Isaiah had envisioned a time when God's Temple at Jerusalem would become a "house of prayer for all nations," providing a spiritual center for humanity (Isaiah 56:7).

Jesus' activities that day were not intended to change things or to spark a revolution. Like his ride down the Mount of Olives on the foal of the donkey, he intended to *signal* something—namely that the imminent overthrow of the corrupt Temple system was at hand and the vision of the Prophets would be fulfilled. He began to overturn the tables of the money changers and topple the pay stations of those who sat taking money for the sale of the animals. He then quoted the words of Jeremiah and Isaiah as an explanation for his actions. Mark also adds that he "would not allow anyone to carry anything through the Temple" (Mark 11:16). There were certain narrow gates through which goods had to pass to support the exchange and sales activities and Jesus stationed several of his rugged Galilean men at these posts and told them business was closed for the day.

The priestly leadership heard about the ruckus. They already had been looking for a way to have Jesus arrested and killed. They were more determined than ever to stop him but they feared the people. The crowd must have been immense that Monday morning and the crush of people cheered on Jesus. This was not a riot for which the priests might call in the Romans. They would be reluctant to do that anyway since the governor Pontius Pilate was known for his brutal handling of Temple crowds and his disdain for the Jews in general. Jesus' actions were a symbolic "prophetic protest" and he had the support of the people, who were likely tired of paying the prices demanded to fulfill these ritual requirements. Mark indicates the "siege" lasted the entire day and it was only at evening that Jesus and his men left the city and went back to Bethany for the night.

Tuesday was an important day for Jesus and his Council of Twelve. They openly went back to the Temple early that morning and Jesus spent the entire day verbally sparring with various segments of the Temple establishment, including the Sadducean priests, leading Pharisees, and the Herodians—the political supporters of Herod's dynasty. The priests asked him "by what authority are you doing these things?" They apparently referred to his two "prophetic" activities on Sunday and Monday. He said he would tell them if they would state in front of the crowds who were intently following the exchange whether John the Baptizer had been a prophet of God or a charlatan. Although the priests had not responded positively to John's call of repentance and baptism, the people had, by the masses, and the priests feared to answer, knowing John's immense popularity. The Pharisees and Herodians asked Jesus whether he supported Roman taxation—perhaps the most sensitive political and religious issue of the day. Holding up a Roman coin he replied with his now famous but ambiguous retort: "Render to Caesar the things that are Caesar's and to God the things that are God's" (Mark 12:17).

Jesus said two things that day that seem to epitomize his entire view of "true religion," especially vis-à-vis what was going on in the Herodian Temple. A man asked Jesus which of the commandments of the Torah was the greatest. Jesus quoted the Shema—that great confession of the Jewish faith: "Hear O Israel, Yahweh our God, Yahweh is One, and you shall love Yahweh your God with all your heart, and with all your soul, and with all your mind, and with all your strength." He added that the "second" greatest commandment was to love one's fellow human being as oneself. The man agreed and observed that if one loved God, and loved one's fellow as oneself, that would be "much more than all whole burnt offerings and sacrifices." Jesus then made a surprising statement to the man: "You are not far from the Kingdom of God" (Mark 12:28–34). This indicates that Jesus' view of the Kingdom of God involved not only the revolutionary overthrow of the kingdoms of the world, but also a certain spiritual insight into what God most desires from human beings. One would not be complete without the other.

Toward the end of the day, as people were lined up to bring their monetary contributions into the Temple treasury, Jesus observed a poor widow who had come with two copper coins. It was all she had. He told the crowds, "This poor widow has put in more than all of these" (Mark 12:43). The coin was called a *lepton* and it took one hundred of them to make a denarius—an average day's wage for a laborer.

Throughout the day the crowds were amazed and thrilled at all Jesus said and they marveled at the way he seemed to be able to handle his challengers no matter their rank or power. The gospels report repeatedly that Jesus' enemies wanted to arrest him but feared the crowds. Luke says that people were pouring into the Temple to hear him as word spread through the city about the excitement he had caused (Luke 21:38). The Temple officials knew that if they acted publicly they would provoke a riot among the people and the Romans would step in, possibly blaming them for the disturbance. Their only hope was to arrest Jesus somehow when he was alone, maybe at night, with only a few of his followers around. Passover was two days away and they had no idea what Jesus had in mind or of what he might be capable. They determined that they had to act fast.

A FINAL EVENING MEAL

On Wednesday Jesus began to make plans for Passover. He sent two of his disciples into the city to prepare a large second-story guest room where he could gather secretly and safely with his inner group. He knew someone with such a room available and he had prearranged for its use. Christian pilgrims today are shown a Crusader site known as the Cenacle or "Upper Room" on the Western Hill of Jerusalem that the Crusaders misnamed "Mount Zion." This area was part of the "Upper City" where Herod had built his palace. It is topographically higher than even the Temple Mount. It was the grandest section of ancient Jerusalem with broad streets and plazas and the palatial homes of the wealthy. It is very unlikely that this was the place.[7]

The "Upper Room" was more likely located in the lower city, the original "Mount Zion," where the poor lived, just north of the pool of Siloam. In fact Jesus tells his two disciples to "follow a man carrying a jug of water," who will enter the city, and then enter a certain house. The only water source was in the southern part of the lower city of Jerusalem. In fact the authentic site of the pool of Siloam was uncovered quite by accident in 2004. We can now pinpoint the precise area mentioned in the gospels.

Later Christian tradition put Jesus' last meal with his disciples on Thursday evening and his crucifixion on Friday. We now know that is one day off. Jesus' last meal was Wednesday night, and he was crucified on Thursday, the 14th of the Jewish month Nisan. The Passover meal itself was eaten Thursday night, at sundown, as the 15th of Nisan began. Jesus never ate that Passover meal. He had died at 3 P.M. on Thursday.

The confusion arose because all the gospels say that there was a rush to get his body off the cross and buried before sundown because the "Sabbath" was near. Everyone assumed the reference to the Sabbath had to be Saturday—so the crucifixion must have been on a Friday. However, as Jews know, the day of Passover itself is also a "Sabbath" or rest day—no matter what weekday it falls on. In the year A.D. 30, Friday the 15th of the Nisan was also a Sabbath—so *two* Sabbaths occurred back to back—Friday *and* Saturday. Matthew seems to know this as he says that the women who visited Jesus' tomb came early Sunday morning "after the Sabbaths"—the original Greek is plural (Matthew 28:1).

THE EVENTS SURROUNDING JESUS' CRUCIFIXION

Date	April 3/ Nisan 13	April 4/ Nisan 14	April 5/ Nisan 15	April 6/ Nisan 16	April 7/ Nisan 17
Weekday	Wednesday	Thursday	Friday (Sabbath)	Saturday (Sabbath)	Sunday
Events	Jesus' Last Supper & Gethsemane arrest	Crucifixion 9 A.M. Death at 3 P.M. Passover meal after sunset	Passover Day Jesus in tomb	Jesus in tomb	Empty tomb discovered

As is often the case, the gospel of John preserves a more accurate chronology of what went on.[8] John specifies that the Wednesday night "last supper" was "*before* the festival of Passover." He also notes that when Jesus' accusers delivered him to be crucified on Thursday morning they would not enter Pilate's courtyard because they would be defiled and would not be able to eat the Passover *that* evening (John 18:28). John knows that the Jews would be eating their traditional Passover, or Seder meal, Thursday evening.

Reading Mark, Matthew, and Luke one can get the impression that the "last supper" *was* the Passover meal. Some have even argued that Jesus might have eaten the Passover meal a day early—knowing ahead of time that he would be dead. But the fact is, Jesus ate no Passover meal in A.D. 30. When the Passover meal began at sundown on Thursday, Jesus was dead. He had been hastily put in a tomb until after the festival when a proper funeral could be arranged.

There are some hints outside of John's gospel that such was the case. In Luke, for example, Jesus tells his followers at that last meal: "I earnestly wanted to eat this Passover with you before I suffer but I won't eat it until it is fulfilled in the kingdom of God" (Luke 22:14–16). A later copyist of the manuscript inserted the word "again" to make it say "I won't eat it again," since the tradition had developed that Jesus did observe Passover that night and changed its observance to the Christian Eucharist or Mass. Another indication that this is not a Passover meal is that all our records report that Jesus shared "a loaf of bread" with his disciples, using the Greek word (*artos*) that refers to an ordinary loaf—not to the unleavened flatbread or *matzos* that Jews eat with their Passover meals. Also, when Paul refers to the "last supper" he significantly does not say "on the night of Passover," but rather "on the night Jesus was betrayed," and he also mentions the "loaf of bread" (1 Corinthians 11:23). If this meal had been the Passover, Paul would have surely wanted to say that, but he does not.

As late as Wednesday morning Jesus had still intended to eat the Passover on Thursday night. When he sent his two disciples into the city he instructed them to begin to make the preparations. His enemies had determined not to try to arrest him during the feast "lest there be a riot of the people" (Mark 14:2). That meant he was likely "safe" for the next week, since the "feast" included the seven days of Unleavened Bread that followed the Passover meal. Passover is the most family-oriented festival in Jewish tradition. As head of his household Jesus would have gathered with his mother, his sisters, the women who had come with him from Galilee, perhaps some of his close supporters in Jerusalem, and his Council of Twelve. It is inconceivable that a Jewish head of a household would eat the Passover segregated from his family with twelve male disciples. This was no Passover meal. Something had gone terribly wrong so that all his Passover plans were changed.

Jesus had planned a special meal Wednesday evening alone with his Council of Twelve in the upper room of the guesthouse in the lower city. The events of the past few days had brought things to a crisis and he knew the confrontation with the authorities was unavoidable. In the coming days he expected to be arrested, delivered to the Romans, and possibly crucified. He had intentionally chosen the time and the place—Passover in Jerusalem—to confront the powers that be. There was much of a private nature to discuss with those upon whom he most depended in the critical days ahead. He firmly believed that if he and his followers offered themselves up, placing their fate in God's hands, that the Kingdom of God would manifest itself. He had intentionally fulfilled two of Zechariah's prophecies—riding into the city as King on the foal, and symbolically removing the "traders" from the "house of God."

At some point that day Jesus had learned that Judas Iscariot, one of his trusted Council of Twelve, had struck a deal with his enemies to have Jesus arrested whenever there was an opportunity to get him alone, away from the crowds. How Jesus knew of the plot we are not told but during the meal he said openly, "One of you who is eating with me will betray me" (Mark 14:18). His life seemed to be unfolding according to some scriptural plan. Had not David written in the Psalms, "Even my bosom friend, in whom I trusted, who ate of my bread, has lifted the heel against me" (Psalm 41:9). History has a strange way of repeating itself. Over a hundred years earlier, the Teacher of Righteousness who led the Dead Sea Scroll community had quoted that very Psalm when one of his inner "Council" had betrayed him.[9]

When Judas Iscariot realized that the plan for the evening included a retreat for prayer in the Garden of Gethsemane after the meal, he abruptly left the group. This secluded spot, at the foot of the Mount of Olives, just across the Kidron Valley from the Old City, offered just the setting he had promised to deliver. Some have tried to interpret Judas's motives in a positive light. Perhaps he quite sincerely wanted Jesus to declare himself King and take power, thinking the threat of an arrest might force his hand. We simply don't know what might have been in his mind. The gospels are content simply to call him "the Betrayer" and his name is seldom mentioned without this description.

Ironically our earliest account of that last meal on Wednesday night comes from Paul, not from any of our gospels. In a letter to his followers in the Greek city of Corinth, written around A.D. 54, Paul passes on a tradition that he says he "received" from Jesus: "Jesus on the night he was betrayed took a loaf of bread, and when he had given thanks, he broke it and said, 'This is my body that is broken for you. Do this in remembrance of me.' In the same way he took the cup also, after supper, saying, 'This cup is the new covenant in my blood. Do this, as often as you drink it, in remembrance of me' " (1 Corinthians 11:23–25).

These words, which are familiar to Christians as part of the Eucharist or the Mass, are repeated with only slight variations in Mark, Matthew, and Luke. They represent the epitome of Christian faith, the pillar of the Christian Gospel: all humankind is saved from sins by the sacrificed body and blood of Jesus. What is the historical likelihood that this tradition, based on what Paul said he "received" from Jesus, represents what Jesus said at that last meal? As surprising as it might sound, there are some legitimate problems to consider.

At every Jewish meal, bread is broken, wine is shared, and blessings are said over each—but the idea of eating human flesh and drinking blood, even symbolically, is completely alien to Judaism. The Torah specifically forbids the consuming of blood, not just for Israelites but anyone. Noah and his descendants, as representatives of all humanity, were first given the prohibition against "eating blood" (Genesis 9:4). Moses had warned, "If anyone of the house of Israel or the Gentiles who reside among them eats any blood I will set my face against that person who eats blood and will cut that person off from the people" (Leviticus 17:10). James, the brother of Jesus, later mentions this as one of the "necessary requirements" for non-Jews to join the Nazarene community—they are not to eat blood (Acts 15:20). These restrictions concern the blood of animals. Consuming human flesh and blood was not forbidden, it was simply inconceivable. This general sensitivity to the very idea of "drinking blood" precludes the likelihood that Jesus would have used such symbols.

As we discussed earlier, the Essene community at Qumran described in one of its scrolls a "messianic banquet" of the future at which the Priestly Messiah and the Davidic Messiah sit together with the community and bless their sacred meal of bread and wine, passing it to the community of believers, as a celebration of the Kingdom of God. They would surely have been appalled at any symbolism suggesting the bread was human flesh and the wine was blood.[10] Such an idea simply could not have come from Jesus as a Jew.

So where does this language originate? If it first surfaces in Paul, and he did not in fact get it from Jesus, then what was its source? The closest parallels are certain Greco-Roman magical rites. We have a Greek papyrus that records a love spell in which a male pronounces certain incantations over a cup of wine that represents the blood that the Egyptian god Osiris had given to his consort Isis to make her feel love for him. When his lover drinks the wine, she symbolically unites with her beloved by consuming his blood.[11] In another text the wine is made into the flesh of Osiris.[12] The symbolic eating of "flesh" and drinking of "blood" was a magical rite of union in Greco-Roman culture.

We have to consider that Paul grew up in the Greco-Roman culture of the city of Tarsus in Asia Minor, outside the land of Israel. He never met or talked to Jesus. The connection he claims to Jesus is a "visionary" one, not Jesus as a flesh-and-blood human being walking the earth. When the Twelve met to replace Judas, after Jesus had been killed, they insisted that to be part of their group one had to have been with Jesus from the time of John the Baptizer through his crucifixion (Acts 1:21–22). Seeing visions and hearing voices were not accepted as qualifications for an apostle.

Second, and even more telling, the gospel of John recounts the events of that last Wednesday night meal but there is absolutely no reference to these words of Jesus instituting this new ceremony of the Eucharist. If Jesus in fact had inaugurated the practice of eating bread as his body, and drinking wine as his blood at this "last supper" how could John possibly have left it out? What John writes is that Jesus sat down to the supper, by all indications an ordinary Jewish meal. After supper he got up, took a basin of water and a cloth, and began to wash his disciples' feet as an example of how a Teacher and Master should act as a servant—even to his disciples. Jesus then began to talk about how he was to be betrayed and John tells us that Judas abruptly left the meal.

Mark's gospel is very close in its theological ideas to those of Paul. It seems likely that Mark, writing a decade after Paul's account of the last supper, inserts this "eat my body" and "drink my blood" tradition into his gospel, influenced by what Paul has claimed to have received. Matthew and Luke both base their narratives wholly upon Mark, and Luke is an unabashed advocate of Paul as well. Everything seems to trace back to Paul. As we will see, there is no evidence that the original Jewish followers of Jesus, led by Jesus' brother James, headquartered in Jerusalem, ever practiced any rite of this type. Like all Jews they did sanctify wine and bread as part of a sacred meal, and they likely looked back to the "night he was betrayed," remembering that last meal with Jesus.

What we really need to resolve this matter is an independent source of some type, one that is Christian but not influenced by Paul, that might shed light on the original practice of Jesus' followers. Fortunately, in 1873 in a library at Constantinople, just such a text turned up. It is called the *Didache* and dates to the early 2nd century A.D.[13] It had been mentioned by early church writers but had disappeared until a Greek priest, Father Bryennios, discovered it in an archive of old manuscripts quite by accident. The title *Didache* in Greek means "Teaching" and its full title is "The Teaching of the Twelve Apostles." It is a type of early Christian "instruction manual" probably written for candidates for Christian baptism to study. It has lots of ethical instructions and exhortations but also sections on baptism and the Eucharist—the sacred meal of bread and wine. And that is where the surprise comes. It offers the following blessings over wine and bread:

With respect to the Eucharist you shall give thanks as follows. First with respect to the cup: "We give you thanks our Father for the holy vine of David, your child which you made known to us through Jesus your child. To you be the glory forever." And with respect to the bread: "We give you thanks our Father for the life and knowledge that you made known to us through Jesus your child. To you be the glory forever."[14]

Notice there is no mention of the wine representing blood or the bread representing flesh. And yet this is a record of the early Christian Eucharist meal! This text reminds us very much of the descriptions of the sacred messianic meal in the Dead Sea Scrolls. Here we have a messianic celebration of Jesus as the Davidic Messiah and the life and knowledge that he has brought to the community. Evidently this community of Jesus' followers knew nothing about the ceremony that Paul advocates. If Paul's practice had truly come from Jesus surely this text would have included it.

There is another important point in this regard. In Jewish tradition it is the cup of wine that is blessed first, then the bread. That is the order we find here in the *Didache*. But in Paul's account of the "Lord's Supper" he has Jesus bless the bread first, then the cup of wine—just the reverse. It might seem an unimportant detail until one examines Luke's account of the words of Jesus at the meal. Although he basically follows the tradition from Paul, unlike Paul Luke reports first a cup of wine, then the bread, and then another cup of wine! The bread and the second cup of wine he interprets as the "body" and "blood" of Jesus. But with respect to the first cup—in the order one would expect from Jewish tradition—there is nothing said about it representing "blood." Rather Jesus says, "I tell you that from now on I will not drink of the fruit of the vine until the kingdom comes" (Luke 22:18). This tradition of the first cup, found now only in Luke, is a leftover clue of what must have been the original tradition before the Pauline version was inserted, now confirmed by the *Didache*.

Understood in this light, this last meal makes historical sense. Jesus told his closest followers, gathered in secret in the Upper Room, that he will not share another meal with them until the Kingdom of God comes. He knows that Judas will initiate events that very night, leading to his arrest. His hope and prayer is that the next time they sit down together to eat, giving the traditional Jewish blessing over wine and bread—the Kingdom of God will have come.

Since Jesus met only with his Council of Twelve for that final private meal, then James as well as Jesus' other three brothers would have been present. This is confirmed in a lost text called the *Gospel of the Hebrews* that was used by Jewish-Christians who rejected Paul's teachings and authority. It survives only in a few quotations that were preserved by Christian writers such as Jerome. In one passage we are told that James the brother of Jesus, after drinking from the cup Jesus passed around, pledged that he too would not eat or drink again until he saw the kingdom arrive.[15] So here we have textual evidence of a tradition that remembers James as being present at the last meal.

In the gospel of John there are cryptic references to James. Half a dozen times John mentions a mysterious unnamed figure that he calls "the disciple whom Jesus loved." The two are very close; in fact this unnamed disciple is seated next to Jesus either at his right or left hand. He leaned back and put his head on Jesus' breast during the meal (John 13:23). He is the one to whom Jesus whispers that Judas is the betrayer. Even though tradition holds that this is John the fisherman, one of the sons of Zebedee, it makes much better sense that such intimacy was shared between Jesus and his younger brother James. After all, from the few stories we have about John son of Zebedee, he has a fiery and ambitious personality—Jesus had nicknamed him and his brother the "sons of Thunder." They are the two that had tried to obtain the two chief seats on the Council of Twelve, one asking for the right hand, the other the left. On another occasion they asked Jesus for permission to call down fire from heaven to consume a village that had not accepted their preaching (Luke 9:54). On both occasions Jesus had rebuked them. The image we get of John son of Zebedee is quite opposite from the tender intimacy of the "disciple whom Jesus loved." No matter how ingrained the image might be in Christian imagination, it makes no sense to imagine John son of Zebedee seated next to Jesus, and leaning on his breast.

It seems to me that the evidence points to James the brother of Jesus being the most likely candidate for this mysterious unnamed disciple. Later, just before Jesus' death, the gospel of John tells us that Jesus put the care of his mother into the hands of this "disciple whom he loved"

The Garden of Gethsemane

(John 20:26–27). How could this possibly be anyone other than James his brother, who was now to take charge of the family as head of the household?

Late that night, after the meal and its conversations, Jesus led his band of eleven disciples outside the lower city, across the Kidron Valley, to a thick secluded grove of olive trees called Gethsemane at the foot of the Mount of Olives. Judas knew the place well because Jesus often used it as a place of solitude and privacy to meet with his disciples (John 18:2). Judas had gone into the city to alert the authorities of this rare opportunity to confront Jesus at night and away from the crowds.

It was getting late and Jesus' disciples were tired and drowsy. Sleep was the last thing on Jesus' mind, and he was never to sleep again. His all-night ordeal was about to begin. He began to feel very distressed, fearful, and deeply grieved. He wanted to pray for strength for the trials that he knew would soon begin. Mark tells us that he prayed that if possible the "cup would be removed from him" (Mark 14:36). Jesus urged his disciples to pray with him but the meal, the wine, and the late hour took their toll. They all fell asleep.

13

THE KING IS DEAD

It was no small operation that arrived that night at the Garden of Gethsemane to arrest Jesus. The gospel of John says that Judas arrived at the place followed by the leading priests, a detachment of the Jewish Temple police, and a cohort of Roman soldiers—that is a force of 600 men![1] Though spurred by accusations from the leading priests, this was a Roman operation. Pontius Pilate, the Roman governor, had authorized the arrest. It is obvious when Jesus is later taken to Pilate after his "trial," that his Jewish accusers did not just show up that early morning on an unannounced surprise visit with their condemned prisoner. We have to assume they went to Pilate, reported the potentially seditious activities of Jesus earlier in the week, and told him their plan to arrest Jesus quietly without causing any riots at Passover. Pilate had evidently authorized their plan and made sure that they were backed up by enough Roman troops to forestall anything going wrong. The Emperor Tiberius had already reprimanded Pilate for stirring up the population by his heavy-handed responses to disturbances. Passover had always been a prime time for agitators. The crowds that gathered in Jerusalem from all over the world were immense, providing a ready audience for any would-be Messiah or special cause. Josephus regularly mentions disturbances that took place at this festival. Pilate was anxious to play this one by the book—a quiet arrest, a trial by the representatives of the Jewish Sanhedrin—then he would examine the prisoner himself to determine what to do next.

Although we have no evidence that Jesus resisted arrest, all four of our gospels report that a scuffle ensued, weapons were drawn, and Simon Peter swung a sword at the head of one of the servants of the high priest and lopped off his ear. Resistance would have been futile, and Jesus was apparently convinced that his arrest was part of God's plan. He ordered his disciples to put down their weapons. Whether the intent of the authorities was to arrest the whole group or just Jesus we cannot be sure, but as Jesus was bound and taken away the others all fled into the darkness of the olive groves and escaped. According to the gospel of John, Simon Peter and "another disciple," whom I take to be Jesus' brother James, as I will explain later, followed secretly at a distance to observe what would happen to Jesus.

WHO KILLED JESUS?

Christians were later quite eager to blame the Jews for Jesus' arrest and crucifixion. Although Jesus had his Jewish enemies, they were mainly made up of the Sadducean priestly aristocrats who ran the Temple with some support from among certain Pharisees. Josephus wrote that the Sadducees were "more heartless than any of the other Jews" when they sat in judgment.[2] With the Jewish people as a whole Jesus was incredibly popular. And he also had friends in high places, including on the Jewish Sanhedrin itself—a type of indigenous Jewish senate. That was the whole reason for these stealth activities late through the night and into the early morning. Everyone was busy with Passover preparations, and if things moved quickly Jesus would be on a Roman cross by morning before anyone would know the difference. Jesus' Jewish enemies were certainly the catalysts for the strike but in the end the result was Roman through and through.

The "trial" of Jesus had three phases. He was first taken to a private house in the middle of the night likely belonging to the high priest

Annas. The office of high priest was a political appointment made by the Romans. Joseph Caiaphas officially held that position in A.D. 30 but his father-in-law, Annas, was the one who wielded the power over his shoulder. Annas had officially served as high priest from A.D. 6, until the Romans removed him in A.D. 15, but he never lost his influence. Five of his sons were subsequently to fill that office in an almost unbroken succession. The Romans did not make such choices lightly and one has to assume a high level of political influence and corruption in order for a single figure to hold such power for so long. Other than Herod Antipas, Joseph Annas was the most wealthy and powerful Jewish leader of the time. His was a priestly dynasty and its control of Jewish affairs was near absolute. This is not the last time the Annas dynasty would attack the Jesus dynasty, threatened by its potential to hold sway with the people as the legitimate Davidic authority. As we shall see, Annas's fifth son, his namesake Annas II, was the priest who had James the brother of Jesus brutally killed in A.D. 62. The Jesus dynasty and the Annas dynasty were like water and oil. Both Jesus and James pronounced "woes" upon the rich, warning them of God's impending judgment. And part of the messianic agenda was the prophetic expectation that this corrupt priestly family would be replaced by a line of priests who would teach and practice righteousness at the end of days (Malachi 3).

Caiaphas had married one of Annas's daughters and accordingly served in Annas's shadow, as a puppet priest during his long reign from A.D. 18 to 36. Luke refers to the "high-priesthood of Annas and Caiaphas" as if they held joint office—indicating just how much control the father-in-law wielded (Luke 3:2). The priestly family of Annas controlled untold wealth and lived in splendor. They were able to exercise a monopoly on all trade associated with Temple services. The people despised them. We have an amazing Rabbinic text that laments the abuses of these very priestly families in the time of Jesus: "Woe to me because of the house of Hanin [Annas]; woe unto me for their calumnies . . . Woe is me because of the House of Kathros (Caiaphas), woe is me because of their pens . . . For they are the High Priests, and their sons are treasurers, and their sons-in-law are trustees, and their servants beat the people with staves."[3] By striking at the heart of Annas's operation—Temple trade—Jesus had touched the nerve center of their power.

Since Jesus had openly ridden into the city the previous Sunday afternoon, allowing the crowds to hail him as "King," it would be relatively easy to form a capital case against him. The question about paying Roman taxes was designed to bolster the evidence. In a meeting earlier in the week Caiaphas had already determined that Jesus was to die, and he must have had the backing of his powerful father-in-law. According to the gospel of John these leading priests feared that if they let Jesus continue "everyone will believe in him and the Romans will come and destroy our holy place and our nation" (John 11:48). The decision had been made to eliminate him. The only question was when.

We don't know how many gathered at the high priest's mansion late that night but it surely was not an official meeting of the entire Jewish Sanhedrin. Jesus was taken into the house. Outside in the courtyard a contingent of the Jewish Temple Guard had gathered and built a charcoal fire to cut the chill of the night. Servants and messengers were milling about. According to the gospel of John the mysterious "other disciple," whom I take to have been James, was able to gain entrance into the courtyard and get Peter in as well because the household servant woman who was guarding the gate knew him (John 18:15–18). Someone inside recognized Peter's Galilean accent and accused him of being with Jesus. Peter vehemently denied even knowing him.

The clandestine and illegal nature of this "trial" is indicated by the time as well as the place chosen for the proceedings. The full Sanhedrin of seventy elders met in a special room in the Temple compound during daylight, not in a private house near midnight. And it would have been inconceivable to convene an official meeting of the Sanhedrin on the preparation day for the Passover. This was a covert move on the part of the clan of high priests to remove an enemy, not an official hearing and trial. The idea was to get Jesus to say on the record statements that could then be reported to Pontius Pilate as seditious. Various charges were aired and Jesus remained totally silent during the questioning. His refusal to say anything at all infuriated his accusers. Finally when asked point blank, "Are you the Messiah?" he did reply: "I am—and you will see the Son of man sitting at the right hand of Power and coming with the clouds of heaven" (Mark 14:62). As previously discussed, this reference to the "Son of man" is not to himself, but to the prophecy of Daniel 7:13 that symbolically refers to God's people collectively as "the coming of a Son of Man" before the throne of God, where they are given power over all nations (Daniel 7:27). What Jesus was saying was "Yes, I am Israel's King and you will see the manifestation of God's Kingdom."

Jesus' admission that he was the Davidic King was all they needed. Some of those gathered spit in his face and he was delivered to the guards in the courtyard, who began to mock him and rough him up with blows. They blindfolded him and struck his face, taunting him to "Prophesy who just hit you." At daybreak others who were part of the inner priestly circle gathered, how many we do not know, but Mark's claim that the "whole Council" gathered at dawn on Passover morning appears unlikely. This is clearly an inside operation. Anyone who might have opposed the decision was surely not invited, particularly those on the Sanhedrin who supported Jesus or were at least sympathetic to his cause. There was a tendency in later Christian tradition to put responsibility for Jesus' death on the "Jews" as a whole and the idea that Jesus was condemned to die at an official convocation of the entire Sanhedrin was one way to support such a claim. The gospel of John never makes this claim and even Matthew, who uses Mark as his source, changes the words "whole Council" to the phrase "they took counsel against Jesus to put him to death."

Recently two rather amazing archaeological discoveries have shed new light on this first phase of the "trial" of Jesus that night. As part of the rebuilding of the Jewish Quarter following the 1967 Six Day War, the Israelis carried out extensive excavations, exposing the Herodian city as it was when the Romans destroyed it in A.D. 70. It was in this area that the wealthy high priests had their homes, just to the west of the massive Herodian Temple complex. As chance would have it the archaeologists discovered the ruins of a magnificent palatial mansion that very possibly belonged to Annas.[4] It extends over two thousand square feet and is built on three levels, with easy access to and a magnificent view of the Temple to the east. On the ground floor of the western side is a courtyard, with the gated area still visible. The walls inside have colored frescoes with marble and floral motifs. Mosaic floors were found throughout. Of particular interest is a large reception hall measuring 36 by 21 feet. Other equally lavish houses were adjacent to this one and in the ruins of one just to the north was found a stone weight inscribed in Aramaic "of Bar Kathros," which

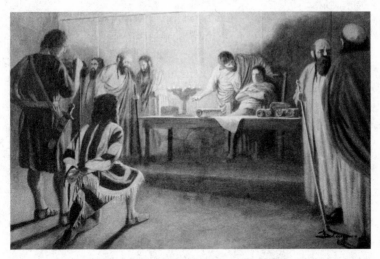

Jesus being judged before Pilate at Gabbatha

means "belonging to the house of Caiaphas." It is certainly possible that the palatial mansion was the house of Annas where Jesus was condemned to die. The large room would have served as a type of "judgment hall" and the courtyard below was visible from within, just as the gospels describe.[5]

In November 1990 an even more chilling discovery was made. Construction crews building a park just south of the Old City accidentally broke through a sealed burial cave, undisturbed since the first century, with bones and ossuaries intact. As unbelievable as it sounds, it turned out to be the family tomb of High Priest Caiaphas. Indeed one of

The Caiaphas Ossuary with its inscription on the side

the ossuaries inscribed "Yehosef bar Qafa" (Joseph son of Caiaphas) held the bones of the man who had officially presided over the "trial" of Jesus.

Sometime early that Thursday morning Jesus was bound and taken under guard by his accusers to the Roman governor Pontius Pilate. Pilate was staying in the royal palace complex that Herod the Great had built on the western edge of the city. Outside the city wall, still visible today, was a stone entranceway and staircase going up to a raised platform in front of the Praetorium or official military headquarters of the governor just inside the wall on the grounds of the royal palace. Since the high priests and their cohorts had ritually purified themselves to eat the Passover at sundown that evening, they did not enter the Praetorium area, which would have been considered defiling.

Instead they stood outside on the steps and Pilate came to meet them. He sat down at a judge's bench on the raised stone platform. This area where official Roman judgments were decreed was called in Hebrew *Gabbatha*—literally "the Stone Pavement." The charges they registered against Jesus were purely political, not religious: that he was a threat to the stability of the nation; that he opposed paying the Roman taxes levied by Caesar; and that he himself claimed to be the rightful King as Messiah of Israel (Luke 23:2). Any one of these charges was enough in Roman eyes to merit death by crucifixion.

The excavated stone staircase of Pilate's judgment platform today

Jesus before Caiaphas in the Priestly Mansion Judgment Hall

Pilate took Jesus into the Praetorium headquarters inside the palace walls to question him. All four New Testament gospels offer elaborate descriptions of how Pontius Pilate found Jesus innocent of these charges and went to extraordinary lengths to release him but was intimidated by the Jewish authorities and their supporters waiting outside, who demanded that he be crucified. He even suggested that Jesus be released in keeping with a Roman custom of freeing a Jewish prisoner during the Jewish festival. Jesus' crowd of accusers rejected the suggestion and demanded instead that another prisoner, named Barabbas, being held for insurrection, receive this gesture of Roman amnesty. Finally Pilate, fearing the Jewish crowds, who kept shouting out, "Let him be crucified," acquiesced and called for a basin of water, washing his hands of the matter, and again declaring Jesus to be innocent. He then delivered Jesus over to them to be crucified. Matthew even adds the assertion that "all the people" responded to Pilate's reluctance with the fateful retort, "Let his blood be upon us and upon our children" (Matthew 27:25).

Scholars are agreed that little in these accounts of Jesus' trial before Pilate is historically credible. They have been completely shaped by a later Christian theological tradition that sought to put the blame for

Jesus' death wholly upon the Jewish people while exonerating the Romans as sympathetic to Jesus, with Pilate doing all he possibly could to save Jesus' life. All four of our New Testament gospels were written after the great Jewish Revolt against Rome (A.D. 66–73). Anti-Jewish sentiments were prevalent in the reign of Tiberius (A.D. 14–37), spurred on by the notorious prefect Sejanus, the most influential Roman citizen of his day. After the costly and bloody Jewish Revolt, such anti-Jewish feelings were fanned to a flame by the Romans and any association of Jesus with Jewish sedition and disloyalty to Rome had to be avoided if the new Christian movement was to be spread among the Romans. That Jesus died by Roman crucifixion was an undeniable and terribly embarrassing fact. But if his crucifixion could be blamed on the obstinacy of the Jews, then perhaps the Christian movement could explain its Jewish origins and the shameful death of its leader in a more favorable—that is, less Jewish—light. This would allow the nascent Christian tradition greater chance of winning converts and acceptance throughout the Roman Empire in which it was spreading.

What we do know is that Pilate was known for his brutality, his cruelty, and his fearless disregard and disdain for his Jewish subjects. Since his arrival in Judea in A.D. 26 his acts of arrogance and violence had become legendary. He doubtless had the support of Sejanus, who after Tiberius's retreat to the island of Capri in A.D. 27, virtually ran the Empire in the emperor's name. Philo of Alexandria, a contemporary Jewish philosopher and historian, described Pilate as "naturally inflexible, a blend of self-will and relentlessness, a man noted for vindictiveness and a furious temper."[6]

Pilate had a reputation of handling arrests without trial and ignoring legal procedures. Even if Pilate thought Jesus to have been a harmless and deluded fool, he would have happily condemned him without the slightest hesitation. The portrait the New Testament gospels present of Pilate is simply historically inaccurate.

Leaving aside all theology, and concentrating on the more probable historical facts, we can say the following: The high priests Annas and Caiaphas with their supporters delivered Jesus to Pilate charging him with sedition. Pilate questioned Jesus privately regarding the charges.

When he learned Jesus was from Galilee he decided to send him to Herod Antipas, who was in town for the Passover and residing nearby in the palace. Herod had been seeking Jesus' death for some time and he was pleased to finally have him in custody. Herod examined him at length but Jesus refused to say anything in response. Jesus' accusers were present and repeated the charges against him. Herod and his soldiers decided to have a bit of sport with Jesus. They clothed him in a royal robe and began to treat him with contempt, mocking him as a so-called "King." Herod then sent Jesus back to Pilate, having endorsed the decision that Jesus be executed by crucifixion. In Jerusalem it was Pilate who had the jurisdiction to have the decision carried out.

Pilate ordered Jesus delivered over to his Praetorium guard, the most trusted and elite Roman troops in Jerusalem. They took Jesus into the courtyard of the palace and flogged him. The Greek words used imply a severe beating with whips. This was standard Roman practice, a type of preliminary punishment for slaves or those sentenced to death by crucifixion. Such a scourging was considered so severe that it was against Roman law to carry it out on a Roman citizen. It was part of the method the Romans used to intimidate and terrorize any who opposed Roman rule. The soldiers did not often get a "Messiah" as a prisoner so they took full advantage of the situation, placing a mock crown of thorns on his head, a reed in his hand, and bowing to him, hailing him sarcastically as "King of the Jews." Pilate ordered a placard or *titulus* written in Latin, Greek, and Hebrew that read: "This is Jesus the King of the Jews." Jesus likely wore it around his neck as he was led away, carrying the *patibulum* or crossbeam, to the place of execution. The placard was then fixed to the cross, above the victim's head, to publicly announce one's crime. This is a very important element of the story as it witnesses to the fact that the Romans crucified Jesus for sedition—that is, for claiming to be a King.

Pilate took advantage of the occasion to have two other Jewish prisoners crucified as *lestai*. This term, traditionally translated as "thief," is regularly used by Josephus to describe the Zealot brigands who had acted against Rome. This is the precise word used to describe the prisoner Barabbas, who had been arrested and slated for crucifixion for leading a violent insurrection. The two men crucified with Jesus were likely part of that recent disturbance. The point is, from Pilate's point of view, the three of them, Jesus included, are all guilty of the same thing—sedition against Rome.

Jesus and the other two victims were led outside the city to a place called Golgotha ("Place of the Skull") that the Romans regularly used for crucifixions. Josephus says they purposely chose locations that would be easily seen by passersby, whether along main roads or atop hills.

THE MOST WRETCHED OF DEATHS

Josephus described Roman crucifixion as the "most wretched of deaths."[7] Anyone growing up in 1st-century Roman Palestine knew the horror of this form of terror by direct experience and observation. The hapless victims of crucifixion, left on the crosses for days, were a common sight to the Jewish population. Josephus reported that during the Roman siege of Jerusalem in the summer of A.D. 70 the number of captives crucified reached five hundred a day—so many that there was no wood left in the area as all the trees had been cut down.

We know quite a bit about the methods the Romans used in crucifying their victims. Not only do we have literary sources but in 1968 the skeletal remains of a Jewish male victim were discovered in a tomb just north of Jerusalem off the Nablus Road. He was in his twenties and his name, Jehohanan, was inscribed on his ossuary. His remains have given us an amazing glimpse into the details involved in Roman crucifixion as it was practiced in 1st-century Roman Jerusalem.

We know that the nails were put through the forearms and not the hands, between the radius and ulna bones. In that manner the arms were securely attached to the *patibulum*. Jehohanan's radial bones were scored from friction between the nail and the bone. Physiologists have shown that nails through the hands will not hold the weight of a body, and nails through the wrists would have ruptured blood vessels. The "science" of crucifixion required that nails be affixed in a way to minimize bleeding, otherwise the victim would quickly pass out and die in a matter of minutes. The references in the gospels to Jesus' "hands" being pierced use a Greek word that can be understood as including the forearms. The feet were nailed through the heel bone. It is the largest bone in the foot and as with the forearm, puncturing this bone will not cause profuse bleeding. In the case of Jehohanan the nail is still intact through his heel bone. When he was removed from the cross the nail had bent on a knot in the wood and whoever removed him simply cut the wood away, leaving it attached to his foot.

Death by crucifixion was a slow process; it could take as long as two or three days. The victims were stripped naked, exposed to the scorching Mediterranean sun. Death resulted from a combination of shock, exhaustion, muscle

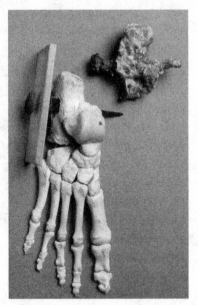

Heel bone with crucifixion nail and reconstructed model

cramps, dehydration, loss of blood, and finally suffocation or heart failure. Depending on the angle in which the arms and legs were nailed, death could be brought on more quickly, or extended. The buttocks were supported by a piece of wood called a *sedecula* that offered some support of the body. Over time, as fatigue set in, breathing became acutely difficult. If there was a reason to hasten death, the legs of the victim could be broken, causing the body to slump and making breathing impossible after just a short time.

Josephus relates a story of seeing among the many crucified captives during the Jewish Revolt three of his former acquaintances in a small village near Jerusalem. He begged the Roman general Titus to allow them to be taken down from their crosses and put in his care. A physician was called, and despite his efforts two of them died, but one was nursed back to health and recovered. The Romans often left the corpses to rot on crosses but the Jews had a law requiring those "hung on a tree" to be buried the same day as they were crucified.[8] When allowed, Jews

The crucifixion scene from the Mount of Olives

removed the bodies before sundown and buried them. Since Jehohanan's legs were broken, his death was likely hastened to allow for burial the same day as his crucifixion.

FORSAKEN BY GOD

Jesus and the other two victims were put on their crosses by 9 A.M. Thursday. Whether Jesus expected God would rescue him before things went that far is impossible to say. If he had identified himself with the Davidic figure who was to be "pierced" in Zechariah 12 it is entirely possible that he thought he was destined to be *nailed* to the cross—but then saved from death itself before it was too late.

What Jesus likely expected was a sudden, dramatic, and overwhelming manifestation of the Kingdom of God—perhaps a great earthquake that would destroy the Herodian Temple, with the sun darkened, the moon turning blood red, the dead being raised, and the appearance of legions of heavenly armies in the sky. During the previous week he had told his disciples who had been admiring the beauty of the massive stones of Herod's Temple complex that the day would come when not one stone would be left on another (Mark 13:2). At his trial one of the charges had been, "We heard him say, 'I will destroy this temple that is made with hands, and in three days I will build another made without hands'" (Mark 14:58). As Jesus had told his disciples the night before at their last meal, "Now is the judgment of the world, now the ruler of the world will be driven out" (John 12:31). The Hebrew Prophets had written vividly about the "Day of Yahweh," when people would cast their gold and silver into the streets and hide in the caverns of the rocks from the "terror of Yahweh and the glory of his majesty when he rises to terrify the earth" (Isaiah 2:21). The kings of the earth were to be toppled and Satan's armies shut up in a pit (Isaiah 24:22). For Jesus the prophetic "third day" had arrived and the coming of "the Son of Man in the clouds of heaven" was imminent.

The gospels report that the chief priests and others who had supported them taunted the victims, aiming particular scorn at Jesus: "Let the King of Israel come down from the cross that we may believe!" Standing at a distance was Jesus' mother, Mary, as well as Mary Magdalene and the other women who had followed him from Galilee on this last journey to Jerusalem. According to the gospel of John the "disciple whom Jesus loved" was also present with Jesus' mother. Late in the day, when Jesus began to think he might die after all, he officially put his mother in the care of this disciple whom I have identified as his brother James—now to be the "eldest" of the family.

According to Mark Jesus was on the cross from the sixth to the ninth hour—that is 9 A.M. to 3 P.M. (Mark 15:33). Toward the end he began to sense his life slipping away. He cried out with a loud voice in his native Aramaic tongue: *Eloi, Eloi, Lama sabachthani?* Those are the opening words of Psalm 22—My God, My God, why have you forsaken me? At that point he bowed his head and breathed his last. Other than the words of the Psalm he quoted we will never know what his last thoughts were. It might well be that as he grew weaker he was reciting that very Psalm. It is the prayer of a dying man, attributed to King David, who in the end is saved from terrible suffering and death. In fact, this is the Psalm that specifically refers to "piercing of the hands and feet" (verse 16). The Psalm ends with the hopeful declaration: "God did not hide his face from me but heard when I cried to him." Up until the last minutes perhaps, Jesus believed that God would intervene, save his life, and openly manifest his Kingdom.

Since the Jewish Passover meal or Seder was to be eaten just after sundown that evening, the high priests had asked the Romans to break the legs of the victims to hasten death. The gospel of John remarks, "They did not want the bodies to remain on the cross during the Sabbath, especially since *that* Sabbath was a high day" (John 19:31). When they came to Jesus he appeared to be completely lifeless. One of the soldiers thrust a spear into Jesus' side just to be sure. He did not flinch. The King was dead.

14

DEAD BUT
TWICE BURIED

JESUS was dead by 3 P.M. on Thursday. His family and his followers were in utter shock. None of them could believe that God would have allowed Jesus, the Davidic Messiah and legitimate King of Israel, to die. There were no preparations for his burial. Jesus' family was from Galilee and owned no family burial cave in Jerusalem. The sun was beginning to set and the Passover meal would begin at nightfall. Something had to be done quickly with Jesus' corpse, lest the family suffer the shame of having it left on the cross overnight.

A TEMPORARY BURIAL

The gospels relate that Joseph of Arimathea, a wealthy and influential member of the Jewish Sanhedrin, intervened to help. Joseph went to the Roman governor Pontius Pilate and using his influence and status as a member of the Sanhedrin got permission to remove Jesus' body from the cross and temporarily bury him. Presumably Joseph had not been called the night before to the hastily convened "trial" at the house of Annas and Caiaphas. He was one of a minority of influential Jewish leaders who supported Jesus. He enlisted the help of a man named Nicodemus, also a member of the Sanhedrin, who shared his sympathetic view of the Messianic Movement. The problem they faced was where to temporarily bury Jesus in such pressing circumstances.

It is commonly assumed that the tomb in which they placed Jesus that late afternoon belonged to Joseph of Arimathea. That was not the case. This misconception is based on one small editorial gloss in the gospel of Matthew and no other source we have supports the assumption (Matthew 27:60).¹ Mark and Luke just say they "took the body and laid it in a tomb hewn out of the rock." The gospel of John supplies an additional important detail: "In the place where Jesus was crucified was a garden, and in the garden a new tomb in which no one was ever yet laid" (John 19:41). It is improbable that a newly cut tomb conveniently located near the place where Jesus was crucified just happened to belong to Joseph of Arimathea. The fact is we have no idea who might have owned this tomb. It had been recently cut out of the bedrock and no one was yet using it, so it suited the emergency situation that Joseph and Nicodemus faced. They could temporarily put the corpse of Jesus inside and after the Passover and Sabbath holidays the family could return and give Jesus his proper funerary rites according to Jewish custom.

Jesus' mother, Mary, and her companion Mary Magdalene followed Joseph and Nicodemus to the tomb, noting carefully its location. There was no time to prepare the body for burial according to the traditional Jewish custom, which included washing and anointing the corpse, and applying various spices and perfumes to control the odor of decay. Joseph and Nicodemus simply wrapped the body in a linen shroud and laid it out on a stone slab as a temporary resting place late Thursday afternoon until the Passover on Friday and the weekly Sabbath on Saturday had passed. They blocked up the small entrance into the tomb with a stone, cut for that purpose, to keep out animals or strangers who might happen by.

The Church of the Holy Sepulchre now encloses the traditional site of Golgotha and the tomb where Jesus' body was placed. In the time of Jesus it was a rock quarry, barely outside the Herodian city wall on the northwest. It has become the holiest site in Christendom. It is located in the Christian Quarter inside the present walls of the Old City of

Jerusalem. It is a site revered since the 4th century A.D. when Helen, the devout Christian mother of the newly converted Roman Emperor Constantine, declared it to be the place. Roman Catholics, Eastern Orthodox, Armenian, and Coptic Christians all share in the veneration of this location. Protestants generally prefer a location outside the walls of the Old City, just north of Damascus Gate, called "Gordon's Calvary" or the "Garden Tomb" next to the modern city bus depot in east Jerusalem. There tourists find an elevated rock outcropping whose craggy surface is said to resemble a "Skull," and since Golgotha means "Place of the Skull" many have become convinced it is the right location. There is a garden there with a tomb that is said to be the tomb of Joseph of Arimathea.

The Church of the Holy Sepulchre today

The authenticity of either site is problematic. The tomb at the Protestant site has been dated to the Iron Age (5th century B.C.), which is much too early to fit the description of a "newly hewn tomb." The Catholic site is based upon traditions from the 4th century, a full three hundred years after Jesus' crucifixion. It is just yards from the ancient northern city wall

Gordon's Calvary

near a deep rock quarry, an unlikely area for new tombs and gardens. Its authenticity was based on relics that Empress Helena claimed to find—such as the true cross of Jesus buried nearby—bolstered by visions and reported miracles. The tomb that Helena chose is very likely that of John Hyrcanus, the 2nd-century B.C. Maccabean ruler.[2] It was mentioned a number of times by Josephus precisely in that location. This site simply does not fit the biblical or historical record.

A more likely site for Jesus' crucifixion is on the Mount of Olives, east of the city, overlooking the Temple compound. One of our earliest sources remembers Jesus' crucifixion as "outside the camp" (Hebrews 13:12–13). The technical expression "outside the camp" was interpreted as a distance of at least two thousand cubits (about half a mile) east of the Temple sanctuary.[3] It was there, toward the summit of the Mount of Olives, where certain purification rituals were performed and criminal penalties were carried out.[4] There was also an attempt, in the 1st century A.D., to locate tombs outside this perimeter, to avoid ritual defilement of the Temple.[5] This suited the Roman purposes well since they preferred to stage crucifixions on hills by main roads so that the population would see the punishment and take heed. The Mount of Olives was visible to those coming into the city on the main roads and it was just far enough removed from the Temple sanctuary so that the corpses would not cause ritual defilement. A 2nd-century Christian text called the *Acts of Pilate* says Jesus was crucified near the place where he had been arrested, that is, the Garden of Gethsemane on the Mount of Olives. Shem-Tob's version of Hebrew Matthew, which I mentioned in Chapter 8, refers to Golgotha as a "mountain" or "hill." There is nothing north of the city one could refer to in this way, but the description fits the Mount of Olives. At the summit of the Mount of Olives was a rounded hillock or dome that might account for the name "Place of the Skull."[6] The entire western side of the Mount of Olives, facing Jerusalem, was an area of gardens and tombs. If this location is correct Jesus spent the last agonizing hours of his life facing the Temple of Jerusalem with a full view of its courts.

The Mount of Olives looking east from the Old City

We are not told where Jesus' family and the core group of his followers ate the Passover meal the evening of Jesus' death but one can only imagine the sad and solemn occasion it must have been. They probably would have gathered in the home of Mary and Martha at Bethany, on the Mount of Olives, where Jesus and his followers had been staying that entire week. They must have been terrified that others of their group might be arrested. The shock of Jesus' death would have been all that was on anyone's mind.

AN EMPTY TOMB

Trying to determine what happened next is probably the most difficult and controversial topic in the study of Christian origins. Here we enter an area where faith and theological dogma are intertwined with probable historical fact in a tangle that seems almost impossible to separate. There are a few things we know with certainty and a lot that we probably will never know. Such is the nature of our sources and evidence. The standard Christian proclamation is well known: that Jesus was raised from the dead, that he appeared to many witnesses, and that he ascended into heaven, where he sits as the glorified Christ at the right hand of God, from where he will return at the end of the age to judge the living and the dead. But this familiar message, packaged in this way, was a long time coming.

Three facts appear to be indisputable: first, that Jesus was truly dead; second, that he was hastily and temporarily buried in an unknown tomb; and third, that the movement Jesus began did not end with his death but revived and found new life under the leadership of Jesus' brother James.

All four New Testament gospels report that the tomb in which Jesus was temporarily placed was found empty on Sunday morning. But they don't agree as to who arrived first at the tomb and what subsequently transpired. The gospel of John says that Mary Magdalene went alone, without the others, even before sunrise, when it was still dark, and she was the one who found the stone blocking the entrance removed and the body missing from the slab where it had been placed late Thursday afternoon. She immediately ran back into the city to find Simon Peter and the "disciple whom Jesus loved," exclaiming, "They have taken away the Master out of the tomb and we do not know where they have laid him" (John 20:2). Simon and the unnamed disciple ran all the way to the tomb to verify the report. All they found were the linen wrappings that had been put around the corpse—Jesus' body was gone. No one leaped to any conclusion about Jesus being raised from the dead. At that point it was a matter of a missing corpse.

Mark says that Jesus' mother Mary, Salome, and Mary Magdalene went *together* to the tomb, and instead of seeing Jesus they encountered a "young man" who told them, "Do not be amazed, you seek Jesus of Nazareth who was crucified. He has risen, he is not here; see the place where they laid him." They fled from the tomb in amazement and said nothing to anyone. Matthew reports that Jesus' mother and Mary Magdalene went together to the tomb, there was a great earthquake, and an angel of the Lord came down from heaven and rolled away the stone, telling them "Jesus is not here, he has risen" (Matthew 28:1–7). Luke says that they found the stone already rolled away, went in the tomb, saw that there was no body, and were perplexed. Suddenly two men in dazzling apparel appeared and said to them, "Why do you seek the living among the dead?" (Luke 24:2–5).

Looking out from a 1st-century empty tomb on the Mount of Olives

Some have suggested that Jesus might not have been clinically dead but that he fell into some type of comatose state from which he subsequently recovered.[7] This idea, commonly referred to as the "swoon theory," has many variations, including the idea that Jesus might have plotted the whole thing—having himself drugged so that he could suffer as Israel's Messiah but escape death.[8] Various fantastic theories have emerged based on this idea. One idea is that Jesus traveled east, to India, in search of the "lost tribes," where he eventually died with his grave now located in the city of Srinagar in Kashmir.⁹ Another that has cropped up in recent years in several popular books is that Jesus was married to Mary Magdalene and that after surviving the cross he moved with her and their child to live out their lives in the south of France.¹⁰ One modern author has even argued that Jesus traveled east but then returned to Palestine to join the Jewish Revolt and subsequently died at Masada in A.D. 73.¹¹ None of these theories appear to have any basis whatsoever in reliable historical sources. I think we need have no doubt that given Jesus' execution by Roman crucifixion he was truly *dead* and that his temporary place of burial was discovered to be empty shortly thereafter.

SIGHTINGS OF JESUS

Three of our four New Testament gospels report "sightings" of Jesus to support the idea that he had been raised from the dead—Matthew, Luke, and John. But what about Mark? Here we come to one of the most ignored and underrated facts of our story. As shocking as it may sound, the original manuscripts of the gospel of Mark report no appearances of the resurrected Jesus at all! Mark, our earliest gospel source, ended his Jesus story with the empty tomb. Period. The last verse of Mark's gospel originally read: "And they [the two Marys and Salome] went out and fled from the tomb; for trembling and astonishment had come upon them; and they said nothing to any one, for they were afraid" (Mark 16:8). I say, "originally read," because for obvious reasons such a shockingly abrupt and "incomplete" ending could not be allowed to stand. It must have been deeply troubling to early Christians. Christianity was built upon the idea that Jesus appeared after his death to various individuals and groups. How could Mark have possibly left this out?

What happened was that pious scribes who copied Mark made up an ending for him and added it to his text sometime in the 4th century A.D.—over three hundred years after the original text was composed! This concocted ending became verses 16:9–20, but it is not found in any of our older more reliable copies of Mark.[12] It is in fact a clumsy composite of the sightings of Jesus reported by Matthew, Luke, and John. It contains no independent material that can be identified as specifically from Mark, and the Greek style in which it is written is decidedly non-Markan. Clement of Alexandria and Origen, two of our early Christian scholars, who lived in the 3rd century A.D., do not even know the existence of this "longer" ending. In their day it had not yet appeared. Eusebius and Jerome, Christian writers from the early and late 4th century A.D., know it exists but note that it is absent from almost all Greek manuscripts of which they are aware. Two other "made-up" endings were later put into circulation, as shorter alternatives to this longer traditional ending. Clearly no one could accept that Mark ended his book as he chose to end it—it was just too shocking and problematic for Christian faith.

Modern English translations of the New Testament have handled this ancient problem in various ways.[13] Most of them still include the later ending but insert a footnote, pointing out that Mark ends at 16:8 in the most reliable early manuscripts. I doubt this note is often noticed by the average reader, so that the shock of Mark's original ending has been largely ignored. Others print 16:9–20 in double brackets with notes. The original Revised Standard Version, published in 1946, caused quite a stir by printing the nonoriginal ending in small print in a footnote—separated from the original text. There was such a storm over this that later editions of the RSV put it back in the text with a footnote.

What Mark's original text tells us is that the reports of Jesus appearing to various individuals and groups after his resurrection were not considered a necessary part of the "Gospel" story around A.D. 70 when Mark was written. So how did such reports develop?

Actually our earliest account of "sightings" of Jesus is not in the New Testament gospels but in the letter of Paul we call 1st Corinthians, written around A.D. 54. In the course of defending his own vision of Jesus, Paul reports that he had received the tradition and passed it on to his converts that Jesus died, was buried, and rose on the "third day." According to Paul, Jesus appeared first to Cephas or Peter, then to the Twelve, then to five hundred disciples at one time, then to James brother of Jesus, then to all the apostles, and finally—"last of all he appeared to me." Paul passes on a different tradition, as the list of "sightings" he lists here does not easily fit with what the New Testament gospels report. Also, Paul equates his own "sighting" of Jesus, which was clearly "visionary," with those of the original founders—possibly implying that their experiences were much like his. In Judaism to claim that someone has been "raised from the dead" is not the same as to claim that one has died and exists as a spirit or soul in the heavenly world. What the gospels claim about Jesus is that the tomb was empty, and that his dead body was revived to life—wounds and all. He was not a phantom or a ghost, though he does seem to "materialize" abruptly, and at times is first unrecognized, then suddenly recognized by those who saw him. But Paul seems to be willing to use the term "resurrection" to refer to something akin to an apparition or vision. And when he does mention Jesus' body he says it was a "spiritual" body. But a "spiritual body" and an "embodied spirit" could be seen as very much the same phenomenon.

With Matthew, Luke, and John the reporting of post-empty-tomb "sightings" had become a standard part of bolstering the claim that Jesus had been "raised from the dead." Matthew is usually dated to the 80s A.D., Luke into the 90s, and John just around the turn of the 1st century.

The gospel of John says that Mary Magdalene saw Jesus at the tomb that very morning and that he told her, "I am ascending to My Father and your Father, and My God and your God." Matthew reports that Jesus' mother, Mary, and Mary Magdalene ran from the tomb after seeing the angel come from heaven in order to tell the other followers what had happened. On their way Jesus met them and said, "Do not be afraid, go tell my brothers to go to Galilee and there they will see me." Matthew reports no appearances at all in Jerusalem other than this one. He says the Eleven Apostles went promptly to Galilee, to a certain mountain, where they were told by Jesus to go and make disciples among all nations, "baptizing them in the name of the Father, and of the Son, and of the Holy Spirit" (Matthew 28:16–19).

Luke reports precisely the opposite. Jesus suddenly materialized right before the eyes of his startled disciples, who were gathered in hiding in Jerusalem. That is when he told them not to leave the city (Luke 24:49). He then took them out to the Mount of Olives and as they were standing there he began to rise in the air before their eyes and departed into a cloud and was taken into heaven. There are further stories of sightings of Jesus, including two men walking along a road outside Jerusalem. They talk to him but don't recognize him at first, until "their eyes were open." John reports sightings both in Jerusalem and up in Galilee, where Peter and his associates have gone back to their fishing business.

The accounts become more and more fantastic as time goes on. In the 2nd-century A.D. *Gospel of Peter* two men descend from heaven, the stone is rolled back from the tomb, they enter, and when they come out with Jesus the heads of all three of them reach into the heavens.

There is no credible way to harmonize these accounts, and the language is loaded with theological overtones. What we have to realize is that the gospels of Matthew, Luke, and John were written between forty to seventy years after the death of Jesus by authors who were not original witnesses and who were not living in Roman Palestine. By that time the proclamation of the "resurrection of Christ" had become the fundamental cornerstone of the emerging Christian faith, and Paul's version of the story, which I discuss in more detail later, had largely triumphed. The church was removed in time and place from its Jerusalem roots. James was dead and on the way to being forgotten. Even Peter and Paul were dead, though they were remembered as heroes and founders of the Christian faith.

That does not mean these gospels contain nothing of historical value, but it does mean their purpose in reporting the empty-tomb story and the sightings of Jesus is to proclaim the resurrection of Jesus Christ and his death for the salvation of all humankind. The gospel writers do not seem too concerned with the many contradictions among their accounts, if they did know of one another's work. But they did all know Mark, and they all agreed that his account was deficient and needed to be rather drastically supplemented.

WHAT HAPPENED TO JESUS' BODY?

Historians are bound by their discipline to work within the parameters of a scientific view of reality. Women do not get pregnant without a male—ever. So Jesus had a human father, whether we can identify him or not. Dead bodies don't rise—not if one is clinically dead—as Jesus surely was after Roman crucifixion and three days in a tomb. So if the tomb was empty the historical conclusion is simple—Jesus' body was moved by someone and likely reburied in another location. Historians can report what Paul said, or what reports of "sightings" of Jesus were circulating by the time the gospels were written, but these writings, written decades after the fact, witness more to the development of theological beliefs than to what might have happened. Some scholars have questioned the historical accuracy of the empty-tomb story itself—arguing that it was developed to support the theological claim that Jesus had been raised from the dead. But given the hasty and temporary nature of Jesus' burial we should *expect* that the tomb would be empty. It was never intended that Jesus be left in that tomb. The question is what happened to his body? Where might he have been permanently buried and by whom? The short answer is that we simply do not know and anything one might suggest is speculative. But we do, nonetheless, have some clues in our sources that might allow us to plausibly reconstruct some possibilities.

There are a few alternative stories besides those of our New Testament gospels. Tertullian, a 3rd-century Christian writer, reports a polemic circulating in his time that the gardener of the cemetery moved Jesus' body because he suspected the crowds that would come to visit the tomb would trample his vegetables.[14] In a late medieval text called the *Toledot Yeshu* the gardener took his body and buried it nearby in a stream out of fear his disciples would take the body first and make claims that he was raised from the dead. There is a Coptic text from the 6th century A.D. that even tells us the gardener's name was Philogenes. But in this version the gardener planned to take the body to bury it honorably, but at midnight, when he came to move it, the tomb was surrounded by angels and he witnessed Jesus rising from the dead.[15] All these stories about a gardener seem embellishments on the gospel of John's claim that Mary Magdalene at first thought Jesus was the gardener when she met him at the tomb, asking him, "If you have carried him away tell me where you have laid him" (John 20:15).

It may be that John's account offers us our best clue as to what might have happened to Jesus' body. If Mary Magdalene did in fact go very early to the tomb alone, and it was already empty, someone else must have come before she arrived and moved the body. One is left to guess here but the most likely possibility would be his mother, Mary, and his sister Salome, likely assisted by some of the other women who had come with them from Galilee, and perhaps the sisters Mary and Martha with whom they were staying.

Mark says that after sundown on Saturday, when the Sabbath was over, they "bought spices so that they might go and anoint him" (Mark 16:1). Since Jesus' body had been rushed to a temporary tomb because of the Passover holiday it makes sense that the *family* would complete Jesus' final burial as soon as possible. In Jewish tradition corpses are to be buried within twenty-four hours of death if possible. Washing and anointing the naked body of a loved one was an intimate act of devotion. They might have moved him at dusk Saturday night, taken him to a permanent tomb somewhere in Jerusalem, and prepared the body for burial according to Jewish custom. Tombs are dark and it is common to find oil lamps inside, so their work could have easily been carried out after sundown on Saturday. If we trust John's account, for some reason Mary Magdalene was not present and showed up early Sunday morning before dark only to find the tomb empty.

It is unlikely that Mary and her children would have had a family tomb in Jerusalem, but they were closely tied to others, such as Martha and Mary, who might have made one available to them. The whole area around Jerusalem was a vast necropolis of rock-hewn tombs dating to this period. Some are large and monumental; others are small with room for a half-dozen or so burials. Hundreds of 1st-century family tombs have been found on the Mount of Olives, which is where Mary and Martha lived. And if Jesus was in fact crucified and temporarily buried on the Mount of Olives, the tomb where he was more permanently buried might not be far away.

In this case we do have some archaeological evidence. Quite a cluster of 1st-century tombs that show some evidence of having belonged to followers of Jesus have been discovered on the Mount of Olives, and just to the south on the Mount of Offense, and further south in the area of Tal-

piot.[16] On the Mount of Olives on the grounds of the Franciscan Domi-
nus Flevit sanctuary, over forty ossuaries were found with inscriptions of
names such as Lazarus, John, Joseph, Judah, Martha, Miriam, Matthew,
Salome, Simeon, Yeshua, and most significantly a "Simon bar Jonah," the
precise Aramaic name of Jesus' disciple Peter. The names are common
but this particular grouping, near the village where Mary and Martha
lived, with their brother Lazarus, and perhaps near the place where Jesus
was crucified, seems significant. Mary and Martha are together in a single

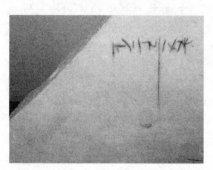

Ossuary fragment with
"Simon bar Jonah" inscribed

ossuary, possibly indicating
they are sisters. There are similar clusters of names at burial
places nearby, but further
south, on the Mount of Offense and in Talpiot. But these
tombs contain more evidence
linking them to Jewish-
Christianity than just the con-
figuration of names. There are
cross marks on some of them,
perhaps added later by pil-
grims, and graffiti such as "Jesus woe!" "Jesus wail!" as well as the Greek
letters Chi and Rho, possibly an abbreviation for *Chr(istos)* or "Christ" in
Greek.[17]

The Tomb of the Shroud, which we discovered in June 2000, is also
quite close to this area, as is the Talpiot tomb found in 1980 that I discussed in the Introduction. If Jesus was moved to another tomb in the
Jerusalem area it well might have been one of these locations.

We can assume that eventually there was a Jesus family tomb somewhere in Jerusalem since the Jesus movement, led by James his brother,
eventually reestablished itself there. We have a tradition that James was
buried in the Kidron Valley, just below the Mount of Olives. There is
also a tradition that Jesus' brothers later buried Mary their mother near
the place where Jesus had been crucified. This area, on and around the
Mount of Olives, and a bit south where the Kidron and Hinnom valleys
intersect, or further south in Talpiot, seems to best fit our evidence.

In this context it is easy to see why the Tomb of the Shroud, the James Ossuary, and the Talpiot tomb discovered in 1980 spark such heated controversy. At the heart of the storm is the unspoken possibility that such a tomb might contain the remains of Jesus himself. Neither Christianity nor Judaism welcomes that proposition.

BACK TO GALILEE

But there is a possible alternative to the final burial of Jesus being located in Jerusalem. Jesus and his family were from Galilee. And surprisingly, there is an emphasis on Galilee in our records of the events following the death of Jesus.

When one reads the New Testament gospels it sounds as though the tragic and brutal death of Jesus was hardly much of a shock or crisis at all. After all, he was raised from the dead three days later and the apostles immediately began to build the Church, preaching that Jesus was now "heavenly King" enthroned at the right hand of God. This might have been how Christian believers wanted to remember things fifty years later but it surely was not the case in the sad days that followed Jesus' death.

It is interesting that within the complexity of the contradictory accounts in the gospels as to what happened after Jesus died, Matthew and John have the disciples *go back to Galilee.* This is a vital point that should not be missed. Everyone thinks of the Church beginning with great power in Jerusalem following Jesus' glorious resurrection from the dead. But if that were the case why would the followers have gone back to Galilee at all? This is certainly not the picture that Luke gives in the book of Acts, where the apostles are gathered in Jerusalem with a united focus on starting the Church. In fact Luke insists, in direct contradiction to both John and Matthew, that they never left the city (Acts 1:4).

The gospel of John reports that after the empty tomb was discovered with various "sightings" of Jesus in Jerusalem, Simon Peter, the sons of Zebedee, Thomas, Nathanael, and two others went back to the Sea of Galilee and *returned to their fishing business* (John 21). It is as if they had not even experienced the resurrected Jesus at all. The 2nd century *Gospel of Peter* also knows this tradition. It reports that after the eight-day festival of Passover the disciples "wept and mourned, and each one, very grieved at what had come to pass, went to his own home" back in Galilee, including Peter and Andrew, who resumed their fishing business. This tradition does not fit well in John, given his reports of Jesus appearing to his disciples in Jerusalem, but that actually contributes to the Galilee story's potential veracity. It appears to be an alternative tradition, added to the very end of John's gospel, and based, he says, upon the eyewitness account of the "beloved disciple."

And here is where Mark becomes very important. Remember, Mark, our earliest gospel, has *no* "sightings" of Jesus at all. But he does know a tradition where Jesus tells the Twelve at that last meal before his arrest, that he will "go before them to Galilee" (Mark 14:28). This ties in with his cryptic remarks about being "raised on the third day," which, as we have seen, refers to the resurrection of Israel the nation, not to Jesus' own individual resurrection. Perhaps it was in Galilee that the followers of Jesus found the renewal of their faith that the Kingdom of God was indeed at hand.

Matthew builds upon this Galilean tradition. He reports that the Eleven Apostles "see" Jesus on a specific mountain in Galilee. Surprisingly, Matthew notes that some even in this inner group doubted it was really him that they saw and Matthew recounts no other appearances of Jesus to the group but this one (Matthew 28:17). One wonders, why Galilee and why this specific mountain? Is it possible that they might have been visiting Jesus' grave in Galilee and Matthew's story is a modified theological recasting of an older tradition that ties the followers of Jesus to a "mountain" in Galilee where they experienced the presence of Jesus?

Surprisingly, there is a tomb of Jesus that almost no one knows or visits in Galilee. The revered 16th-century Kabbalistic Rabbi Isaac ben Luria (known as "the Ari") passed on a tradition that the grave of Jesus of Nazareth ("Yeshu ha-Notzri") was located in the north, in Galilee outside the city of Tsfat (Safed). This tradition, known in Jewish mystical circles, is seldom mentioned to outsiders since Rabbi ben Luria included the Jesus tomb in a list of the tombs of various Jewish sages and saints he terms the "burial places of the righteous." Jesus is a very sensitive subject within Judaism. If one of the greatest spiritual leaders in Jewish history,

Rabbi Isaac ben Luria, not only included Jesus among the "righteous," but claimed to know where he was buried, the repercussions could be troubling. From a Christian point of view Jesus rose from the dead, so that any claim to know where he is buried would be viewed as an expression of Jewish disbelief and slander. But from an orthodox Jewish point of view Jesus has traditionally been seen as a "false Messiah," even a negative figure, so how could it be that someone of the stature of ben Luria would revere him in this way?

The location of the tomb, just north of Tsfat, is quite explicit, so some years ago I decided to drive up into Galilee and see if I could locate it. It turned out to be fairly easy to spot, up on a ridge overlooking the main highway. The tomb was not in a rock-hewn cave but is level with the ground, piled with rocks, and oriented toward Jerusalem to the south. Its appearance reminded me very much of the Essene graves found in the graveyard at Qumran, where the Dead Sea community lived.

Even though our first reference to this tomb comes very late, from a 16th-century rabbinic source, it is the case that Rabbi Shimon bar Yochai and several other famous rabbis from the Roman period were buried in this area. Tsfat had become a center for Jewish mystical teaching in the

James Tabor kneeling over the Tsfat grave in Galilee

2nd century A.D., and perhaps earlier. Was it even remotely possible that Jesus' family took him back to Galilee for burial? Tsfat is located in the low mountainous area north of Capernaum. Jesus had made the area his headquarters for three years. The gospels report that he often went up into those mountains to get away from the crowds so he could pray. Might they have chosen this secluded location so that his body could lie undisturbed, far removed from the political dangers still brewing in Jerusalem? Is it possible that the memory of the location of the grave was passed down in Jewish circles through oral tradition over the centuries?

The Galilee tradition found in Matthew and Luke seems to merit some consideration, whether the rabbinic tradition about a Jesus tomb at Tsfat has any historical validity or not. These gospel stories involving Galilee seem to preserve a bit of the doubt and disappointment that must have characterized the dark days following the death of their beloved Teacher. Although the followers of Jesus reshaped themselves under the new leadership of James, and eventually returned to Jerusalem, there might well have been a period in which they retreated to Galilee in order to sort things out, and that is just what these gospel traditions appear to reflect. If that was the case then the more idealized account of the Jesus movement in the early chapters of the book of Acts is Luke's attempt to recast things in a more triumphant way.

The death of Jesus had to have been every bit as devastating to the group as the death of John the Baptizer had been the previous year. How could it be that the Two Messiahs were both dead? Was the Kingdom of God truly near? The promise of sitting on thrones and ruling over all Israel must have begun to appear quite remote. It was James, the brother of Jesus, the disciple whom Jesus loved, who began to turn things around. Jesus was dead but his dynasty had survived, and the cause for which he lived and died was still to be realized.

Part Five

WAITING FOR
THE SON OF MAN

15

GO TO JAMES THE JUST

WHEN the charismatic leader of a movement is violently killed one expects chaos, confusion, and disintegration to follow. Josephus mentioned at least a dozen other 1st-century A.D. messianic aspirants and revolt leaders whom the Romans executed. In each case the movements they started were crushed or faded away. There was clearly something different about the Jesus movement. After all, they had lost both their leaders, first John and then Jesus—the Two Messiahs in whom there was so much hope. But the movement did not die out; in fact it began to grow and spread.

The traditional view is that Jesus appeared in resurrected glory the Sunday after his Friday crucifixion turning his death into celebration and triumph. This is what Christians celebrate at Easter. But if Jesus truly died, and was buried, and his family and followers no longer had him physically present, and they went through a period of horrible grief and loss, as a more historical reading of the evidence suggests, how was it that the movement survived at all? As we have seen, there is a tradition preserved in the gospel of John, in the very last chapter, as if it is tacked on, that Peter and several of the Twelve returned to their fishing nets in Galilee, resuming a normal life for a time. The *Gospel of Peter* knows of this tradition as well. This sounds more like what one might expect. So what accounted for the transformation from despair to hope and renewal of faith?

I would attribute the survival and the revival of the Jesus movement to three factors. First, there is James himself, as well as Jesus' mother and brothers. Jesus was gone but James, as we will see, became a towering figure of faith and strength for Jesus' followers. To have Jesus' own brother with them, his own flesh and blood, and one who also shared Jesus' royal Davidic lineage, had to have been a powerful reinforcement. And this would be the case with Jesus' family as a whole. They became the anchor of his movement. Mary has been revered for her role as the "Mother of God" for centuries, but historically speaking, her role as the very *human* mother of this extraordinary family of six sons and two daughters seems to have been lost. Unfortunately, we don't have many details about how James was able to accomplish what he did as leader of the movement, since as we will see, his role has been almost totally marginalized in our New Testament records, but the results are evident. He was quite young when he took charge and must have grown into the role with time, as he matured into a man who earned the respect of his contemporaries. A second factor was the message that both John and Jesus had preached, the "good news of the Kingdom of God" and all that it implied. However revered the messengers might have been, what they advocated and proclaimed lived on and was in no way destroyed or lost by their deaths. They had spoken out against injustice and oppression, they had issued a call for repentance and proclaimed forgiveness of sins, and they embodied the messianic hope and faith rooted in the Hebrew Prophets. The *cause* of the Two Messiahs remained and survived. Finally, both Jesus and John had proclaimed that the "end of the age" had drawn near. The apocalyptic perspective that they embodied was reinforced, as we shall see, by the social and political events of their time. It was as if all that the Hebrew Prophets had predicted was in the process of being fulfilled before their eyes. The instability in Rome, the threat of wars and revolt, and even the opposition they faced from the authorities were all seen as further signs that the "appointed time" had grown very short—just as Jesus had proclaimed. They were an intensely apocalyptic community that expected to see the Kingdom of God manifested in its fullness. After all,

Jesus had expected the arrival of the "Son of Man" even before his death. When he had sent out the Twelve he had told them that they would not have "gone through all the towns of Israel before the Son of Man comes." In Daniel's dream the "coming of the Son of Man in the clouds of heaven" was a symbol for the time when the people of God would be given rule over all the nations (Daniel 7:13–14, 27). Jesus had declared that his casting out of demons was a sure sign that the "kingdom of God had arrived"; he compared this work to storming the fortress of a "strong man," namely Satan, and overpowering him (Luke 11:20–22). Jesus' death was surely a terrible shock to all who loved and followed him, but they continued to believe fervently in the central message that both Jesus and John the Baptizer before him had proclaimed: "Repent, for the Kingdom of God is at hand."

The main body of Jesus' core followers, including those who had been with the Messianic Movement from the time John the Baptizer had begun his work, gathered in Jerusalem in the late spring as summer neared. The festival of Pentecost or Shavuot fell the last week of May that year. There were not too many left, just over a hundred who had stayed loyal through the dark and trying days of Passover (Acts 1:15). They clustered in the area of lower Jerusalem, in the city of David. The guesthouse with the "Upper Room" where Jesus ate his last meal became their center of operations. The choice of location might have been more than a matter of convenience. Jesus had deliberately chosen that area of the city for his final meeting with the Twelve. King David had written a Psalm where God declared "I will set my king on Zion, my holy hill," referring to "Mount Zion" in the city of David (Psalms 2:6). Since many were from Galilee and other areas of the country, the community pooled their resources and began to live a loosely communal life, sharing their meals together, with those from out of town staying in the homes of those who lived in Jerusalem (Acts 2:46). There must have been a sense of danger but also one of excited expectation—since surely God would not allow the death of his Righteous Ones, John and Jesus, to go unpunished. Shortly before the day of Pentecost the group gathered to deliberate their situation. They needed a new leader and had to replace Judas Iscariot on the Council of Twelve. He had committed suicide.

What happened next is one of the greatest "untold" stories of the past
two millennia. The tradition most people remember is that the apostle
Peter took over leadership of the movement as head of the Twelve. Not
long afterward the apostle Paul, newly converted to the Christian faith
from "Judaism," joined Peter's side. Together, the apostles Peter and Paul
became the twin "pillars" of the emerging Christian faith, preaching the
gospel to the entire Roman world and dying gloriously as martyrs in
Rome—the new divinely appointed headquarters of the Church. This

Peter and Paul by El Greco

view of things has been enshrined in Christian art through the ages and popularized in books and films. Indeed, Peter's primacy as the first pope has even become the cornerstone of Roman Catholic dogmatic teaching. We now know that things did not happen this way.

Peter did rise to prominence in the group of the Twelve, as we shall see, but it was James the brother of Jesus who became the successor to Jesus and the undisputed leader of the Christian movement. Jesus, their Davidic ruler, had been removed from their midst. James was next in the royal Davidic bloodline. Jesus' death was not the end of the movement politically nor spiritually. The Jesus dynasty would continue for over a century after his death. But if this is the case, how could James, the heir to the Jesus dynasty, have been almost entirely left out of the story of Christian origins—and more important—why? James hardly even appears in Christian art and iconography. It is as if his very existence has been all but forgotten. But he emerges in a history hidden from view. This history is a startling and inspiring story with important implications for our understanding of Jesus and the cause for which he lived and died.

We must begin our search for James by looking at our New Testament sources—for it is from here that his memory was largely erased. We only have one substantial account of the history of the early Christian movement following the death of Jesus—the New Testament book we know as Acts of the Apostles. The same author who wrote the gospel of Luke wrote Acts as a second volume to his literary work. The book of Acts is largely responsible for the standard portrait of early Christianity in which Peter and Paul assume such a dominant role and James is largely left out. The presentation of Acts has become *the* story, even though Luke's version is woefully one-sided and historically questionable. Luke surely knew but was not willing to state that James took over the leadership of the movement after Jesus' death. In his early chapters he never even mentions James by name and casts Peter as the undisputed leader of Jesus' followers. But his major agenda in the book as a whole is to promote the centrality of the mission and message of the apostle Paul. Although Acts has twenty-four chapters, once Paul is introduced in chapter nine the rest of Luke's account is wholly about Paul—even Peter begins to drop out of the picture. Rather than "Acts of the Apostles" the book might better be named "The Mission and Career of Paul."

This is not to say that Acts lacks historical value. We would be immensely diminished in our understanding of the early development of the Christian movement without it. And ironically, Luke has unwittingly left clues in the book of Acts that allow us to verify what we know from other sources—that James, not Peter, became the legitimate successor of Jesus and leader of the movement. We have to learn to read the book of Acts carefully, aware at all times of the scarcely veiled "spin" that Luke put on the story.

Luke more than any of the other gospels marginalizes the family of Jesus. Remember, Luke is the gospel that deliberately avoided even mentioning the brothers of Jesus, much less *naming* them, even though his source Mark plainly listed them as James, Joses, Judas, and Simon (Mark 6:3). Once when a woman in the crowd that followed Jesus cried out "Blessed is the womb that bore you and the breasts that you sucked," Luke alone had Jesus reply, "No, rather blessed are those who hear the word of God and keep it" (Luke 11:27–28). Even at the cross, when Mark plainly said that "Mary the mother of James and Joses" as well as Jesus' sister Salome were present, Luke changed this to read "the *women* [unnamed] who had followed him from Galilee" (Luke 23:49). At the burial scene he did the same. Rather than name "Mary Magdalene and Mary the mother of James" as present at the tomb as his source Mark did, he changed the account to read "the *women* [again unnamed] who had come with him from Galilee followed and saw the tomb" (Luke 23:55). In most cases Luke followed Mark rather closely as a source, much more so than Matthew, who constantly added his own editorial revisions. But Luke departed from Mark when it came to the mother and brothers of Jesus. I think he did this to avoid raising questions about Peter's leadership of the Twelve or the superiority of Paul's mission to the Gentiles. Such bold editing could not be accidental; there is something very important going on here. It is part of Luke's overall agenda to recast the history of the early movement so that Paul comes out ahead of possible rivals including James. But what was their rivalry about?

Luke was a Gentile. In fact he was the only non-Jewish writer in the entire New Testament. He emphasizes the Gentile version of Christianity that Paul espoused. He cannot deny that Jesus was a Jew, or that all of Jesus' original followers were Jewish, or that the early Christian movement as a whole was an apocalyptic movement within Judaism. But he wrote at a time, two decades after the Jewish-Roman revolt, when those Jewish origins of the movement were becoming marginalized and deemphasized and the imminent apocalyptic hope had faded.

Luke was also pro-Roman. Paul, his hero, was a Roman citizen and he wants his Gentile Roman readers to know and value that about him, and thus look with favor on the growing Gentile Christian movement. In his account of the trial of Jesus, Luke goes beyond Mark, his primary source, to emphasize that Pontius Pilate was a reasonable and just ruler who went to extraordinary lengths to get Jesus released. He removes the reference to Pilate having Jesus scourged and even omits the horrible mocking and abuse that Jesus suffered at the hands of Pilate's Roman Praetorium guard (Luke 23:25). According to Luke, again following the theology of Paul, Jesus could not possibly have died "forsaken by God" since his death was part of God's plan to bring forgiveness of sins to the world (Luke 24:47). Luke removed the agonizing final cry of Jesus and instead had Jesus pray directly for the Roman soldiers carrying out his crucifixion, "Father forgive them they know not what they do" (Luke 23:34). Luke was not writing history; he was writing theology. With that in mind we have to take what he tells us with extreme caution and keep in mind at all times his pro-Paul and pro-Roman agenda.

THE JESUS DYNASTY IN JERUSALEM

The primary reason that an understanding of the Jesus dynasty was lost to later Christian memory was that the book of Acts deliberately suppressed its existence. For Luke there was *no* possibility that the followers of Jesus retreated to Galilee in sorrow and despair after Jesus' death. He puts *all* the "sightings" of Jesus in Jerusalem. He does not even mention Galilee and what might have happened there. These "sightings," according to Luke, happened on Sunday, the very day the empty tomb was discovered, so that any doubts the apostles must have had in response to the brutal and horrible death of their leader were immediately dispelled. The new Pauline "Gospel" they were to preach to the Gentile world was put before them by Jesus himself. Luke explicitly said that Jesus told the Eleven "not to leave Jerusalem" (Acts 1:4). For Luke, Galilee represents the native, indigenous, Jewish origins of Jesus and his family. But something did happen in Galilee after the empty-tomb experience and it surely must have involved Jesus' mother, his brothers, and the entire entourage that had followed Jesus to Jerusalem from Galilee. As I described earlier, according to Matthew and John it was in Galilee that the followers found a renewal of their faith and the determination to carry on the movement. Luke would have none of that.

Luke presents quite a different story. According to Acts, about forty days after Jesus' death the Eleven Apostles gathered together in Jerusalem in the Upper Room where they had had their last meal with Jesus to choose a successor to Judas. Luke carefully listed those leaders who were present:

> Peter, and John, and James, and Andrew
> Philip and Thomas, Bartholomew and Matthew
> *James son of Alphaeus, and Simon the Zealot, and Judas brother of James*

He then carefully added a fateful qualifying sentence that has served to marginalize the Jesus family for two thousand years:

> "All these [the Eleven] were constantly devoting themselves to prayer, together with certain women, *including Mary the mother of Jesus as well as his brothers.*" (Acts 1:13–14)

By separating here the Eleven from "Mary the mother of Jesus as well as his brothers" Luke has effectively managed to recast things so that James and Jesus' other brothers played no leadership role at this crucial juncture of the movement. They are mentioned in passing, as if to say, "Oh yes, by the way, they were present but really not significant."

But of course Luke felt obligated to include them as present. He did not dare to completely write them out of the account, knowing as he did the absolutely crucial role that they played. It is more than ironic that in listing the Eleven he mentions by name James, and Simon, and even notes that Judas is the brother of James. As we shall see, the book of Acts was written around a basic undeniable fact—James had assumed leadership of the movement, and Simon his brother took over after James's death in A.D. 62. Luke wrote Acts in the 90s A.D., at least thirty years after James was dead, and Luke was surely aware that Simon, also of the royal bloodline, had succeeded James and was head of the church in Jerusalem even as Luke was writing. Luke purposely ended his account in the book of Acts with Paul's imprisonment in Rome around the year A.D. 60. For him that is the end of the story—Paul in Rome preaching his gospel to the Gentile world. By choosing that cutoff date he had no obligation to record either the death of James or the succession of Jesus' brother Simon. Luke's story in Acts became *the* story of early Christianity for subsequent generations. What he chose not to tell was forgotten.

It is ironic that our earliest evidence regarding the leadership role that James and the brothers of Jesus played after Jesus' death comes to us directly from Paul. Jesus was crucified in the year A.D. 30. Paul's letters date to the 50s A.D. For this twenty-year gap we have no surviving records. These are the silent years in the history of earliest Christianity. What we can know we have to read backward from the records that survive. Fortunately, in Paul's letter to the Galatians, written around A.D. 50, he reached back at least fourteen years in recounting his own autobiography.[1] This gives us an original first-person source, the most valuable tool any historian can work with, reaching back into the decade of the 30s A.D.

In the letter to the Galatians Paul related that three years after joining the movement he made his first trip to Jerusalem, where he saw Peter, whom he calls by his Aramaic nickname Cephas. Paul stayed with him fifteen days. He then wrote, "But I did not see any other apostle except James the Lord's brother" (Galatians 1:19). Not only did he call James an apostle but he clearly identified him as Jesus' brother. The Nazarenes understandably distrusted Paul since he had so recently been at the forefront of those persecuting them, allied with the very leaders who had had Jesus killed. Paul saw Peter but he knew that it was essential that he meet with James, who was in charge. That Paul mentioned this in passing is all the more significant. He does not need to explain to anyone why he would have met with James.

Paul next related that fourteen years after his conversion, very close to A.D. 50, he made a return trip to Jerusalem to receive authorization for his mission to the Gentiles from those he designated as the three "pillars" of the movement—namely *James, Peter, and John* the fisherman (Galatians 2:9). That James is even named is significant, but that he is named *first* by Paul, before Peter and John, is absolutely critical for our understanding. The order of the names indicates an established order of authority. The Council of Twelve, with James at the head, governs the Nazarenes, but of the Twelve three exercise the primary leadership—James, Peter, and John. James the brother of Jesus, sharing the royal lineage of King David, occupies the central position, but one on the right and another on the left flank him as "pillars." Jesus, who had previously occupied the royal position, had been asked by the Twelve who among them would receive the privilege to "sit one on your right and one on your left" when the Kingdom arrived (Mark 10:37). Jesus had died without ever designating any of them for these two positions. Now, with James as the center, Peter and John had filled these roles as part of the messianic governing body that Jesus had inaugurated. We know this pattern from the Qumran community in the Dead Sea Scrolls. The *Community Rule* had stipulated: "In the Council of the Community there shall be twelve men and three priests, perfectly versed in all that is revealed of the Torah".[2]

Even though Luke had related nothing in Acts about James being one of the apostles, much less succeeding Jesus as leader of the group, when he reports this meeting of Paul with the Jerusalem apostles in A.D. 50 in his account in Acts 15 he also felt obligated to relate that James was in full charge of the proceedings. In the early chapters of Acts, Luke had mentioned Peter and John repeatedly, as a pair, indicating that they were in positions of leadership over the Nazarene movement.[3] He had put these two first in his listing of the Twelve—indicating that they had been chosen for the "right and left" positions (Acts 1:13). This was a change from his earlier listing of the Twelve in his gospel, where he had a different order for the first four: Peter, Andrew, James, and John (Luke 6:14). That he has shifted the order in Acts, putting Peter and John in first and second place, fits with what we know from Paul about the "pillars" of the church, namely James, Peter, and John. Prior to this Jerusalem Council meeting in A.D. 50 the only time that Luke identifies Jesus' brother James by name is when Peter is released from prison and he tells a group of Jesus' followers gathered in a private home to "Go tell James and the brothers" that he had been set free (Acts 12:17). Here we have a hint that Peter is inclined to report things to James and the brothers of Jesus, but nothing more is said and no elaboration is given. This report seems to come out of the blue.

Thus in Luke's account in Acts, when James suddenly appears out of nowhere as leader of the Nazarene movement at the Jerusalem Council, we can see that Luke is well aware of James's position. At this critical juncture he dared not leave James out of the story. Coupled with Paul's passing references in Galatians regarding James as the leading "pillar" of the movement we can begin to piece together our evidence. More than a few readers of Acts have puzzled over this anomaly. Who is this mysterious "James" who emerges in chapter 15 without explanation but with such power and authority?

The Jerusalem Council was convened to address a critical and controversial issue that had threatened to split the Messianic Movement. Upon what basis should Gentiles be accepted into the group? Both John the Baptizer and Jesus had proclaimed the imminent arrival of the Kingdom of God. According to the Prophets, God's judgment was to fall not only upon Israel but also upon all humankind. Accordingly, Jews as well as non-Jews were called upon to repent of their sins and turn to God in order to be saved from the "wrath to come." Yahweh was the Creator, the only "true and living God," and worship of any other deities was termed idolatry. But what was to be required of those non-Jews who did respond to this proclamation—the "good news" of the imminent arrival of the Kingdom of God? There was a conservative wing of the Nazarene movement that maintained that these Gentiles should begin to live fully as Jews—which would include circumcision for males, and the observance of all the laws of the Torah. Paul stoutly resisted this position, and he had the support of Peter, who, next to James, was the most influential of the Nazarene leaders. After much discussion and dispute Luke reported that it was James, the brother of Jesus, who arose and rendered his decision:

> Therefore I have made the judgment that we should not trouble those Gentiles who are turning to God, but that we write to them that they abstain from the pollutions of idols, and from fornication, and from what is strangled, and from blood. For in every city, for generations past, Moses has had those who proclaim him, for he has been read aloud every Sabbath in the synagogues. (Acts 15:19–21)

Here Luke feels compelled to give James his rightful place with full authority—even though he offers no explanation for how this might have come to be. The pivotal decision that James decreed was in keeping with the general practice of Jewish groups throughout the Roman world. If non-Jews were attracted to the synagogue they were welcomed as "God-fearers," or "righteous Gentiles," and were not expected to become circumcised and keep the entire Torah as required of Jews. They were, however, expected to follow the ethics of the Torah that were applicable to all human beings. Idolatry and various forms of sexual immorality, widely condoned in Roman society, were strictly condemned. The eating of meat that still contained the blood of the slaughtered animal had been universally forbidden to all human beings from the time of Noah (Genesis 9:4). Beyond these more specific areas of conduct that divided Jew from non-Jew, one was expected to live a life of justice and righteousness. The decision James rendered here was in general harmony with a common Jewish approach toward Gentiles that we know from other sources.[4] But it is not so much the decision itself as the unambiguous authority James wielded over the Nazarene movement that makes this account in Acts so significant. Taking this as our starting point the cumulative evidence outside the New Testament that James took up the mantle of Jesus and occupied his "seat" or "throne" is quite remarkable. Some of this evidence is buried in ancient texts that we have had for centuries and some has emerged just in the past few decades.

JAMES THE JUST ONE

The *Gospel of Thomas* was discovered in upper Egypt in 1945 outside the little village of Nag Hammadi, as I have already explained. Although the text itself dates to the 3rd century, scholars have shown that it preserves, despite later theological embellishments, an original Aramaic document that comes to us from the early days of the Jerusalem church.[5] It provides us a rare glimpse into what scholars have called "Jewish Christianity," that is, the earliest followers of Jesus led by James. As you will recall, the *Gospel of Thomas* is not a narrative of the life of Jesus but rather a listing of 114 of his "sayings" or teachings. Saying 12 reads as follows:

> The disciples said to Jesus, "We know you will leave us. Who is going to be our leader then?" Jesus said to them, "No matter where you go you are to *go to James the Just*, for whose sake heaven and earth came into being."

Here we have an outright statement from Jesus himself that he is handling over the leadership and spiritual direction of his movement to James. Jesus' extravagant and unqualified statement reminds one of the honor that he paid to his kinsman John the Baptizer as "more than a prophet" and the greatest "among those born of women" of his generation. We should keep in mind that the *Gospel of Thomas* in its present form comes to us from a later period, when the matter of "who is going to be our leader" had become a critical one for the followers of Jesus. The phrase "no matter where you go" implies that the authority and leadership of James is not restricted to the Jerusalem Church or even to Roman Palestine. According to this text James the brother of Jesus had been put in charge over *all* of Jesus' followers. The phrase "for whose sake heaven and earth came into being" reflects a Jewish notion that the world exists and is sustained because of the extraordinary virtues of a handful of righteous or "just" individuals.[6] James the brother of Jesus acquired the designation "James the Just" both to distinguish him from others of that name and to honor him for his preeminent position.

The *Gospel of Thomas* provides us with our earliest and most clearly stated evidence that James succeeded Jesus as leader of the movement, but it is confirmed by many other sources.

Gospel of Thomas

Clement of Alexandria, who wrote in the late 2nd century A.D., is another early source who confirms this succession of James. At one point he wrote: "Peter and James and John after the Ascension of the Savior did not struggle for glory, because they had previously been given honor by the Savior, but chose James the Just as Overseer of Jerusalem."[7] In a subsequent passage Clement elaborated: "After the resurrection the Lord [Jesus] gave the tradition of knowledge to James the Just and John and Peter, these gave it to the other Apostles, and the other Apostles to the Seventy."[8] This passage preserves for us the tiered structure of the provisional government that Jesus left behind: James the Just as successor; John and Peter as his left- and right-hand advisors; the rest of the Twelve; then the Seventy.

Eusebius, the early-4th-century Christian historian, wrote in commenting on this passage, "James whom men of old had surnamed 'Just' for his excellence of virtue, is recorded to have been the first elected to the *throne* of the Oversight of the church in Jerusalem."[9] The Greek term *thronos* refers to a "seat" or "chair" of authority and is the same term used for a king or ruler.

Eusebius also preserves the testimony of Hegesippus, a Jewish Christian of the early 2nd century, who he says is from the "generation after the Apostles":

> The succession of the church passed to James the brother of the Lord, together with the Apostles. He was called the "Just" by all men from the Lord's time until ours, since many are called James, but he was holy from his mother's womb.[10]

The Greek word that Hegesippus used here, *diadexomat* ("to succeed"), is regularly used for the passing on of a genetic inheritance, for example, when Philip king of Macedonia passes on his rule to Alexander the Great.[11]

We also have a recently recovered Syriac source, *The Ascents of James*, that is embedded in a later corpus known as the *Pseudo-Clementine Recognitions*, which reflects some of the earliest traditions related to the Jerusalem church under the leadership of James the Just.[12] It records events in Jerusalem seven years following the death of Jesus, when James is clearly at the helm: "The church in Jerusalem that was established by our Lord was increasing in numbers being ruled uprightly and firmly by James who was made Overseer over it by our Lord."[13] The Latin version of the *Recognitions* passed on the following admonition: "Wherefore observe the greatest caution, that you believe no teacher, unless he bring from Jerusalem the testimonial of James the Lord's brother, or of whosoever may come after him" (4:35). The *Second Apocalypse of James*, one of the texts found with the *Gospel of Thomas* at Nag Hammadi, stressed the intimate bond between Jesus and James, in keeping with the idea that he was the "beloved disciple." In this text Jesus and James are said to have been "nursed with the same milk" and Jesus kisses his brother James and says to him, "Behold I shall reveal to you everything my beloved" (50.15–22). I have already noted in Chapter 12 that the *Gospel of the Hebrews* puts James at the Last Supper, thus implying he was one of the Twelve, and making it all the more likely that he is the "disciple whom Jesus loved." Although we don't have the entire text, and it is preserved for us only in quotations by the 4th-century Christian writer Jerome, this gospel was originally written in Hebrew. Some scholars have maintained it might predate even our New Testament gospels.

What is impressive about these sources is the way in which they speak with a single voice, yet come from various authors and time periods. The basic elements of the picture they preserve for us are amazingly consistent: Jesus passes to James his successor rule of the Church; James is widely known, even by Josephus, an outsider, because of his reputation for righteousness both in his community and among the people; Peter, John, and the rest of the Twelve look to James as their leader.

Given what we now know we are in a position to investigate the type of Christianity that James the Just inherited from his brother Jesus and passed on, and what the existence of this Jesus dynasty reveals to us about the hidden and forgotten cause for which Jesus lived and died. But before I turn to that we need to look at Paul. His dominant influence in the New Testament offers the greatest challenge to any attempt to recover the legacy of the Jesus dynasty.

16

THE CHALLENGE
OF PAUL

SAUL of Tarsus, known better by his Roman name Paul, was a young man when Jesus died, probably, like Jesus, in his thirties.[1] The name Saul is Hebrew, honoring the first king of Israel, who like Paul was of the Israelite tribe of Benjamin. Paul (*Paulus*), his Roman surname, means "small." According to Luke, Paul was born and grew up in the city of Tarsus in the Roman province of Cilicia, in Asia Minor (Acts 22). His parents were Jewish but had obtained Roman citizenship, which he thus inherited by right of birth. Jerome, the 4th-century Christian writer, knew a different tradition. He wrote that Paul's parents were from Gischala, in Galilee, a Jewish town about twenty-five miles north of Sepphoris, and it was there that Paul was born. When the revolts broke out following the death of Herod the Great in 4 B.C., Jerome reports, Paul and his parents were captured, and as part of the large-scale exile of Galilean inhabitants from Palestine, were sent to Tarsus in Cilicia.[2] I am inclined to value Jerome's account since he must have thought it was based on good evidence to be willing to contradict the book of Acts, which says that Paul was born in Tarsus.

If Jerome is correct, and Paul was born sometime before 4 B.C., he would have been close to the age of Jesus. It is interesting to think that

both Paul's family and Jesus' family, living just a few miles apart were af-
fected by the revolts in Galilee in different ways. Mary and Joseph had
moved to Nazareth or they might well have been exiled along with the
rest of the inhabitants of Sepphoris, while Paul and his parents apparently were forced out of the country. It is possible that this Galilean ori-
gin of Paul's family can shed some light on Paul's later motivations. After
witnessing such devastation and destruction brought on by those in
Galilee and Judea who sought to oppose Rome, perhaps Paul and his
family learned to be much more accommodating to the social and political realities of their Roman world. In Paul's letter to the Christians at
Rome, written around A.D. 56, when Nero was emperor, Paul instructed
them to pay taxes and honor all Roman officials, including the emperor,
who he says is God's agent for good (Romans 13:6). This is surely opposite from the revolutionary message that Jesus had preached. As we shall
see, the "Kingdom of God" for Paul was a spiritual kingdom, not on earth
but in heaven. Although he expected an apocalyptic judgment in the future, he counseled his followers to fit into society, to be good citizens, and
to wait patiently until Jesus appeared in the clouds of heaven to take his
followers away from heavenly realms.

Somehow Paul's parents had obtained Roman citizenship, possibly for
some kind of loyal service to Rome, or perhaps by an accumulation of
wealth and influence in their new province of Cilicia. Luke says Paul was
a "tent maker," a trade Paul would have learned from his father. The
Greek word can refer to one who works with leather products in general,
including weaving rough goat hair into the famous Cilicium textiles that
were used for tents and were prized for warmth by soldiers and sailors
(Acts 18:3). Luke also says that Paul's father was a Pharisee (Acts 23:6).
Apparently the family had the means, determination, and influence to
send its son to Jerusalem to study with Gamaliel, the leading Pharisee
and rabbi of the day.

Paul had connections to the high priestly family of Annas and cooper-
ated in efforts to suppress and even arrest the followers of Jesus following
his crucifixion. How Paul obtained or maintained such high connections
in Jewish aristocratic society we don't know. Paul mentions a relative
named Herodion, who lived in Rome (Romans 16:11). This might have

provided him some possible connection to Herod's family, which was so prominent in Rome during that time. His sister also lived in Jerusalem and the family appears to have had access to the Roman authorities in Jerusalem (Acts 23:16). Later in life Paul had the means to appeal to the Emperor Nero for a legal hearing regarding charges that had been brought against him, and his Roman citizenship allowed him safe passage and protection, even when under arrest (Acts 25:11; 23:23–24). When in Rome under "house arrest," Paul had connections to those in Nero's household, as well as to members of the powerful Praetorian guard that ended up forcing Nero into suicide (Philippians 1:13; 4:15–18). He mentions specifically Epaphroditus in this context, possibly referring to the court secretary by that name under Nero and Domitian.

Around the year A.D. 36 Paul had a "conversion" experience in which he claimed to have "seen" the risen Jesus. He said he had received both a revelation and a commission—that Jesus was the heavenly exalted "Christ" and that he, Paul, was to preach the good news of salvation through faith in Jesus to the Gentile world. He began to see himself as the Thirteenth Apostle, last but not least, and he referred to himself as the "Apostle to the Gentiles." Just as Jesus had chosen his Council of Twelve to preside over the people of Israel, Paul claimed to be given authority over the non-Jewish or Gentile world to prepare them for a "Second Coming" of Jesus as Messiah, this time from heaven.

There are two completely separate and distinct "Christianities" embedded in the New Testament. One is quite familiar and became the version of the Christian faith known to billions over the past two millennia. Its main proponent was the apostle Paul. The other has been largely forgotten and by the turn of the 1st century A.D. had been effectively marginalized and suppressed by the other. Even within the documents of the New Testament itself one has to look carefully to detect its presence. Its champion was none other than James the brother of Jesus, leader of the Jesus movement from A.D. 30 until his violent death in the year A.D. 62. The two versions of the "faith" are quite distinctively different both in values and in practice. The concept behind the Jesus dynasty, that is, that Jesus was succeeded by a series of leaders who were his own brothers, is not just about royal lineage and pedigree. It has to do with the matter of which version of the Christian faith best represents the original beliefs and teachings of Jesus of Nazareth and John the Baptizer—founders of the Messianic Movement.

There is little doubt that the apostle Paul was accepted into the inner circles of Jesus' original followers. Indeed, in the year A.D. 58 he was arrested and brought before the Jewish High Priest Ananias, accused of being "a ringleader of the sect of the Nazarenes" (Acts 24:5). According to Paul's report, and also that of Luke, James the Just, Peter, and John, the three "pillars" of the church, gave him the "right hand of fellowship" and publicly endorsed his missionary preaching to the Gentile Roman world (Galatians 2:9). It was *what* he preached and taught that began to create problems.

A HEAVENLY CHRIST

Paul was a Jew and in fact, according to his own testimony, as a Pharisee studying in Jerusalem he had "advanced in Judaism" beyond many of his contemporaries (Galatians 1:14). There is no evidence that he had never met or heard Jesus. If he was witness to the events surrounding Jesus' crucifixion at Passover in A.D. 30 he never mentioned it. His connection to Jesus was based on his own visionary experiences in which he claimed to have "seen" Jesus several years after his crucifixion.[3] Paul believed that his "calling" had been foreordained: "He set me apart before I was born and called me through his grace . . . that I might preach him among the Gentiles" (Galatians 1:15–16). He also claimed to hear a disembodied "voice" that he identified as "words" of Jesus.[4] In fact he took pride in his claim that unlike James and the rest of the Twelve, who had known Jesus "according to the flesh," he had received his authority and his commission directly from the heavenly Christ and needed no earthly human approval or authorization.[5] As he wrote his Greek followers at Corinth: "From now on we know no man according to the flesh, even if we once knew Christ according to the flesh, yet now we know him so no more" (2 Corinthians 5:16).

Paul taught that Jesus was a divine preexistent heavenly being, created as the "firstborn" of all God's creation.[6] He existed in the "form of God"

Paul's heavenly vision by Parmigianino

and was "equal to God" (Philippians 2:6). It was by the agency of Christ that God had brought the world into existence.[7] In his heavenly glory Christ was before all things and he was glorified and worshipped by the angelic hosts. He subsequently "emptied himself" and took on human form, being "born of a woman" and sent into the world from heaven.[8] His purpose was to live without sin and to die on the cross as atonement for the sins of the world. As Paul put it: "For our sake he [God] made him to be a sin offering, who knew no sin, so that in him we might become the righteousness of God (2 Corinthians 5:21). God then raised Christ from the dead and transformed him back into his glorious heavenly body. Christ ascended into heaven and was seated in power and glory at God's right hand.[9]

In this way God was able to "reconcile" a sinful world, both Jews and Gentiles, to himself. According to Paul, those who accepted the atoning sacrifice of Christ's blood were forgiven of all their sins and given the "gift" of eternal life. They were made right with God by faith and not by good deeds.[10] Paul expected that he and most of his followers would live to see Christ return from heaven in power and glory. Paul wrote that Jesus had taught him that followers were to reenact a "Lord's Supper" in which they would drink wine as Jesus' "blood" and eat bread as his "body," without which they could not escape the judgment. He claimed that the improper observance of this sacred meal could cause illness and even death.[11] Those believers who had died before Christ's arrival, God would raise from the dead in gloriously transformed spiritual bodies. Those alive at the time would likewise be instantaneously changed from flesh to spirit. Paul took this quite literally. He assured his followers that at Christ's appearance both the living and the dead would rise in the air to meet Christ in the clouds of heaven.[12] There they would sit in judgment over angels and humans, sharing heavenly glory and exaltation with Christ forever.[13] Paul's entire orientation and focus was toward the heavenly world. As he wrote his followers at Corinth: "We look not to the things that are seen, but to the things that are unseen; for the things that are seen are passing, but the things that are unseen are eternal" (2 Corinthians 4:18). His view of the Kingdom of God was heavenly as well. He explicitly declared: "Flesh and blood will not inherit the kingdom of God" (1 Corinthians 15:50).

Paul has sometimes been accused of developing his version of Christianity by drawing upon Hellenistic or "pagan" ideas, as if he had to move outside of Judaism for his inspiration. This is really a misconception with an oversimplified view of the various forms of Judaism in the Roman world. We have many Jewish texts predating Paul that have already begun to develop a dualistic orientation toward the heavenly world with speculations about levels of heaven, hierarchies of angels and demons, magical rites, life after death in unseen spiritual realms with both rewards and punishments, and heavenly glorification. Even speculative ideas related to pre-existent cosmic redeemer figures whose realm is more heavenly than earthly are not unknown.[14] Paul developed his views of "Christology" based on his own mystical experiences but he would have been able to draw upon a complex set of speculative Jewish traditions as well.

Paul referred to his message of the heavenly exalted Christ and the gift of forgiveness and eternal life made available by his death on the cross as "my gospel." He pronounced a formal "curse" upon anyone who preached "any other gospel" than the one he preached (Galatians 1:6–9). He called his "gospel" a "revelation of a secret" hidden for ages, but now revealed to him by the heavenly Christ as the apostle to the Gentiles.[15] Since he realized he could never effectively make the case that Jesus "in the flesh" had taught what he was preaching, his only possible defense was that the heavenly Christ had now revealed these things to him as a "final word." Paul seldom mentioned anything that Jesus taught and said little about Jesus' life other than his death on the cross.[16] The message that Jesus had preached became transformed, for Paul, into Jesus *as* the message.

The most unsettling aspects of Paul's mystical "gospel" for members of the Messianic Movement that John the Baptizer and Jesus had inaugurated was his view of the temporary nature of the Torah or Jewish Law and a "spiritual" redefinition of who constituted the people of Israel. Judaism in the Roman world was quite diverse but in all its forms there were two common elements: the central place of the Torah and the belief that the people of Israel were God's chosen nation. The Torah was revealed to Moses by God and as such represented an eternal covenant binding upon the people of Israel, that is the descendants of Abraham, Isaac, and Jacob. The last of the Hebrew prophets, Malachi, had closed his book with the words "Remember the Torah of my servant Moses" followed by the promise to send "Elijah" with his message of repentance before the great day of Judgment. The observance of the Torah and the expectation of the end of days were intrinsically bound together.

By the early 50s A.D. Paul had begun to propound a version of his new "Christ faith" that entailed the essential abrogation of the Jewish faith by repudiating the validity of God's Torah revelation and redefining "Israel" as all those with faith in Christ. Israel "according to the flesh" as Paul put it, was no longer truly "Israel." Jesus and John the Baptizer had lived and died as Jews faithful to the vision of Israel's historic destiny as declared by all the Hebrew Prophets. The Nazarene movement, led by James, Peter, and John, was by any historical definition a Messianic Movement *within* Judaism. Even the term "Jewish-Christianity," though perhaps useful as a description of the original followers of Jesus, is really a misnomer since they never considered themselves anything but faithful Jews. In that sense early Christianity *is* Jewish. Gentiles had been welcomed into the movement on the basis of Judaism's universal ethical message to all humankind, but no one remotely imagined that John the Baptizer or Jesus had annulled God's covenant with the people of Israel or the eternal Torah upon which it was based. No one in the Jesus movement was thinking about a "new religion" but rather a restoration and fulfillment of the promises that God had anciently made to Israel. This included the promise of a New Covenant that Jeremiah had predicted—but it was a *renewed* covenant with the "house of Israel and the house of Judah," as the Prophet Jeremiah had stated, and as Jesus had expected in choosing his Twelve Apostles, one to rule over each of the twelve tribes of a regathered Israel (Jeremiah 31:31; Luke 22:30).

Paul began to see things differently. Whether he developed his views over time or held them from the start we cannot say. As we will see, Paul was willing to work within a system with which he disagreed in order to bring about change. That he was accepted and endorsed by James at the Jerusalem Council of A.D. 50 indicates that he did not reveal publicly all that he believed. His letter to the Galatians clearly shows the radical implications of his views, and it was written shortly after the Jerusalem Council.

He opened the letter by insisting that he got his authority directly from revelations of "Christ," not from any human being, and he stressed that his contact even with Peter and James had been very minimal. He then related that he had been present at the Council in Jerusalem but had essentially received an endorsement for preaching "his gospel" to the Gentiles. He referred to the Jerusalem leaders, namely James, Peter, and John, as the "reputed" pillars of the church and adds that "what they were means nothing to me" (Galatians 2:6, 9). The entire opening of the letter was intended to say, in effect, that whatever the Jerusalem leaders decided or did not decide was beside the point since his authority was from Christ, not from men.

Paul then went on to argue in the Galatian letter that the Torah or Law given to Israel in the time of Moses was only a *temporary* revelation that had now been annulled by the coming of Christ. He wrote: "The Torah was our custodian until Christ came, that we might be justified by faith. But now that faith has come we are no longer under a custodian" (Galatians 3:24–25). That he used the first person here indicates that he believed that he as a Jew was also no longer "under the Law." Paul further said that the Torah had not even been given directly by God in the first place but was delivered to Moses through an angelic mediator as a temporary measure.[17] He warned his Gentile followers that if they began to observe Jewish holy days they would risk falling into slavery to "spirits" of a lesser rank than God.[18] Paul further maintained that the covenant made with Israel at Mount Sinai under Moses was a system of slavery, and that the Jewish people, as "children born according to the flesh," were now cast out unless they accepted Christ as Savior.[19] Those with faith in Christ were part of a "new creation" in which the distinctions between being "Jewish" or "Gentile" were no longer valid.[20] Paul's implications are clear. God's covenant with Israel has been nullified by "faith in Christ," so that "being Jewish" and following the commandments of God set forth in the Torah had become obsolete.

Paul stoutly and adamantly insisted that his Gentile converts were not required to be circumcised and live as Jews under the Torah. James and the Jerusalem Council had fully agreed. James had ruled that non-Jews who joined the Nazarenes were only required to observe the universal ethical requirements that the Torah prescribed for all humankind. But that was not to say that Gentiles were forbidden to follow the Torah. The door was always open and Jews did in fact accept Gentiles who wanted to undergo circumcision (in the case of males), and fully adopt all the commandments of Israel. James had made this point at the Jerusalem Council when he said, "For from early generations Moses has had in every city those who preach him, for he is read every Sabbath in the synagogues" (Acts 15:21). Gentiles were free to associate or affiliate as closely with the Jewish people as they wished and to follow whatever parts of the Jewish Law that they found spiritually attractive.

Paul insisted otherwise. At times he became quite rabid about this point, as when he wrote his followers at Philippi:

> Look out for the dogs! Look out for the evil-workers! Look out for those who whack off the flesh! For we are the true circumcision who worship God in spirit and glory in Christ Jesus and put no confidence in the flesh. (Philippians 3:2–3)

He sternly warned the Galatians that if any of them underwent circumcision they were "cut off from Christ" and "fallen from grace" (Galatians 5:4). He said that he wished those undergoing circumcision would slip with the knife and "cut themselves off" (Galatians 5:12). His tone was so strident and bitter because there were Jews in the Nazarene movement who had visited Paul's congregations and encouraged those who were so attracted to move further toward a full observance of the Torah. Paul characterized them as "false brethren who slipped in to spy out our freedom" (Galatians 2:4). His use of the first-person "our" seems to indicate that he had quite fully identified with a Gentile way of life himself, even as a Jew. It is unlikely these Nazarenes were *requiring* that Gentiles take up a Jewish way of life, since the Jerusalem Council had made its decision otherwise, but they might have encouraged such a choice as more fully pleasing to God.

As far as James and the Jerusalem leaders were concerned, the status of Gentiles was not really at issue. They had welcomed and accepted them fully into the Nazarene movement. Accordingly Paul's preaching to non-Jews was not objectionable as such. What James and the Jerusalem leaders became concerned about was whether Paul was teaching Jews that they could forsake the Torah and live as Gentiles, no longer observing the commandments given to the people of Israel.

The book of Acts records a subsequent visit of Paul to Jerusalem in
A.D. 58 when the issue was raised directly. Paul appeared before James,
who was still clearly in charge, as well as the "elders" of the community.
They confronted him with a report they had received that he was teaching "the Jews who are among the Gentiles to forsake Moses, telling them
not to circumcise their children or observe the traditions of Judaism"
(Acts 21:21). Luke never really records Paul's answer but presumably he
did not elaborate the views he had been expounding among his converts.
According to Acts, Paul tacitly allowed James and the others to assume
that he, as a Jew, was dedicated to Torah observance. He even joined a
group of Nazarenes who were fulfilling a Torah-required ritual in the
Temple to show his adherence to Judaism. But from what we read in his
letters we have to question whether that was the case. Paul had written
his followers at Corinth, explaining the complexities of his mode of operation among various groups, whether Jews or Gentiles:

> To the Jews I became as a Jew, in order to win Jews; to those under
> the Torah, I became as one under the Torah—though not actually
> being under the Torah—that I might win those under the Torah;
> to those outside the Torah [Gentiles], I became as one outside the
> Torah—not being without law, but under the Torah of Christ—
> that I might win those outside the Torah. (1 Corinthians 9:20–21)

Paul saw himself as under a "higher Torah," that of Christ, but he was
willing to adapt to whatever circumstances in which he found himself.
Presumably, among Gentiles he was willing to "live as a Gentile," which
certainly no Jew observant of the Law could ever do.

Paul was willing to suffer physical persecution for what he preached
and believed and he recounted to his followers the list of things he had
endured—beatings, shipwrecks, hunger, imprisonments, and even near
death by stoning (2 Corinthians 11:20–29). There is no doubting Paul's
sincerity and his passion for what he believed. He was gripped by the visions he had had and his unshakable conviction that he, as "last" of the
apostles, was in no way inferior to any of the Twelve. In fact, as he puts it,
"I labored harder than all of them" (1 Corinthians 15:10). Paul often com-

pared himself to Christ and he believed that like Christ he was destined to suffer and offer his life as a sacrifice for his followers (Philippians 2:17). He saw his own sufferings as "filling up what was lacking in Christ's suffering" (Colossians 1:24). According to later Christian tradition, Paul was beheaded in Rome during the reign of Nero, which would be sometime before A.D. 68.[21]

We don't really know whether Paul ever made a decisive break with James and the Jerusalem leaders or they with him. Again, all we have is the account in the book of Acts and what Paul tells us in his own letters. Acts ends Paul's story abruptly in A.D. 58 and Luke wants to project a picture of reconciliation and harmony in his final scene between James and Paul.

Luke also presents a picture of harmony between Paul and Peter (Acts 15). This seems quite unlikely. Paul in his letter to the Galatians recalls an occasion where he said he "opposed Peter to his face because he stood condemned" over a dispute involving Jewish and Gentile table fellowship (Galatians 2:11). Paul labels Peter a hypocrite and charges that James and his associates influenced him. One can doubt whether we are getting the entire story here since Paul's tone throughout Galatians is so vitriolic. One can safely assume that Peter as well as John, as the intimate associates of James, acknowledged even by Paul as the "pillars" of the movement, worked in harmony and shared the common vision of faith that they had received directly from Jesus in his lifetime.

Paul's legacy is a formidable one, since his version of the gospel was gradually accepted by more and more Christians scattered throughout the Roman world. After A.D. 70, as we shall see, when the Jerusalem center of the movement had been destroyed and its leaders killed or scattered, the influence of the message of the original Twelve Apostles began to diminish. By A.D. 150, intellectually astute Christian leaders such as Justin Martyr, living in Rome, had championed the ideas of Paul and had begun to develop a systematic theological system built around his basic ideas. Paul's triumph, to some degree, was a literary one—that is, his letters and the influence of his ideas as embedded in the New Testament writings, including the gospels, became so persuasive that they came to constitute what was viewed as the only authentic Christianity. If the writings of the original Jerusalem followers of Jesus had survived we would not so easily have lost the vision that James, Peter, John, and the rest of the Twelve had perpetuated. Even the two letters in the New Testament attributed to Peter sound so much like Paul that many scholars see them as either interpolated or even composed by followers of Paul.

Fortunately we do have some sources, few and precious as they are from which we can recover that original message of James and the Twelve. By diligent and careful research, and the boon of some new discoveries, we should be able to reasonably reconstruct the legacy of the Jesus dynasty.

17

THE LEGACY OF THE JESUS DYNASTY

ALTHOUGH James has been all but written out of our New Testament records he nonetheless remains our best and most direct link to the historical Jesus. However one evaluates Paul's "gospel" it is nonetheless a fact that what Paul preached was wholly based upon his own mystical experiences. Paul never met Jesus. He was likely one of those Pharisees who rejected the preaching and baptism of John. James was Jesus' own beloved brother. They literally grew up together in the same household and in the same family and James was accordingly a witness of everything that transpired from start to finish. This is a historical fact, even recognized by Josephus the Jewish historian, who knew James as the brother of Jesus. So, what would result if we were to heed the admonition in the *Gospel of Thomas*—"Go to James the Just for whom heaven and earth came to be"? What was the lost "gospel" that James and the original Jerusalem church proclaimed, irrespective of anything claimed by Paul? Can it possibly be recovered?

The difficulty we face is that Paul's influence within our New Testament canon of documents is pervasive. I would go so far as to say that the New Testament itself is primarily a literary legacy of the apostle Paul. Paul is named as author of thirteen of the twenty-seven "books" of the

New Testament. The book of Acts is almost wholly a defense of his central place as the "thirteenth" apostle. Mark was written around A.D. 70,
after Paul's death. It is a primary carrier of the message that Paul
preached, projected back into the life of Jesus. Both Matthew and Luke,
who use Mark as their main narrative source, then passed on Mark's core
message. The gospel of John, in theology at least, also reflects Paul's essential understanding of Jesus. Paul's view of Christ as the divine, preexistent Son of God who took on human form, died on the cross for the sins
of the world, and was resurrected to heavenly glory at God's right hand
became *the* Christian message. In reading the New Testament one might
assume this was the only message ever preached and there was no other
gospel. But such was not the case. If we listen carefully we can still hear a
muted original voice—every bit as "Christian" as that of Paul. It is the
voice of James, echoing what he received from his brother Jesus.

The most neglected document in the entire New Testament is the letter written by James. It has become so marginalized that many Christians
are not even aware of its existence. And yet it is part of every Christian
Bible, now found as the twentieth book of the New Testament, well to
the back of the collection. It was almost left out entirely. When the
Christians began to canonize the New Testament in the 4th century—
that is, to authoritatively determine which books would be included and
which would not—the status of the letter of James was questioned. It
was not included in the *Muratorian Fragment,* our earliest list of New Testament books that were accepted as Scripture in Rome at the end of the
2nd century.[1] The 3rd-century Christian scholars Origen and Eusebius
both listed it among the disputed books.[2] Even the great Western Christian scholars Jerome and Augustine accepted the letter only reluctantly.
Fortunately, it was finally included in the New Testament canon of sacred
Scripture.

There were two major reasons that some later Christians questioned
the letter of James. The first has to do with what James said and did not
say about his brother Jesus. He only mentioned the name of Jesus two
times in a passing way and either reference could easily be removed without affecting the content of the letter or the points James was making
(James 1:1; 2:1). In addition, the letter lacked any reference to Paul's view

of Jesus as the divine Son of God, his atoning death on the cross, or his glorified resurrection. How could a New Testament document that lacked such teachings really be considered "Christian"? The second factor that put the letter in disfavor with some was that James directly disputed Paul's teaching of "salvation by faith" without the deeds of the Law while strongly upholding the positive nature of the Torah as well as its enduring validity:

> What does it profit, my brothers, if a man says he has faith but has not works? Can his faith save him? . . . So faith by itself, if it has no works, is dead. (James 2:14, 17)

> For whoever looks into the perfect Torah [Law], the Torah of liberty, and perseveres, being no hearer that forgets but a doer that acts, he shall be blessed in his doing. (James 1:25)

> For whoever keeps the whole Torah but fails in one point has become guilty of all of it. (James 2:10)

James addressed his letter to the "Twelve Tribes in the Dispersion" (1:1). This is a direct reference to the scattered "Twelve Tribes" of Israel over which Jesus had promised the Twelve Apostles would rule. The letter reflects an early Palestinian Jewish cultural context. For example, James referred to the local meeting or assembly of Christians as a *synagogue*, reflecting his understanding of the movement as fully a part of Judaism (James 2:2). Even though the letter is written in Greek, at least as we have it today, linguistically it reflects numerous Aramaic and Hebrew expressions and recent research has revealed its Palestinian Jewish milieu.[3]

What is most amazing about the letter of James is that the ethical content of its teaching is directly parallel to the teachings of Jesus that we know from the Q source. The Q source is the earliest collection of the teachings and sayings of Jesus that scholars date to around the year A.D. 50. As I have previously discussed, it has not survived as an intact document but both Matthew and Luke use it extensively. By comparing Matthew and Luke and extracting the material they use in common but do not derive from Mark, we are able to come to a reasonable construction of this lost "gospel of Q." It consists of about 235 verses that are mostly but not entirely the "sayings" of Jesus. The Q source takes us back to the original teachings of Jesus minus much of the theological framework that the gospels subsequently added.[4] Perhaps the most striking characteristic of the Q source in terms of reconstructing Christian origins is that it has nothing of Paul's theology, particularly his Christology or view of Christ.

The most familiar parts of Q to most Bible readers are in Matthew's Sermon on the Mount (Matthew 5–7) and Luke's Sermon on the Plain (Luke 6). What is amazing is that the letter of James, short as it is, contains no fewer than *thirty* direct references, echoes, and allusions to the teachings of Jesus found in the Q source! A few of the more striking parallels are the following:

JESUS' TEACHINGS IN THE Q SOURCE	TEACHINGS OF JAMES
Blessed are you poor for yours is the kingdom of God (Luke 6:20)	Has not God chosen the poor to be rich in faith and heirs of the kingdom (2:5)
Whoever relaxes one of the least of these commandments . . . shall be [called] least in the kingdom (MATTHEW 5:19)	Whoever keeps the whole Torah but fails in one point has become guilty of it all (2:10)
Not everyone who says "Lord, Lord" shall enter the kingdom . . . but he who does the will of my Father (MATTHEW 7:21)	Be doers of the word and not hearers only (1:22)
How much more will your Father . . . give good gifts to those who ask him (MATTHEW 7: 11)	Every good gift . . . coming down from the Father (1:17)

Woe to you that are rich, for you have received your consolation (LUKE 6:24)	Come now, you rich, weep and howl for the miseries that are coming upon you (5:1)
Do not swear at all, either by heaven for it is the throne of God, or by earth for it is his footstool . . . let what you say be simply "Yes" or "No" (MATTHEW 5:34, 37)	Do not swear, either by heaven or by earth or with any other oath but let your yes be yes and your no be no (5:12)

The letter of James has other important connections to the message of Jesus and John the Baptizer beyond these characteristic ethical teachings. James knows about the practice of anointing the sick with oil, as Jesus had practiced and taught his disciples (James 5:14). Both John and Jesus had taught that one is forgiven of sins and "justified" before God through repentance and prayer—that is, directly calling upon God. James wrote that confession of sins and prayer were the way to salvation (James 5:15–16). This is in keeping with Jesus' teaching in the Q source. Jesus related a story in which two men were praying in the Temple, one who was proud of his righteousness and the other who considered himself so unworthy he would not even lift his eyes to heaven. This one struck his breast and cried out "God be merciful to me a sinner." Jesus declared "this one went up justified before God rather than the other" (Luke 18:14). This is in keeping with the general teaching of the Hebrew Bible regarding forgiveness of sins. As the Psalms express: "Have mercy upon me O God, according to your steadfast love, according to your abundant mercy blot out all my transgressions and cleanse me from my sins" (Psalm 51:1). Judaism does not teach "salvation" by human merit as sometimes assumed, but rather that all human beings are "justified" by grace, finding forgiveness from their sins by repentance and prayer—"calling upon the name of the Lord" (Joel 2:32). Even the animal sacrifices of the Jewish Temple were never understood to atone for or cover sins unless one first turned in faith to God and asked for grace and forgiveness (Psalm 51:16).

The letter of James contains the most direct possible link to the teachings of Jesus himself. James is essentially echoing and affirming what he had learned and passed on from his brother Jesus, who had in turn learned and heard from John the Baptizer. It is important to note that James did not directly quote Jesus or attribute any of these teachings to Jesus by name—even though they are teachings *of* Jesus. For James the Christian message is not the person of Jesus but the message that Jesus proclaimed. James's letter lacks a single teaching that is characteristic of the apostle Paul and it draws nothing at all from the tradition of Mark. What we have preserved in this precious document is a reflection of the original gospel proclamation of Jesus—the "Gospel of the Kingdom of God" with its full political and social implications.

OTHER WITNESSES

Several additional witnesses to this original non-Pauline version of Christianity have survived. One of them, surprisingly, is from a second brother of Jesus, namely the apostle Jude. As with the letter of James, 4th-century theologians debated whether the letter of Jude should be included in the New Testament. Although it was finally declared part of sacred Scripture it was put next to last in the New Testament collection and not a single verse of Jude is ever read in the Roman Catholic cycle of lectionary readings. Many Bible readers today would be surprised to learn that we in fact have within the New Testament itself letters from not one but two of Jesus' brothers. The Protestant Reformer Martin Luther, a great champion of the apostle Paul, moved the letters of James and Jude to the very end of his 1522 edition of the New Testament asserting that they were of lesser quality than "the true and certain books of the New Testament."[5] He commented that James in particular was a "strawy epistle," indicating his view that it provided little spiritual nourishment.

Jude's letter likely dates to the last decades of the 1st century A.D. He warned his readers of certain "intruders" who had stolen in among the movement and he urges them to "struggle earnestly for the faith that was once for all passed on" to the original believers (Jude 3). The Greek verb Jude uses here (*paradidomai*) refers to a formal passing on of an authorized tradition. The phrase "once for all" implies that no subsequent tradition is to replace the original one. Jude saw a struggle under way and feared that his readers might lose sight of the original message of Jesus. He does not identify by name those he has in mind but he does say that such teachers had turned the notion of "grace" into a license for lawless behavior.

Both James and Jude shared the apocalyptic outlook that Jesus and John the Baptizer had proclaimed. James had written that "the coming of the Lord is at hand" and that "the Judge is standing at the doors" (James 5:8–9). Jude quoted the book of Enoch which survives in Ethiopic, and also in Aramaic fragments among the Dead Sea Scrolls. Enoch was the seventh generation from Adam and according to this apocryphal work he had prophesied, "The Lord comes with ten thousand of his holy ones, to execute judgment on all, and to convict everyone of all the deeds of ungodliness that they have committed." The reference to the "coming of the Lord" was to "the only God our Savior," as Jude puts it, not to the Second Coming of Jesus (Jude 25). What these early Christians expected was drawn from the Hebrew Prophets who had predicted the *coming* of the Lord God, that is Yahweh, not a "Second Coming" of the Messiah. Notice carefully the language in the following texts:

> Then the LORD [Yahweh] your God will come and all the holy ones with him. (Zechariah 14:5)

> Behold the LORD [Yahweh] God comes with might, and his arm rules for him; behold his reward is with him, and his recompense before him. (Isaiah 40:10)

> For behold the LORD [Yahweh] will come in fire, and his chariots like the storm wind, to render his anger in fury, and his rebuke with flames of fire. (Isaiah 66:15)

James and Jude refer to their brother Jesus as the "Lord" but they don't use the term to refer to the "Lord God" but to Jesus as their respected "Master" who had given his life for the cause of the Kingdom of God.

The Greek word for "Lord" is *kurios* and it is a term of respect, something akin to "Sir" or "Mister" in older English usage.

One of the pivotal moves that Paul had made was to equate Jesus as "Lord" with passages in the Hebrew Bible that referred exclusively to the "Lord God" of Israel—thus effectively making Jesus *equal* Yahweh.[6] For example, through the prophet Isaiah God had declared:

> Turn to me and be saved all the ends of the earth! For I am God, and there is no other. By myself I have sworn . . . to me every knee shall bow, and every tongue shall swear allegiance. (Isaiah 45:22–23)

Paul quotes this very verse but shifts its reference to the "Lord" Jesus as the Christ: "So that at the name of Jesus every knee should bow . . . and every tongue should confess that Jesus Christ is Lord" (Philippians 2:10–11). This is an enormous change that eventually became commonplace among orthodox Christians who began to easily equate Jesus of Nazareth, the man, with the Lord God of Israel. Jesus was "God in the flesh" and accordingly his mother Mary became the "holy mother of God." Since Christians maintained that they were nonetheless monotheistic, that is, they adhered to the *Shema*—the great confession of Judaism, "Hear O Israel, the Lord our God, the Lord is One"—the conclusion became inescapable. If Jesus were truly "God," and there is one God not two, then he is nothing less than an incarnation of the Lord God of Israel. To put things bluntly, God became a man.

Paul regularly uses the expressions "Jesus Christ" and "the Lord Jesus Christ" as if the term "Christ," which was a Greek term for the Messiah or anointed Davidic King, were a proper name rather than a designated title. He is well aware of Jesus' claim to Davidic lineage but he downplays that aspect of his "human" background. He wrote to the church at Rome that Jesus Christ our Lord "was born of the seed of David, *according to the flesh*," but was declared the Son of God with power "by the resurrection from the dead" (Romans 1:2–4). For Paul anything "according to the flesh" is "earthly" and thus unimportant, so that Jesus' claim to be the Davidic Messiah is essentially marginalized in order to assert his status as the divine "Son of God" and *heavenly* Christ. If Jesus' Davidic lineage meant so little to Paul, James's claim to that same pedigree would mean even less.

This is something that few Jews could accept and James, Jude, and the original followers of Jesus never dreamed of such an idea. For them Jesus was the revered "Master," and the anointed Messiah or Christ, but as a faithful Jew, Jesus himself confessed the *Shema* and highlighted it as the "great commandment" (Mark 12:29). The gospel of Mark preserves a saying of Jesus in this regard where a man comes up to Jesus and addresses him as "Good Master," to which Jesus replies: "Why do you call me good, there is One who is good, God alone" (Mark 10:18). Jesus had been heralded as King of Israel and was in fact executed for this claim before he could formally assume the Davidic throne. According to all the Hebrew prophets the Davidic Messiah was to rule from the city of Jerusalem not in heaven; he was to gather the Twelve Tribes of Israel to the Holy Land from all the nations to which they had been dispersed; and he was to usher in a universal era of peace and justice for the entire world. The phrase "kingdom of heaven" does not refer to a kingdom *in* heaven, as the prayer that both John the Baptizer and Jesus taught makes clear: "Let your kingdom come; let your will be done *on earth* as it is in heaven." In contrast Paul taught that the "earthly Jerusalem" was no longer relevant but a new spiritual "Jerusalem above" was where Christ now ruled as King (Galatians 4:26). For Paul the people of Israel, the city of Jerusalem, and the Davidic Messiah were all transferred from the literal to the symbolic, from earth to heaven. James, Jude, and the Q source stand as witness to an original version of the Christian faith that takes us back to Jesus himself, with firm historical links reaching back to John the Baptizer.

Fortunately there are other witnesses that have surfaced in recent times that allow us to trace more clearly this forgotten trajectory through earliest Christianity. Perhaps the most important is the lost source called the *Didache*, which was discovered quite by accident in 1873 as I previously explained in Chapter 12.[7] This document dates to the beginning of the 2nd century A.D. or even earlier, making it as old as some of the books included in the New Testament canon. Indeed, among certain circles of early Christianity it had achieved near canonical status.

The *Didache* is divided into sixteen chapters and was intended to be a

"handbook" for Christian converts. The first six chapters give a summary
of Christian ethics based on the teachings of Jesus, divided into two
parts: the way of life and the way of death. Much of the content is similar
to what we have in the Sermon on the Mount and the Sermon on the
Plain, that is, the basic ethical teachings of Jesus drawn from the Q
source now found in Matthew and Luke. It begins with the two "great
commandments," to love God and love one's neighbor as oneself, as well
as a version of the Golden Rule: "And whatever you do not want to happen to you, do not do to another." It contains many familiar injunctions
and exhortations, but often with additions not found in our Gospels:

> Bless those who curse you, pray for your enemies, and fast for
> those who persecute you. (1.3)

> If anyone slaps your right cheek, turn the other to him as well and
> you will be perfect. (1.4)

> Give to everyone who asks, and do not ask for anything back,
> for the Father wants everyone to be given something from the
> gracious gifts he himself provides. (1.5)

Many of the sayings and teachings are not found in our New Testament
gospels but are nonetheless consistent with the tradition we know from
Jesus and from his brother James:

> Let your gift to charity sweat in your hands until you know to
> whom to give it. (1.6)

> Do not be of two minds or speak from both sides of your mouth,
> for speaking from both sides of your mouth is a deadly trap. (2.4)

> Do not be one who reaches out your hands to receive but draws
> them back from giving. (4.5)

> Do not shun a person in need, but share all things with your
> brother and do not say that anything is your own. (4.8)

Following the ethical exhortations there are four chapters concerning baptism, fasting, prayer, the Eucharist, and the anointing with oil. The Eucharist in the *Didache*, as we saw in our Chapter 12, is a simple thanksgiving meal of wine and bread with references to Jesus as the holy "vine of David." It ends with a prayer: "Hosanna to the God of David." The Davidic lineage of Jesus is thus emphasized. There are final chapters on testing prophets and appointing worthy leaders. The last chapter contains warnings about the "last days," the coming of a final deceiving false prophet, and the resurrection of the righteous who have died. It ends with language similar to that used by Jude, but taken from Zechariah and Daniel: "The Lord will come and all of his holy ones with him" and "Then the world will see the Lord coming on the clouds of the sky." Both references to the "Lord" here are to Yahweh, the God of Israel.

The entire content and tone of the *Didache* reminds one strongly of the faith and piety we find in the letter of James, and teachings of Jesus in the Q source. The most remarkable thing about the *Didache* in terms of the two types of Christian teaching—that of Paul and that of the Jesus dynasty—is that there is *nothing* in this document that corresponds to Paul's "gospel"—no divinity of Jesus, no atoning through his body and blood, and no mention of Jesus' resurrection from the dead. In the *Didache* Jesus is the one who has brought the knowledge of life and faith, but there is no emphasis whatsoever upon the *figure* of Jesus apart from his message. Sacrifice and forgiveness of sins in the *Didache* come through good deeds and a consecrated life (4.6).

The *Didache* is an abiding witness to a form of the Christian faith that traces directly back to Jesus and was carried on and perpetuated by James, Jude, and the rest of the Twelve Apostles.

JAMES AND JESUS

There is no evidence that James worshipped his brother or considered him divine. His emphasis in his letter was not upon the person of Jesus but upon what Jesus taught. So we might well ask, what then was James's view of his brother? James believed that God had anointed Jesus as the Davidic Messiah. But he also understood, as Jesus did, that the *suffering of the righteous*, even the suffering and death of a Messiah, could be one's lot.

John had been beheaded. Jesus had been crucified. Many of Israel's leaders in past times had died violent deaths at the hands of wicked enemies. At one point in his letter James chastises those of power and wealth who oppress the poor and he lays a very specific charge against the establishment of his day: "You have condemned, you have killed the *just one*, and he does not resist you" (James 5:6). James's use of the specific term the "just one" is significant here. In biblical thought there is the concept of the *Zaddik*—that is, the "righteous one" or the "just one." Such a one can be a Jew, or a Gentile, a king or a peasant, a prophet or a Messiah. Judaism has the phrase "the righteous of the nations" referring to any and all human beings who aspire to God's ways of justice, love, and righteousness. James's contemporaries, as we have seen, gave him that designation— James the Just. When James referred here to the authorities condemning and killing the "just one" who did not resist them, I believe he had his brother Jesus in mind, but not only his brother. Jesus was a *Zaddik*, but so was John the Baptizer. Jesus had told the Twelve, on their way to Jerusalem, that *all* of them, in order to follow him, must "take up a cross" and fulfill the same role he saw for himself—that of suffering for righteousness sake. James ended his own life in testimony to the same idea— speaking out boldly and opposing all evil, but then facing whatever persecution or suffering the message entailed. James saw Jesus as a model to follow. As Jesus' successor James sought to emulate Jesus' faith, his ethical teachings, and his courage in the face of evil.

Christians and Jews later debated whether the prophecy of the Suffering Servant of Isaiah 53 referred to Jesus or to the people of Israel. The answer I think James would have given is the same as the one Jesus gave—the path is open to all willing to follow. Jesus, by his willingness to "go to the cross," became such a suffering servant, but he was one among many. Countless "just ones" through the ages have courageously given their lives for the cause of righteousness. James had once quoted a passage from the Hebrew Prophets that signified that the "rebuilding of the tents of David," that is, the reestablishing of the Davidic messianic line that he and his brothers now represented, was that "so that all other people may seek Yahweh, even all the Gentiles over whom my name has been called" (Acts 15:16–17). This is the lasting legacy of the Jesus dynasty.

18

THE END OF THE AGE

JAMES took leadership of Jesus' followers at his death in A.D. 30 and ruled from the city of David in Jerusalem for the next three decades. It should come as no surprise that his main enemies were the same as those who had had his brother executed—namely the Sadducean high priestly families that were in charge of the Temple. It is surely an irony of history that the high priest Annas, son of the Annas who had presided at the trial of Jesus, was behind the murder of James, also at the season of Passover in the year A.D. 62. The story of what happened is one of the most intriguing of that time.

Josephus is our best historical source for James's death and his testimony is of immense value considering that he was a contemporary of James and that he had himself risen to prominence in Jewish society. According to Josephus, the younger Annas was rash in temper and unusually daring, being heartless in judgment toward any who opposed him. Judea at that time was still ruled directly by a Roman governor but the emperor Claudius had put the remainder of the country under the last ruler of the Herodian dynasty, Herod Agrippa II, great-grandson of Herod the Great. When the Roman governor Festus died and his replacement Albinus was on his way from Rome, Annas took advantage of the opportunity and had James arrested and brought before the Sanhedrin, which he and his henchmen controlled. He charged James and some others, presumably Nazarenes, with transgressing the Jewish law and delivered them to be stoned. Josephus's own words are worth quoting:

> He [Annas] convened the judges of the Sanhedrin and brought before them James the brother of Jesus (called Christ), and some others, on the accusation of breaking the law and delivered them to be stoned. And those inhabitants of the city who were considered the most fair-minded and who were strict in observance of the law were offended at this.[1]

It is surely significant that Josephus, who was a Pharisee and not part of the Nazarene movement, not only recorded the execution of James but also knew that James was the brother of Jesus. A delegation of leading Jewish citizens traveled to Caesarea, where Agrippa II held court, and complained about the murder of James. Some of them even went to meet Albinus, who was making his way from Alexandria. Albinus was furious and wrote to Annas threatening punishment. In the meantime Agrippa had him stripped of the priesthood that he had only held for three months. All of this was because of his move against James.

Eusebius, the early-4th-century Christian historian who lived in Palestine, claimed that Josephus mentioned James again in a later passage, which he quotes: "And these things happened to the Jews to avenge James the Just, who was the brother of Jesus (called Christ), for the Jews killed him in spite of his great righteousness."[2] Even though this passage is not found in our late-14th-century copies of Josephus it is possibly authentic, as it was also known to Origen, a 3rd-century Christian scholar.[3] The "things" to which Josephus referred, in context, are the events surrounding the Jewish Revolt and the Roman destruction of Jerusalem in A.D. 70.

We also have a more detailed account of the death of James from Hegesippus, a 2nd-century Jewish Christian who wrote that "he [James] was believed by all men to be most righteous" and thus was called "Just" by all men from Jesus' time to his own.[4] Hegesippus added other details that may well be historically true. He wrote that James was "holy from his mother's womb" and like his kinsman John the Baptizer neither drank wine nor ate any meat. Hegesippus also reported that James wore the linen of a priest and constantly prayed in the Temple, kneeling so much of the time that his knees grew hard like a camel's. According to Hegesippus, James was continually praying for the forgiveness of the people. Epiphanius, a 4th-century Christian writer, asserted that James, as a descendant of David, also exercised the "priesthood" on behalf of his community, entering into the holy areas of the Temple where only priests could go and functioning as a "high priest" to his followers.[5] We saw in Chapter 2 that Mary, mother of Jesus and James, represented both the Davidic royal family as well as a priestly Aaronic lineage. There is a very ancient tradition in the Hebrew Bible that "David's sons were priests" (2 Samuel 8:18). These ancient traditions may indicate that the followers of James looked to him as fulfilling a priestly role, representing his community of Nazarenes in the Temple, as well as a royal Davidic one.

James's death by Luiken

Both Hegesippus and Epiphanius offer more details about how James's death came about. They reported that before James was stoned he was pushed over the southeast wall of the Temple complex and fell into the Kidron Valley. Barely alive, he was then stoned and beaten to death with a club. Epiphanius recorded that "Simon son of Clophas," the brother of James and half-brother of Jesus, was present at the murder and tried to intervene. They note that James was buried in that area, not far from the Temple itself, and Hegesippus claimed that the location of the grave was known in his own day. The massive Herodian stones of the southeast corner of the Temple compound are still in place today, towering over the Kidron Valley. Just to the east is the Mount of Olives with its many ancient tombs and just to the south is our Tomb of the Shroud, where the Kidron turns into the Hinnom Valley. If I am correct that Jesus was crucified outside the eastern wall of Jerusalem, both he and his brother James died in very close proximity to each other, both at Passover, and both at the hands of the Annas family of priests.

Southeast corner of Temple Mount today

Hegesippus believed that James's death, like that of Jesus, was a fulfillment of prophecy. This was a common view among the early Christians. Most often they referred to the Greek translation of Isaiah 3:10 that read: "Let us bind the Just One, for he is a burden to us." It is chilling to note that James himself, probably with the brutal death of his brother Jesus in mind, wrote in his letter: "You have condemned and murdered the Just One and he does not resist you" (James 5:6). He likely had no idea how prophetic his words would prove to be regarding his own death.

One important, though puzzling, element in Hegesippus's account is his assertion that the authorities who condemned James first demanded that he tell them "What was the Gate of Jesus." The phrase has made little sense to scholars but I think it might represent a mistranslation of an older Aramaic or Hebrew account. The name "Jesus" in Hebrew is *Yeshua'* and the word "salvation" is *yeshuah*—they are pronounced the same and their spelling is nearly identical. If the authorities were asking James "What is the gate of salvation" the exchange begins to make sense. According to Hegesippus they wanted him to tell the people, increasing numbers of whom were believing in Jesus, "not to err concerning Jesus." If James had for over thirty years been proclaiming his brother as the *gate* of salvation then the demand that he answer their question and thus dissuade the crowds from believing in Jesus makes little sense. His answer is revealing. According to Hegesippus, James replied: "Why do you ask me concerning the Son of Man? He will come in the clouds of heaven." Hegesippus is of course quite convinced that James refers here to Jesus as "Son of Man," but such is not necessarily the case. If this was, in fact, James's reply about the "Gate of salvation," and he pointed to the "Son of Man coming in the clouds of heaven," he was echoing precisely what Jesus told Caiaphas when questioned at his own trial—"You will see the Son of Man coming with the clouds of heaven" (Mark 14:62). As I have discussed earlier, based on Daniel 7:13-14, this "coming of the Son of Man in the clouds of heaven" represented to the early Christians not the coming of Jesus, but the triumph of the people of God—just as it was interpreted to Daniel.

SIMON TAKES OVER:
THE DYNASTY CONTINUES

Following the death of James in A.D. 62, Eusebius reported that the remaining apostles gathered with those left of the *family of the Lord* and they took counsel together as to who would succeed James. He wrote that "they all unanimously decided that Simeon the son of Clophas, was worthy of the throne."[6] Eusebius noted that this Clophas, mentioned in the gospel of John, was the brother of Joseph, husband of Mary, and thus also of Davidic lineage. As I argued in Chapter 4, there is good evidence that Clophas, legally the uncle of Jesus, was the second husband of Mary his mother, based on Levirate law. Eusebius wrote in the 4th century A.D. but he based his information on the writings of Hegesippus, taking us back to the 2nd century A.D.—much closer to the time of Simon's succession.

We can presume Peter was still alive when James died. As part of Jesus' inner circle, and having served as the "right-hand man" to James as one of the "pillars" of the movement for over thirty years, we might expect that he would have taken over the leadership of the group. That the apostles chose Simon shows just how important the Jesus dynasty was in their thinking. But what about Peter? What do we know about him?

Unfortunately, we have very little reliable history regarding Peter from the death of Jesus to the death of James. There are a few early stories in the book of Acts as well as two New Testament letters attributed to Peter, but these sources are so heavily influenced by Paul's theology that Peter's authentic voice has been lost. In the book of Acts Peter speaks, acts, and has the same ideas as Paul; even his "sermons" parallel those of Paul thought for thought. It is possible to simply extract the Pauline elements from Peter's letters, particularly 1 Peter, and find a core that might be original, but the process is highly subjective. The best we can do is take Paul at his word—that Peter was allied with James, and thus we can assume he shared the legacy of the Jesus dynasty and endorsed and preached its message—the message he too had received from Jesus.

In the gospel of Matthew, Peter is told by Jesus that he will be given the "keys of the kingdom," which Roman Catholics take to indicate that he was put in charge of the Jesus movement, but we have no indication that was the case (Matthew 16:19). The transition from Jesus, to James, to Simon appears to be well documented. So what were the keys of the kingdom? The image is a biblical one, taken from the book of Isaiah, where Eliakim, son of Hilkiah, is promised: "I will place on his shoulder the key of the house of David; he shall open and no one shall shut; he shall shut and no one shall open" (Isaiah 22:21–22). Eliakim is not a king but an official over the household of King Hezekiah, who ruled in the 8th century B.C. (2 Kings 18:18). Hezekiah was of the lineage of David. To have the "key of David" is to be like a "chief of staff" over a royal household or administration. What Jesus was promising Peter was that he would occupy the "right-hand" position of responsibility—which he did, in service to James, who was of the house of David. According to Paul, James had determined that Peter would primarily function as a teacher, taking Jesus' message to Jewish groups scattered throughout the Roman world (Galatians 2:7). Apparently Peter, along with Jesus' brothers, regularly traveled, taking their wives with them, to various regions of the Empire (1 Corinthians 9:5). The letter of 1 Peter is addressed to the exiled Jews of the "Diaspora" (Jews living out of the Land of Israel) in the provinces of Asia Minor, namely Pontus, Galatia, Cappadocia, Asia, and Bithynia. One assumes these are some of the regions to which Peter had traveled.

There is a tradition that Peter died side-by-side with Paul in Rome during the reign of Nero. Eusebius says Peter was crucified but later legends circulated that he insisted on being nailed upside down to his cross, since he was unworthy to die in the manner Jesus had died.[7] It is difficult to know how much weight to give to this tradition that Peter died in Rome, since the Roman Catholic Church subsequently made such claim to him as its first bishop or pope. One has to wonder whether stories about Peter as a martyr in Rome are more theological than historical. I have already mentioned the ossuary found on the Mount of Olives inscribed with Peter's full Aramaic name: Simon bar Jonah. This name is otherwise unknown in any Jewish record. Whether Peter's or not, Jerusalem seems a more likely resting place for Peter, in the area where Jesus, James, and the Jesus family were all buried.

It is worth noting that Eusebius and Epiphanius offer us independent lists of the successors of James the Just.⁸ They both record Simon as second, and one named Jude or Judas as third. But then they follow with a list of *twelve* men, who they say all ruled over the Jerusalem church in succession down to the reign of the Emperor Hadrian (A.D. 135). The problem is, we know that Simon himself continued his rule until at least A.D. 106, when he was crucified as a descendant of David by Emperor Trajan. It is hardly possible that thirteen different men successively took charge over the next twenty-five years. What is more likely is that this list of twelve represent a "Council of Twelve," who held office as a group, following the model that Jesus had established.⁹

The names of these twelve men are most interesting. After James, Simon, and Jude we have Zachariah, Tobiah, Benjamin, John, Matthew, Philip, Senikus, Justus, Levi, Vaphres, Jose, and Judas. It is entirely possible that the next to last might be Jesus' remaining brother Joseph, still remembered by the unusual nickname that Mark preserved—Jose or Joses. It is also possible that John, Matthew, and Philip are the aged but original members of the Twelve whom Jesus had chosen. We do have reliable traditions that John in particular lived on well past age one hundred.¹⁰

The *Apostolic Constitutions*, related to our *Didache* but compiled much later, in the 4th century A.D., says that the third person in line, the Jude who succeeded Simon, was a third brother of Jesus. The possibility is quite significant in that it would trace the Jesus dynasty through *four* successive brothers: Jesus, James, Simon, and Judas! But one has to wonder about the chronological possibilities that such could have been the case. If Simon was crucified under Trajan in about A.D. 106, and according to Epiphanius he was over one hundred years old at the time, is it likely that a younger brother, Jude, could have possibly taken over? Would he not have been too old?

What we don't know is the birth years of Jesus' siblings. It is possible that after Jesus was born in 5 B.C., a good number of years passed until the births of James and the others. Mary might have been as young as fifteen or sixteen when she had Jesus. Indeed, if the others were the children of Clophas and not Joseph, one would need to allow time lapsing from Joseph's marriage to Mary and his death. Joseph seems to disappear from the scene by the time Jesus is an adult at age thirty. Since James is referred to as "the younger" (literally, "the little one" Mark 15:40), he is an adult, but perhaps in his twenties, which would mean that Mary had the four brothers and two sisters during her twenties, which surely makes some sense. That would put James's birth around A.D. 5 with the rest to follow. He would have been in his late fifties when he died in A.D. 62, and Simon could have then been nearly one hundred when Emperor Trajan crucified him, as Epiphanius claimed. It is then conceivable, despite these chronological uncertainties, that Jude, a third brother of Jesus, even though in his nineties, would have been chosen to carry on the Jesus dynasty at Simon's death because of the great honor and respect these early Christians had for the royal family. The brother Joses, or Joseph, who would have been second in line to succeed James, very possibly had died by the time Simon took over leadership.

We simply cannot know, but what we can know, with some certainty, is that the royal family of Jesus, including the children and grandchildren of his brothers and sisters, were honored by the early Christians well into the 2nd century A.D., while at the same time they were watched and hunted down by the highest levels of the Roman government in Palestine.

THE OTHER DYNASTY

The decades of the 40s, 50s, and 60s A.D., both in Palestine and the larger Roman Empire, were years of chaos and instability, with political unrest, violence, rebellions, and wars. This provided a backdrop, in Palestine in particular, for a messianic fervor the likes of which had never before been seen. It seemed obvious to all who had an eye and ear for what the Hebrew Prophets had predicted that the "last days" were swiftly drawing to a close and the long-anticipated Kingdom of God had drawn near.

Rome was ruled by the Julio-Claudian Dynasty, a succession of the first five emperors beginning with Augustus and ending with Nero, thus stretching from 27 B.C. to A.D. 68. Despite all attempts to establish a legitimate bloodline succession, no pair of these five emperors were related as father and son. Augustus (27 B.C. to A.D. 14) was the adopted son of his great-uncle Julius Caesar, who had been assassinated in 44 B.C. Tiberius

(A.D. 14–37), who succeeded Augustus, was the son of his second wife, Livia, but by a previous husband, so there was no blood link between them. It was only shortly before his death that Augustus passed the reign on to Tiberius, whom he had adopted as his son. The reigns of Augustus and Tiberius were comparatively long and peaceful, with a good degree of prosperity and expansion of the Empire. Both died in old age by natural causes. But all that was soon to change.

Caligula (A.D. 37–41) was a grandson of Augustus and was adopted as son by Tiberius. Caligula was a crazed megalomaniac who declared himself a "god," married his sister Drusilla, and murdered countless senators and members of the Roman aristocracy. In A.D. 41 he ordered a statue of himself to be set up in the Temple in Jerusalem. The Syrian governor Petronius, who had been ordered to carry out the order, purposely delayed the operation, knowing its potential to spark a full-scale Jewish revolt. In the meantime Caligula's own palace guard assassinated him. Claudius (A.D. 41–54), an uncle of Caligula and adopted son of Tiberius, became emperor, installed more or less by those who had murdered Caligula. His reign was comparatively long and stable compared to that of Caligula, but he did order all Jews to leave the city of Rome in response to growing unrest and messianic fervor among various Jewish groups. Claudius's fourth wife, Agrippina, murdered him by poisoning, in order to put her son Nero, whom Claudius had adopted, into power. Agrippina tightly controlled Nero (A.D. 54–68) until he finally had her clubbed to death at the urging of his mistress Poppaea, who began to rule behind the scenes. The early years of his reign were somewhat stable but the latter years were characterized by drunken revelries and dissipation. When a fire broke out in Rome in A.D. 64, destroying three quarters of the city, Nero blamed the Christians and had many of them in Rome arrested and killed. Tacitus, the Roman historian, offers us the gruesome details. Those captured were torn to death by dogs, crucified, and set on fire on the grounds of the imperial palace while Nero invited in the populace for the display and rode around in his chariot."

A full-scale Jewish Revolt had broken out in Palestine in A.D. 66 under the rule of the Roman governor Gessius Florus. Jerusalem fell into the control of several rebel factions. Nero had appointed a Spanish general,

Vespasian, to crush the revolt and several legions poured into the country. Josephus was put in charge of the Jewish forces in Galilee but by A.D. 68 Vespasian had crushed all opposition and moved south into Judea to lay siege to Jerusalem. Josephus surrendered and ended up on intimate terms with Vespasian, even advising him in the war effort, having become convinced that Jewish opposition was futile and disastrous. When Nero committed suicide in A.D. 68 three successive Roman generals made a bid to become emperor. General Galba marched in from Spain, and the Senate accepted him as emperor, but Otho, an influential senator, had him assassinated by the palace guard and declared himself emperor. General Vitellius, recognizing the opportunity, immediately marched down from Germany to Rome with his legions, forcing Otho to commit suicide, and becoming emperor himself. In the meantime Vespasian decided to act. He left the war in Judea and the siege of Jerusalem in the hands of his son Titus and traveled to Rome to challenge Vitellius. Vitellius tried to flee but was killed by troops loyal to Vespasian and the Senate declared Vespasian emperor. In the summer of A.D. 69 the new emperor Vespasian returned to Jerusalem, rejoining his son Titus, to personally conduct the final stages of the siege.

THE END OF THE AGE

Jerusalem was surrounded by four Roman legions—the Fifteenth that Titus had brought up from Egypt, and the Fifth, Tenth, and Twelfth that Vespasian had mustered from Syria. Including auxiliary troops the Roman forces numbered over 50,000. The city was cut off from supplies and by the spring of A.D. 70 severe famine had set in. Josephus reports that some even resorted to cannibalism, and chaos reigned inside the besieged city. Those who sought to escape were captured and crucified. According to Josephus, who had now joined Vespasian camped on the Mount of Olives before the city, as many as five hundred per day were captured and crucified in order to terrorize those inside and force surrender. Vespasian's troops had stripped the land all around Jerusalem of trees in order to get enough wood for all the crosses. The Zealots that controlled the local population trapped inside refused all offers. By summer the Romans had constructed ramps and were able to breach the walls and enter the city by stages. They set fire to the city and razed the walls to the ground. Finally the Temple itself, with its vast complex of buildings and courts, was burnt and utterly demolished.

The Roman Destruction of Jerusalem by David Roberts

Tourists can view the excavated ruins of Jerusalem's destruction in the Old City. The archaeologists have left much of the destruction debris, including the huge Herodian stones that once formed the walls of the vast Temple compound, lying in place, unmoved after nearly two

Herodian stones remaining from the Roman destruction

Western wall left standing from Roman destruction

thousand years. The steps that led up into the Temple have been uncovered under thirty or forty feet of accumulated debris. The modern Jewish
Quarter is built over the excavated destruction layers but in nearly every
basement of every home, as well as in the museums in the area, the ruins
tell the story more vividly than the pages of Josephus. Josephus wrote
that Vespasian destroyed the entire city as an example to the Jews who
had dared to oppose Rome. He left standing just three towers, the bases
of which are still visible near Jaffa Gate, as a testimony, he said, to the former splendor of the city he had conquered.

The Jewish-Roman war was a tragedy beyond measure for the religion
of Judaism and for the nation. The destruction of Jerusalem and the Temple left the Jewish people without a national and religious center. Thousands were taken prisoner and tens of thousands died by one means or
another. There was a great triumphal march in Rome to celebrate the victory of Vespasian, with Jewish captives and booty from the Temple, includ-

ing its sacred vessels, paraded through the streets. The
Romans minted a special silver coin that was inscribed IVDAEA CAPTA
("Judah is Defeated"). The scene is
captured for us today on Titus's
Arch in Rome, which was erected
by the Roman Senate in A.D. 81,
following Titus's death and deifi-
cation. It has panels depicting the
victory of Vespasian and Titus
and its inscription reads: "The
Roman Senate and People to Deified Titus, Vespasian Augustus,
son of Deified Vespasian." The

Roman coin "Judaea Capta"
celebrating the Roman victory

arch was erected soon after the completion of the famous Roman Colosseum, and new inscriptional evidence indicates that the Colosseum had
been built largely with Jewish slave labor and funds extracted from Judea.[12]

The Arch of Titus and the Colosseum in Rome

The causes of the war were of course complex but Josephus, having lived through it all, drew a most startling conclusion when he wrote:

> But what more than all else incited them to the war was an am-
> biguous oracle, likewise found in their sacred scriptures, to the
> effect that *at that time one from their country would become ruler of the*
> *world.* This they understood to mean someone of their own race,
> and many of their wise men went astray in their interpretation
> of it. The oracle, however, in reality signified the sovereignty of
> Vespasian, who was proclaimed Emperor on Jewish soil.[13]

What Josephus asserts here is that the chief cause of the war was a religious one involving the expectation of the coming of the Jewish Davidic Messiah. According to Josephus it was a messianic fervor that fueled the fires of revolt. The population was convinced that God would intervene and not only rout the Romans from Palestine, but, as the Hebrew Prophets had predicted, establish his chosen King as ruler over all nations. The specific "oracle" Josephus had in mind was evidently the "Seventy Weeks" prophecy of the book of Daniel that had marked out a final apocalyptic period of 490 years that included the coming of an "anointed prince" or Messiah figure (Daniel 9:25). But in retrospect, after the disaster of the war and the destruction of the city of Jerusalem, Josephus charged that his pious countrymen had misread or overlooked a key portion of Daniel's prophecy, namely its surprising conclusion:

> After the sixty-two weeks (i.e., 483 years) an *anointed one* shall be
> cut off and shall have nothing, and the troops of *the prince* who is
> to come shall destroy the city and the sanctuary. (Daniel 9:26)

The "world ruler" who comes is none other than the emperor Vespasian, who does indeed "destroy the city and the sanctuary"—not the awaited Jewish Messiah. So who then would be the "anointed one" or "messiah" who is "cut off"? Josephus says nothing about that but the followers of Jesus had read Daniel's prophecy in a similar way—even before the disaster of the Roman war. Their interpretation was likely spurred by the tragic and unexpected murder of their leader James the Just in A.D. 62.

James, descended from the royal line of David, and thus aptly called a "messiah" or "anointed one," had indeed been killed precisely seven years before the Romans laid siege to the city of Jerusalem in the summer of A.D. 69. That was seven years short of the completion of the 490-year period—precisely as Daniel had predicted. The "end of the age" could not be long following.

Eusebius and Epiphanius preserved a tradition that the Jerusalem followers of Jesus, now led by Simon son of Clophas, fled the city of Jerusalem just before siege in response to an "oracle given by revelation before the war."[14] They reported that the followers settled in the area of the Decapolis city of Pella—on the other side of the Jordan in the mountains of Gilead. Although some scholars have questioned the historical reliability of this tradition there is strong evidence in its favor. As we have seen, the book of Revelation, dating to the time of Nero and the Jewish Revolt, portrays the church as a "woman" who flees into the wilderness "to her place" where she is nourished for three and a half years (Revelation 12:14). In the book of Revelation Nero is the "Beast" with the mysterious number 666 and it was indeed Nero who both persecuted the Christians after the fire in Rome and sent Vespasian to quell the Jewish Revolt in A.D. 66.[15] When James was killed in A.D. 62, based on Daniel's predictions, the followers of Jesus had calculated a final *seven-year* period. They evidently left the city halfway into that period, or in the year A.D. 66, calculating that the "end" would come three and a half years later—in A.D. 69.

The gospel of Mark preserves a long discourse by Jesus that scholars call the "Little Apocalypse" that basically offers a running interpretation of Daniel's Seventy Weeks prophecy. It is built around the expectation that Jerusalem and the Temple would someday be surrounded by armies and destroyed, just prior to "the Son of Man coming in the clouds with great power and glory" (Mark 13:26). The followers of Jesus are told that those who are in Judea are to "flee to the mountains" before the siege, as a terrible time of trouble is to follow. Whether Jesus predicted these things or not, and most scholars have concluded they were likely put in his mouth shortly after the destruction of Jerusalem by the Romans in A.D. 70, they nonetheless offer strong support to the flight from Jerusalem tradition. It is unlikely that Mark, writing shortly after the Jewish Revolt, would have had Jesus telling his followers to do something that they in fact never did. Mark can be read backward, as "history" in the mouth of Jesus written after the fact.

Further, as we saw in Chapter 12, Pella, the region to which they are said to have fled, is just a few miles north of the biblical "Wadi Cherith," the traditional place where Elijah hid from danger and very likely the area where Jesus had spent the last winter of his life hiding from Herod Antipas—the "Jesus hideout" in Jordan. If Simon, leader of the group at this time, was in fact the brother of Jesus as I have argued, the flight in A.D. 66 would be a return visit for him after forty years.

How many of these Jerusalem Christians might have followed Simon northeast across the Jordan into the Decapolis region we cannot say. It is moving to imagine this band of loyal followers of the Jesus dynasty making their way to "their place," living in those caves surrounded by the steep cliffs, and awaiting the hope that had been kindled by John the Baptizer forty years earlier. Josephus reports that refugees fled the advancing Roman armies in all directions. This is the period when the Essene settlement at Qumran was abandoned and the Dead Sea Scrolls were hidden in the surrounding caves. We know that 960 Jewish refugees ended up in the Judean desert to the south, at the fortress of Masada. It was there that they committed suicide in the spring of A.D. 73 after a prolonged Roman siege. Masada became the "last stand" of Jewish resistance. It is possible, even likely, that Jewish followers of Jesus were included in that group. Some archaeological evidence points in that direction. In November 1963, during the first season of excavations at Masada, in a remote cave at the southern end of the fortress, the skeletons of twenty-four men, women, and children were discovered—seemingly removed from the main body of Zealot rebels who occupied the northern area. They appear to be a sectarian group, and it is possible that they were a group of Essenes or Nazarenes who had joined the others in flight.[16]

We can be fairly certain that not only the followers of Jesus, James, and Simon but many other Jews who understood the prophecies of Daniel were convinced that the "end of the age" was shortly to come and the "Son of Man" was imminently to appear. The destruction of the city and Temple of Jerusalem, and the resulting Roman occupation of that holy site, now dedicated to the Roman god Jupiter, was labeled by pious Jews as the "desolating sacrilege" spoken of by Daniel (Mark 13:14). It was understood to be *the* sign of the end.

THE JESUS DYNASTY LOST AND FORGOTTEN

We have no good historical record for these early Palestinian Christians during the period from the flight to Pella in A.D. 66 to the execution of the aged Simon during the reign of Trajan, probably around A.D. 106. It is like a curtain has descended over the history of the original followers of John the Baptizer, Jesus, James, and Simon for forty years. There are records of what was transpiring in those areas of Christianity to the West that had been influenced by Paul—but details of what transpired among those who had followed the Teaching represented by the Jesus dynasty were not preserved. We can assume that some might have returned to Jerusalem and tried to recover what measure of normalcy they could but many more must have been scattered, most likely to areas east of the Jordan River. Those were not normal times and the dangers were acute for any who might still maintain any type of messianic hope.

Eusebius reported that after the revolt the emperor Vespasian "ordered a search to be made for all who were of the family of David, that there might be left among the Jews no one of the royal family, and for this reason a very great persecution was again inflicted on the Jews."[17] Simon and any other relatives of the family of Jesus were probably in hiding or at least maintaining a low profile. Vespasian was succeeded by his natural born sons Titus (A.D. 79–81) and Domitian (A.D. 81–96), forming the short-lived "Flavian" dynasty. Domitian followed in his father's footsteps and gave direct orders that any of the bloodline of David be executed. Hegesippus related a fascinating story, preserved by Eusebius, in which two grandsons of Jesus' brother Jude were arrested, questioned, and released, during the reign of Domitian.[18] Hegesippus wrote that they were brought before the emperor Domitian himself, which seems unlikely though it is possible, given the high profile of the Davidic family and the tensions of the times in Palestine. They were asked if they were of David's line, which they acknowledged, but they insisted they had no political aspirations and were men of modest means, making a living by farming. Hegesippus's account survives in a few other sources in which these two descendants of Jude are said to be *sons* rather than grandsons. In Greek the words "son" and "grandson" (*huioi* and *huionoi*) can easily be confused, differing by two letters. Their names are given as Zoker, a shortened form of Zechariah, and James. Hegesippus further wrote that they were "leaders in the churches" because of their "witness" to the origins of the movement and their "relation to the Lord."[19] They were called *desposyunoi*, which means, "belonging to the master," that is members of the Jesus dynasty.[20] Simon's crucifixion was part of a roundup of any of "the royal house of the Jews."[21] We have no record of Jude's manner of death, but we do know that during the early decades of the 2nd century A.D., in Palestine at least, identification with the Davidic family and its messianic expectations could have serious consequences.

Being Jewish at all was becoming increasingly unpopular in the Roman world. During the years A.D. 132–35 a second, even more bloody, Jewish Revolt erupted in Palestine during the reign of the emperor Hadrian. It was led by Simon bar Kosiba, known subsequently in history as Bar Kochba, who had been accepted by many Jews as the Davidic Messiah. As punishment the Romans forbade Jews to even enter the city of Jerusalem and Hadrian completely rebuilt the city, turned it into a Roman colony, and renamed it *Aelia Capitolina* in honor of Jupiter Capitolinus, the patron deity of Rome. A temple dedicated to Jupiter was built over the site of the ruins of the Jewish temple.[22] Any hope of the Kingdom of God being realized on earth had begun to fade and Jewish messianic fervor grew cold. Paul's "gospel," which rejected "Israel according to the flesh" and focused on salvation and a Kingdom of God "not on earth but in heaven," had an increased appeal to many.

We do know that these original Christians survived, mostly in the areas east of Palestine, well into the 4th century A.D. But they were scattered and without power or influence and they had little to no part in influencing what went into the New Testament, which became the official story of early Christianity.

They were known subsequently by the term "Ebionites," which meant in Hebrew "poor ones." Eusebius knows of them, though he considers them heretics in contrast to the Christian orthodoxy that he championed. Among his charges was that the Ebionites made Jesus a "plain and ordinary man," born naturally from "Mary and her husband." Eusebius further stated that the Ebionites insisted on observance of the Jewish Law or Torah and that they maintained that salvation was by "works" as well as faith, as the letter of James affirms. The Ebionites rejected the letters of the apostle Paul and considered him an apostate from the original faith. They used only a Hebrew version of the gospel of Matthew—now lost to us other than in fragments. Eusebius, allied with the emperor Constantine, who had turned to Christianity himself by A.D. 325, classified each of these Ebionite views as heretical. And yet ironically, their views are grounded in the teachings of Jesus himself, and that tradition passed on by his brothers.[23]

A much more positive view of the Ebionite "gospel" is now embedded in the 4th-century documents we call the *Pseudo-Clementines*. A document called the *Kerygmata Petrou* or the Preaching of Peter is particularly valuable in this regard. This document claims to be a letter written by Peter to James the brother of Jesus. Peter complains that his letters have been interpolated and corrupted by those influenced by Paul so that they have become worthless. He urges James not to pass along any of his teachings to the Gentiles, but only to those members of the council of the Seventy whom Jesus had appointed. Paul is sharply censored as one who put his own testimony based on visions over the certainty of the teachings that the original apostles had from Jesus directly.[24] Scholars do not consider such materials as authentic 1st-century documents but they do appear to reflect later legendary versions of the very disputes that did occur during the lifetime of Paul, Peter, and James and thus preserve for us some memory of the conflicts that the New Testament, and particularly Luke, tend to smooth over.

It is only now through the discovery of lost documents, the insights gained by new archaeological discoveries, and a critical reading of the

New Testament and other historical records, that we are in a position to begin to put many of the pieces of the puzzle together. The legacy of the Jesus dynasty is at last coming to light with exciting results for those who wish to hear again the original teachings of Jesus.

I began the story of the Jesus dynasty with a tale of two tombs and their possible relationship to the ancient burial ossuary inscribed in Aramaic "James son of Joseph, brother of Jesus" that came to public view in late 2002. When the James Ossuary story broke worldwide both reporters and the public found themselves wondering—just who is this James? And how is it that Jesus had a brother? It is as if the surfacing of the James Ossuary and the discovery of the two tombs, whatever turns out to be their final disposition, have somehow signaled for us the material reality of a hidden and forgotten story of the utmost significance.

An understanding of the Jesus dynasty offers us much more than an interesting alternative to the standard ways in which Christian history has been presented. It opens for us new avenues of thinking about the significance of Jesus of Nazareth and what his life and teachings can mean to us. Jesus was the most influential figure in human history and who he was and how he is remembered matters greatly to all of us, whether secular or religious, whether Jewish, Christian, or Muslim.

Conclusion

RECOVERING LOST
TREASURES

History is not merely an assemblage of constructed facts. It also involves an attempt to retrieve and imagine a past that we can no longer see or touch. History touches the heart as well as the head. And it is here that material evidence makes a difference. Historical artifacts, authentically connected to the people and places we study in texts, offer us an avenue of linked imagination that is both moving and significant. I felt this acutely when I first viewed the James Ossuary in Toronto in November 2002, and I know that the other historians and academics in the room did as well. It is that tangible touching of the past that stirs the human heart, no matter how learned or reserved one might be. And that is why this book begins with the "Tale of Two Tombs," describing the discoveries of the Tomb of the Shroud and the Talpiot tomb with its unusual cluster of six names corresponding to those of the Jesus family.

At this point there is no proof that the James Ossuary, even if authentic, came from either of these tombs, though more evidence might come to light if DNA testing is carried out. But what is significant about these tombs is that they represent to us the 1st-century cave burial of a family, which if not Jesus' actual family, reflects the same customs and practices of remembering the dead. To crawl into one of these tombs, as I have done, is to join with the past in a way that affects one far more than at an intellectual level. It is a way of touching the reality of ancient Jewish history at the time of the birth of Christianity. The aristocratic male, whose remains we found still shrouded in the Hinnom tomb, might have been a witness to the last days of Jesus. In other words, this man lived and died in that time, at that place. The ossuary of Caiaphas held the bones of the man who presided at the trial of Jesus. Looking at the nail-pierced heel bone of Jehohanan brings a chilling image of the horrors of Roman crucifixion. And if it does turn out that the James Ossuary did come from the tomb of the "Jesus family"—then much more might result from our study of these remains. Although our mute artifacts speak no words, they powerfully bond us to a past that continues to have deep meaning for our present. Here, at the end of this book, I want to explore some of the lost treasures of this past, and their relevance for our present and our future.

The history of Jesus, his royal family, and the birth of Christianity, as I have presented it in this book, was hidden partly as a result of intentional efforts of some segments of the early Christian movement, and partly through the loss of documents and records that are only now coming to light. According to the version of the birth of Christianity that became dominant, the important role of John the Baptizer was reduced to that of a forerunner of Jesus, while the existence and role of James, the brother of Jesus, who took over leadership of the movement following Jesus' death, was muted or in some cases denied. Jesus himself, as "God in the flesh," was transformed into a figure hardly human, who had appeared briefly among humankind, died, was resurrected, and returned to heavenly glory. The message that Jesus preached was transformed into the person of Jesus *as* the message—the proclamation that Christ had come and died for the sins of the world. By the middle of the 3rd century A.D. a new religion had been born, shaped by these theological perceptions, and completely separated from all forms of Judaism. Christianity, as such, has become the world's largest religion and its message has had a profound impact on billions of lives over the past two millennia of Western civilization. And yet, at the core of all forms of Christianity are the teachings of Jesus, and more than any other factor, it is the compelling portrait of

Jesus that has attracted so many to this faith. That makes it all the more tragic that what was lost, marginalized, and largely forgotten was the *original* story, which was Jesus' own story—what he in fact was in his own time and place, as a 1st-century Jewish Messiah who lay claim to the throne of David and inaugurated a Messianic Movement with the potential to change the world. Only with this understanding of Jesus can Christianity—and Christians—recapture the passion and fervor of the revolutionary message that Jesus proclaimed and seek to live according to his radical teachings.

That original story and Jesus' original message, fortunately, can be recovered. Its essential elements remain embedded in the New Testament documents, particularly in the Q source. Once recognized and coupled with other ancient texts, and the rich assortment of archaeological data now coming to light, they can provide us with an authentic voice, long ago muted but still possessing the power to transform lives and even to challenge modern culture and society, as Jesus did in his own day.

It is the case that such a recovery challenges many sacred dogmas of Christian orthodoxy, but as we have seen, what became the dominant Christian story was really built upon Paul's revelations, more than upon Jesus' teachings. The process of recovery through a critical reading of our ancient evidence that I have undertaken in this book is essentially an attempt to find the Christian story that most faithfully represents Jesus. This is the desire of millions of Christian believers, as well as countless others who admire Jesus as an historical figure. Many are readily prepared to listen to the voice of Jesus, but reluctant to equate orthodox Christian theology with Jesus' life and message.

I see this recovery process as primarily a building up, rather than a tearing down. It involves a process of rehabilitation—of John the Baptizer, of Jesus, of James, and of Jesus' entire family. The results are positive rather than negative, constructive rather than destructive. They take us back to Jesus himself, and to the people he most loved and the cause for which he died. It is an amazingly touching and inspiring story, by any measure, but it also offers us insights into what is most enduring and provocative about the historical figure of Jesus.

Jesus, his mother Mary, and to a lesser degree, all of the apostles, have been so enshrined within Christian theology that their existence as real historical characters is easily lost. Their lives as human beings, who lived and breathed on planet earth, within their very particular social, cultural, and political contexts, can become blurred and phantomlike. Humans through the ages share a commonality that links us together across time and space. Our hopes and our dreams, our joys and our disappointments, our sufferings and our tragedies, tie us all together. If our understanding of Jesus develops out of that common humanity we will be in a position to better understand Jesus and his early followers and to identify with them on levels that might otherwise be missed. In the end, the Jesus story is a thoroughly *human* story, but one bursting with spiritual potential and direction even at the beginning of the third millennium.

THE JESUS STORY RECOVERED

In *The Jesus Dynasty* I have sought to present the reader with the relevant evidence regarding our recovery of the historical Jesus. There is much we can never know, given both the nature of the sources and their scarcity. With regard to some areas we are left to guess or speculate based on the evidence that we do have. I have touched on subjects that are as sensitive as they are controversial—the paternity of Jesus, the possibility that Mary remarried after the death of Joseph, the reburial of Jesus in a tomb—these are all matters where faith and history find a tense meeting place. I have sought to present a chronology that seems reasonable, and to locate places where things we read of in our texts might have taken place. At every point I have wanted to present the *human* side of the Jesus story, set in its real historical context and free of any theological agenda. The bare results are the following.

Jesus had a human father and a human mother. It is most likely that Mary, his mother, while set to marry an older man Joseph by family arrangement, became pregnant by another man before the wedding. Mary eventually bore six other children, four boys and two girls, whether by Joseph or by his brother Clophas. John the Baptizer, not Jesus, was the initiator of the Messianic Movement that became Christianity. Jesus valued his kinsman John as highly as anyone could value another—as a

Prophet and Teacher, and inaugurator of the Kingdom of God. Jesus joined the movement John had begun, being baptized by John, and working with him to advance the Messianic Movement. John and Jesus filled expectations of the coming of Two Messiahs current in their time—one as priestly descendant of Aaron, the other as royal descendant of David. Their joint message was a simple one: a call to repent of sins in view of the imminent arrival of the Kingdom of God. Those who responded were baptized in water as a sign of their participation in the movement and its message. Theirs was an apocalyptic movement that expected God to soon intervene in history to establish the Kingdom of God as described in detail by all the Prophets. It was to be a new era of justice, righteousness, and peace for all humankind, centered on the reconstituted nation of Israel with Jerusalem as the new world capital from which would radiate the knowledge of God and the universal ethics of the Torah to all the nations of the world.

John and Jesus proclaimed justice for the poor and oppressed and pronounced warnings of judgment upon those who refused to turn from their unrighteous ways. They taught an intimacy with God as a heavenly Father, God's care for all creatures, and the forgiveness of sins, as exemplified in the prayer they began to spread among their followers. Neither John nor Jesus had any idea of beginning a new religion, but both lived as Jews according to the Torah or Jewish Law. They issued the call to both Jews and non-Jews to turn to the revelation of the Torah of Moses and the Hebrew Prophets.

The preaching and baptizing efforts of John and Jesus led to John's arrest by Herod Antipas, ruler of Galilee. Following John's arrest Jesus continued the work they had begun. He chose the inner Council of Twelve, including four of his brothers, to whom he promised rule over the Twelve Tribes of Israel, which he expected to be gathered back to the Land of Israel. He initiated a campaign throughout Galilee, and eventually through most of the regions of Roman Palestine. He became known as a healer and an exorcist as well as a preacher of the Kingdom of God and a teacher of Torah ethics. Jesus was convinced that the downfall of Satan, the unseen ruler of the world, was imminent. His activities stirred bitter opposition among certain leaders among the Herodians, the Pharisees, and the Sadducees—particularly those who shared a measure of political power with the Romans in Jerusalem.

When Herod Antipas unexpectedly and brutally murdered John, Jesus believed that his destiny was to go to Jerusalem, enter the Temple, and directly confront the religious and political authorities with his message of radical reform. He likely realized that this encounter might well lead to his own arrest, and possibly even his execution. Here we have no way of knowing the inner thoughts and motivations of Jesus, but I am convinced, based on the biblical passages that apparently became his guide, that he expected God would intervene to save him from his enemies at the final moment, and usher in the Kingdom of God. Unlike others of his generation, who had armed followers to resist Roman military occupation, Jesus was convinced that if he acted in faith, God would intervene.

Like his kinsman John, Jesus died in faith that his cause would be realized. His followers were devastated and for a time returned to Galilee in fear and disappointment. Their faith had been severely tried—the Two Messiahs were dead. It was under the leadership of James, linked with Peter and John, that the community regained its faith. They believed that Jesus, though dead, had triumphed in his cause, and would in the end be vindicated, as would be all the righteous martyrs for the Kingdom of God. James, also of Davidic ancestry, was understood to be a successor of Jesus, ruling over the nascent messianic "government" that Jesus had initiated with his Council of Twelve.

The message and teachings of James, Peter, John, and the Twelve was a continuation of that of John the Baptizer and Jesus. They expected the imminent manifestation of the Kingdom of God, and they preached a message of repentance from sins, baptizing their followers into what they believed was the core of a newly constituted and reformed nation of Israel. Non-Jews were invited to join them in the cause, as long as they turned from the worship of idols and adhered to the minimum ethics prescribed in the Torah for Gentiles.

The message that Paul began to preach in the 40s and 50s A.D., as Paul himself so adamantly insisted, was in no way dependent upon, nor derived from, the original group of Jesus' apostles in Jerusalem led by James.

It was based upon his own visionary experiences of a heavenly Christ. It was Paul's message that became the foundation of Christian theological orthodoxy. In contrast, the message of James and the original Jerusalem apostles was not derived from the revelations that Paul claimed to receive, but was based on what the group had been taught directly from John the Baptizer and Jesus during their lifetimes.

Accordingly, James and his successors provide us our best historical link to Jesus and his original teachings. That we find no trace of Paul's gospel, nor of Pauline theology, in the Q source, or in the letter of James, or in the *Didache*, should not surprise us. James and his successors represent an original version of Christianity, linked more directly to the historical Jesus, that has every claim of authenticity. And that is what the Jesus dynasty represents. It is more than an interesting alternative twist on Christian history that allows us to fill in a missing minor piece of the story. An understanding of the Jesus dynasty opens the way for us to recover an original Christianity and its potent message for our own times.

FOR WHAT DID HE LIVE AND DIE?

Given what I have presented in *The Jesus Dynasty* one might be tempted to classify Jesus with other "failed messiahs" whose hopes and dreams were never realized as they expected. But the cause is always greater than the person. Jesus' cause was the Kingdom of God. But he defined it most elegantly: "Let your Kingdom come, let your will be done *on earth* as it is in heaven." The second phrase is an explanation of the first. The Kingdom coming is when the will of God is realized on earth, not in heaven. The Kingdom Jesus expected was not an *earthly* Kingdom, but it was a Kingdom *on* earth. It involved nations and peoples, politics and power, governments and structures of authority. This is in keeping with all the Hebrew Prophets who pioneered the vision of the Kingdom of God— that the *earth* would be filled with the knowledge of God as the waters cover the sea. On the wall across the street from the United Nations building in New York is a large carved stone monument with the words of Isaiah written upon it: "They shall beat their swords into plowshares, and their spears into pruning hooks, and nation shall not lift up sword against nation, neither shall they learn war any more." The quotation is taken from Isaiah chapter 2, one of the main passages of the Hebrew Bible that sketches a vision of the Kingdom of God. The Jesus dynasty reminds us of a Christianity that never escapes this world, and retains a cutting message against all forms of injustice, unrighteousness, and oppression while setting forth the ideal of the Kingdom of God realized on earth.

But Jesus not only proclaimed the arrival of the Kingdom of God, he pinpointed a set of central ethical and spiritual values, based upon the message of the Hebrew Prophets, that still find powerful resonance among Christians and non-Christians alike. From texts such as the Q source, the letter of James, the *Didache*, and the *Gospel of Thomas*, we can recover and emphasize these insights and realize their potential power and their challenging appeal.

Love God first, and your fellow human as yourself, and whatever you find hateful to yourself, do not do to another, but do to others as you would have them do to you. This is the essence of the Torah and the Prophets. Don't think I came to destroy the Torah and the Prophets; I came to fulfill. Whoever relaxes one of the least of the commandments will be considered "least" by those in the Kingdom of God. Be doers of the Torah and not hearers only, for faith without works is dead.

When you give charity do not let your left hand know what your right hand is doing. Let your gift to charity sweat in your hands until you know to whom you give it. When you pray go to your room and shut the door and pray to your Father who sees in secret. The first will be the last, and the last will be first. For nothing hidden will fail to be revealed.

Do not be of two minds or speak from both sides of your mouth, for speaking from both sides of your mouth is a deadly trap. Above all, you are always under oath. If you say "yes," then it is "yes," and "no," then it is "no."

Give to one who asks you, and from one who would borrow turn not away. Whoever has two coats must share with him who has none, and whoever has food must do likewise. Lend, expecting nothing in return. Take no interest.

Forgive and you will be forgiven, give and it will be given to you, for the measure you give will be the measure you get back. Confess your sins one to another and pray for one another. Care for those who oppose you, pray for those who mistreat you, do good to those who hate you, bless those who curse you. Cast the plank from your own eye so you can see to remove the splinter from that of your fellow human. In the same manner as you judge others, you will be judged. For judgment will be without mercy to one who has shown no mercy.

Draw near to God and God will draw near to you. Cleanse your hands you sinners and purify your hearts you double-minded. Lament and mourn and weep. Humble yourselves before God and he will exalt you.

It is impossible to mount two horses or to stretch two bows — you cannot serve God and the system of this world. Following the path of righteousness leads to the cross. Beware when all humans speak well of you. A prophet is not without honor except in his or her own circles. He who is not for me is against me.

For Jesus and his early followers these and many other core teachings represented more than a set of pious platitudes. Rather they mapped a social and political program to be put into operation in order that the Kingdom of God might be realized on earth as it is in heaven. Both its challenges and its dangers in a world system that operates on opposite principles were well understood by that generation. John was beheaded. Jesus and Simon were crucified. James was stoned to death. The cost of hearing the Voice and seeking to follow was a high one.

THE FAITH OF ABRAHAM

An understanding of the Jesus dynasty also offers new avenues of understanding between Jews, Christians, and Muslims. Christian persecution of Jews has understandably done much to marginalize Jesus within Jewish history. Over the centuries Jews found it difficult to think about Jesus without associating him with the bad conduct of those who acted in his name. In the last century, and into our own time, much of that is changing with a recovery of the Jewishness of Jesus and a fruitful attempt by historians to place Jesus in his proper historical context. As Martin Buber, the great Jewish philosopher of the 20th century, put it, "I do not believe in Jesus but I believe with him. I firmly believe that the Jewish community in the course of its renaissance will recognize Jesus; not merely as a great figure in its religious history, but also in the organic context of a Messianic development extending over millennia, whose final goal is the Redemption of Israel and of the world." What Jews have rejected is not so much Jesus as the systems of Christian theology that equated Jesus with God, that nullified the Torah, and that displaced the Jewish people and their covenant. Jews are acutely aware of the unredeemed nature of the world. If Jesus can never be *the* Messiah for Jews, as a descendant of David who inaugurated a yet unfinished messianic program, he is surely, by historical measures, *a* messiah. That seems to be Buber's great insight. A recovery of the perspectives of James and Jesus' other original followers, who continued to hope and strive for messianic redemption, and who espoused a set of biblical ethics based on the Hebrew Prophets, even after Jesus' death, offers a point of unity and understanding hitherto neglected between Jews and Christians.

For Christians an understanding of the Jesus dynasty opens a way for recovering and appreciating the Jewish roots of Jesus. There have been significant developments along these lines in recent years across a wide spectrum of Christian groups—whether traditionally "liberal" or "conservative." More and more Christians have become familiar with basic Jewish customs and holidays in an effort to understand Jesus better as a Jew in his own time. It is not uncommon for Passover observances to be conducted in churches, with rabbis invited in to teach, in an effort to better understand Jesus in his own time and place. In the academic study of Christian origins at any major college or university the Jewishness of Jesus is a given, and courses on the New Testament and early Christianity approach Jesus and his movement as an integral part of the history of the varieties of Judaism in Roman Palestine. If Christians can give James his rightful place as successor to Jesus' movement, and begin to realize that his version of the faith represents a Christianity with claims to authenticity that override those of Paul, even more doors of understanding between Christians and Jews will be opened. But just as important, in terms of Christian mission and purpose in the world, the unfinished agenda of John, Jesus, and James can find new life and relevance in modern times.

Muslims do not worship Jesus, who is known as *Isa* in Arabic, nor do they consider him divine, but they do believe that he was a prophet or messenger of God and he is called the Messiah in the Qu'ran. However, by affirming Jesus as Messiah they are attesting to his messianic message, not his mission as a heavenly Christ. There are some rather striking connections between the research I have presented in *The Jesus Dynasty* and the traditional beliefs of Islam. The Muslim emphasis on Jesus as messianic prophet and teacher is quite parallel to what we find in the Q source, in the book of James, and in the *Didache*. To be the Messiah is to proclaim a message, but it is the same message as that proclaimed by Abraham, Moses, and all the Prophets. Islam insists that neither Jesus nor Mohammed brought a *new* religion. Both sought to call people back to what might be called "Abrahamic faith." This is precisely what we find emphasized in the book of James. Like Islam, the book of James, and the teaching of Jesus in Q, emphasize *doing* the will of God as a demonstration of one's faith. Also, the dietary laws of Islam, as quoted in the Qu'ran, echo the teachings of James in Acts 15 almost word for word: "Abstain from swineflesh, blood, things offered to idols, and carrion" (Qu'ran 2:172).

Since Muslims reject all of the Pauline affirmations about Jesus, and thus the central claims of orthodox Christianity, the gulf between Islam and Christianity on Jesus is a wide one. However, there is little about the view of Jesus presented in this book that conflicts with Islam's basic perception. The prophet Mohammed was in contact with Christian groups in Arabia, and there is evidence to suppose that the Christians he met might have been closer in their beliefs to the Ebionites than to the Western church. If that be the case then one of the most fascinating turns of history would be that the view of Jesus represented by the Jesus dynasty, has survived, ironically, in aspects of Islamic tradition as well.

The Christianity we know from the Q source, from the letter of James, from the *Didache*, and some of our other surviving Jewish-Christian sources, represents a version of the Jesus faith that can actually unite, rather than divide, Jews, Christians, and Muslims. If nothing else, the insights revealed through an understanding of the Jesus dynasty can open wide new and fruitful doors of dialogue and understanding among these three great traditions that have in the past considered their views of Jesus to be so sharply contradictory as to close off discussion.

A FINAL WORD

When I stood in the Garden of Gethsemane that night in my youth, I could not possibly have imagined the four-decade journey upon which I was embarking. For me as an historian it has been a fascinating investigative journey filled with unanticipated results and significant disclosures. My goal at every turn has been to get as close as one can, given our evidence, to the historical Jesus as far as he might be recovered in our own time. Modern historians are acutely aware that neither our sources, nor our own attempt to make sense of them, are transparent windows. Our view of the past, accordingly, is never a clear one. It is impossible to gaze upon "facts" without interpretation. All historians come to their investigations with selective criteria of judgment forged by both acknowledged and unrecognized predisposed interests and cultural assumptions. There is no absolutely objective place to stand. As long as we recognize our limitations of method and resist equating our own reconstructions with an absolute truth we can at least seek to approximate a standard of best evidence. When it comes to the quest for the historical Jesus our need to be aware of our own prejudices seems particularly acute. No other figure in history elicits such passionate responses nor engenders such opposite conclusions. A conscious humility before the evidence is absolutely essential. I have tried in this study to incorporate these high standards. To the degree I have succeeded I am pleased and with every good historian I stand ever open to critique and revision.

I have discovered over the last forty years that there are countless others who share the quest for the historical Jesus and who want to know the truth, wherever it may lead. Our conclusions might differ but I hope that my journey will help them to better glimpse Jesus as he was in his own time and place. I truly believe that an understanding of Jesus and his family, and the dynasty that perpetuated his message, is one of the most important keys to completing our quest to know the historical Jesus and the origins of Christianity.

Timeline of Major Events and Figures

167–64 B.C.	Revolt of the Maccabees against Syrian ruler Antiochus IV
63 B.C.	Roman conquest of Palestine by Pompey; Judea made a Roman province
31 B.C.–A.D. 14	Rule of Augustus, first emperor of Rome
37–4 B.C.	Rule of Herod the Great, King of the Jews, over Palestine
4 B.C.	Death of Herod the Great and uprisings in Galilee and Judea
4 B.C.–A.D. 6	Rule of Archelaus, son of Herod, over Judea
4 B.C.–A.D. 39	Rule of Herod Antipas, son of Herod, over Galilee and Perea
4 B.C.–A.D. 34	Rule of Philip, son of Herod, over eastern territories
5 B.C.	Birth of John the Baptizer and Jesus
A.D. 6	Revolt of Judas the Galilean following removal of Archelaus
A.D. 14–37	Rule of Tiberius, second emperor of Rome
A.D. 26–36	Rule of Pontius Pilate, procurator over Judea
A.D. 26	Preaching of John the Baptizer and the baptism of Jesus
A.D. 29	John the Baptizer beheaded by Herod Antipas
A.D. 30	Crucifixion of Jesus
A.D. 37–41	Rule of Caligula, third emperor of Rome
A.D. 41–54	Rule of Claudius, fourth emperor of Rome
A.D. 54–68	Rule of Nero, fifth emperor of Rome
50s A.D.	Career and preaching of Paul
A.D. 62	Death of James the brother of Jesus
A.D. 63	Traditional date of the death of Peter
A.D. 64	Traditional date of the death of Paul
A.D. 68–69	Attempts of generals Galba, Otho, Vitellius to become emperor

A.D. 69–79	Rule of Vespasian, sixth emperor of Rome
A.D. 66–70	First Jewish Revolt, Roman destruction of Jerusalem in A.D. 70
A.D. 73	Fall of Masada, final Jewish holdout
A.D. 79–81	Rule of Titus, son of Vespasian, seventh emperor of Rome
A.D. 81–96	Rule of Domitian, son of Vespasian, eighth emperor of Rome
A.D. 96–98	Rule of Nerva, ninth emperor of Rome
A.D. 98–117	Rule of Trajan, tenth emperor of Rome
A.D. 106	Crucifixion of Simon, successor to James, the brother of Jesus
A.D. 117–38	Rule of Hadrian, eleventh emperor of Rome
A.D. 132–35	Second Jewish Revolt led by Jewish Messiah Bar Kochba

Notes

Introduction

1. For more information on these and other interesting sites relevant to biblical studies see http://www.tfba.org.
2. The students with me that afternoon were Kaitlyn Cotanch, Lee Hutchinson, Vicki Powell, Jeff Poplin, and Mark Williams.
3. In the Bible the phrase "gathering the bones" of the deceased possibly refers to this practice of secondary burial. The Jewish practice is summarized in the Mishnah, *m. Sanhedrin* 6:6: "When the flesh had decomposed they collect the bones and bury them in their right place."
4. B. Zissu, S. Gibson, Y. Tabor, "Jerusalem—Ben Hinnom Valley," in *Hadashot Arkheologiyot* (Jerusalem: Israel Exploration Society, 2000), vol. III, pp. 70–72, Figs. 138–39.
5. Hershel Shanks and Ben Witherington III, *The Brother of Jesus: The Dramatic Story & Meaning of the First Archaeological Link to Jesus & His Family* (New York: HarperSanFrancisco, 2003).
6. David Samuels's "Written in Stone" (*New Yorker*, April 12, 2004), gave many the erroneous impression that the case was closed.
7. A full regularly updated archive of materials both pro and con on the authenticity of the James ossuary inscription can be found at http://www.bib-arch.org
8. Her official letter is at http://bib-arch.org/bswbOOossuary_yardeni.asp.
9. Their official press release is archived at: http://www.rom.on.ca/news/releases/public.php?mediakey=vhggdo3048.
10. See Gibson's published account of this information based on Rafi Lewis' written affidavit in "A Lost Cause," *Biblical Archaeology Review* (November/December 2004): 55–58.
11. Samuels, "Written in Stone," 51.

12. It is interesting that the initial AP headline, "JESUS" CASKET FOUND IN
ISRAEL, was defensively softened to CASKETS LABELED JESUS, MARY AND
JOSEPH PROBABLY COINCIDENCE within a matter of hours. By the time the
story filed by veteran *Jerusalem Post* reporter Abraham Rabinovich appeared
in *USA Today* on April 3, the Gannett headline read COFFIN IN ISRAEL IS
NOT THAT OF JESUS' FAMILY, EXPERTS SAY. The story had deflated like a
punctured tire.

13. L. Y. Rahmani, *A Catalogue of Jewish Ossuaries in the Collections of the State of
Israel* (Jerusalem: Israel Antiquities and Israel Academy of Sciences and
Humanities, 1994). The ossuary inscribed "Jesus son of Joseph" is catalogue
No. 80.503 in the Israeli warehouse and listed as No. 704 in the Rahmani
publication.

14. The ossuary is catalogued as S 767 in the warehouse and appears as No.
9/Plate 2 in Rachmani. It was "discovered" by Eleazar Sukenik of Hebrew
University, the first Israeli to identify the Dead Sea Scrolls. He found it in a
basement storage area of the Palestinian Archaeological Museum (today the
Rockefeller) in Jerusalem in 1926. Unfortunately it had no archaeological
context. When Sukenik published a report about the ossuary in January
1931, the news that such an inscription existed, it being the only one ever
found until that time, created no small stir in the world press, particularly in
Europe (see L. H. Vincent, "Épitaphe prétendue de N.S. Jésus-Christ," *Atti
della pontificia: academia romana di archaeologie: Rendiconti* 7 [1929–30]: 213–39).

15. For some reason Baruk seems to have misidentified the first one. Instead he
showed them a broken inscribed fragment barely six inches in diameter
that could not have read "Jesus son of Joseph." No such inscribed fragment
exists. The actual 1926 ossuary with this inscription is complete and intact,
pictured clearly in the Rachmani catalogue. Had the crew been shown this
one it would have more than suited their purposes for filming and I doubt
they would have even asked to see the second one. Baruk then brought out
the second one, discovered in 1980.

16. The ossuary from Talpiot with the inscription "Jude son of Jesus" is on permanent display in the Israel Museum for public viewing as part of an exhibit showing the common use of these various Jewish names on burial
ossuaries of the time.

17. *London Sunday Times*, March 31, 1996.

18. Reuters, April 2, 1996.

19. *London Sunday Times*, March 31, 1996. Zias's comments are all the more interesting given his later skepticism about the authenticity and significance
of the so-called "James ossuary" revealed to the public in 2002.

20. Neil Silberman, *The Hidden Scrolls: Christianity, Judaism, and the War for the Dead Sea Scrolls* (New York: Putnam, 1994), p. 129.

21. Associated Press, April 2, 1996.

22. Amos Kloner, "A Tomb with Inscribed Ossuaries in the East Talpiot," *Atiqot* 29 (1996): 15–22. Kloner writes, "The bones within these ossuaries were in an advanced stage of disintegration" (p. 16). He says nothing about the human skulls that Gibson saw and put in his drawing. In a final note in his article he says, "After the completion of the excavation, the bones were reburied" (p. 22). Notice that Kloner did not publish his official report until 1996, sixteen years after the excavation and the same year all the publicity broke. He apparently was not involved in the excavation and writes his report based on the information compiled by the excavator, the late Joseph Gath.

PART ONE: IN THE BEGINNING WAS THE FAMILY

1. A *Virgin Shall Conceive*

1. Mary's parents, Joachim and Anna, are not named in the New Testament. Our earliest source is the 2nd-century A.D. gospel called the *Protoevangelium of James*. A reliable 3rd-century Greek copy, the Bodmer papyrus, was recently discovered. Joachim and Anna became popular figures in Catholic lore and their story was a favorite theme of Renaissance artists. Churches were dedicated to St. Anne as early as the 5th century and are common throughout the world today. The tradition that Mary was born in Sepphoris is much later, and less reliable, first mentioned by the "Piacenza Pilgrim" in A.D. 570. He reports being shown the house of Mary. A Crusader church was built to commemorate the site, but there is some evidence of Byzantine remains on the grounds including a 3rd-century mosaic. Today the Sisters of St. Anne maintain a convent there and maintain the tradition of Mary's family.

2. Josephus, *Jewish War*, Book 1, trans. by H. St. J. Thackeray, Loeb Classical Library (Cambridge, Mass.: Harvard University Press, 1927), 386–97 and *Jewish Antiquities*, Book 15, trans. by Allen Wikgren, Loeb Classical Library (Cambridge, Mass.: Harvard University Press, 1943), 194–201. Subsequent references to Josephus are to the Loeb Classical Library editions, beginning with the book number.

3. Josephus *Jewish War* 7.300. The destruction of the genealogies is reported by Julius Africanus. See Eusebius, *Church History*, trans. by Kirsopp

Lake, Loeb Classical Library (Cambridge, Mass.: Harvard University Press, 1984), 1.7.11–13.

4. See Eusebius *Church History* 3.12, 19. These texts will be analyzed extensively in subsequent chapters.

5. Some have put the death of Herod slightly later but 4 B.C. is the most commonly accepted date.

6. Josephus *Jewish Antiquities* 17.271–85.

7. Varus's rule in Syria was characterized by cruelty and arrogance toward the local population. This is the same Varus responsible for the devastating Roman defeat in the Teutoburger Forest, east of the Rhine, in A.D. 9 by the German Arminius, changing the course of history. The Romans lost three legions in what became known as the "Varus Disaster" (*Clades Variana*). Varus was married to the grand-niece of the emperor Augustus and was well connected in aristocratic Roman circles. According to the Roman historian Seutonius, when Augustus heard the news of the defeat he knocked his head against the doorpost crying out "O Quintilius Varus! Give me back my legions!"

8. Josephus *Jewish Antiquities* 17:285–98, and *Jewish War* 2.66–75.

9. Josephus *Jewish Antiquities* 18.27. The Greek word he uses, *proschema*, could be translated in this context as "showplace."

10. In Jerusalem, just outside the Garden of Gethsemane in the Kidron Valley, there is the Church of the Tomb of the Virgin, sometimes called the Church of the Assumption. Queen Helena, mother of the emperor Constantine, built it in A.D. 326. It supposedly has the graves of Mary, Joseph, and Mary's parents, Joachim and Anna. We have no independent evidence of the deaths of Joseph and Mary's parents in Jerusalem.

11. The Greek verb *mnesteuo* means to be legally pledged to be married. It is the same verb used of Mary in Luke 1:27 and Matthew 1:18. In Jewish tradition "engagement" is a type of preliminary "marriage," but without full consummation, and sexual unfaithfulness is regarded as adultery (*Sanhedrin* 57b).

12. The returning to Nazareth is according to Luke 1:26. Apparently Matthew is unaware of this tradition. He does say that the couple eventually settled in Nazareth, but only after the birth of Jesus (Matthew 2:23).

13. When Jesus returned home to Nazareth as an adult he was invited to speak in the synagogue and his family was known by name (Luke 4:16; Matthew 13:55).

14. "Nazareth Village," http://www.nazarethvillage.com.

15. Some Roman Catholic scholars have maintained that Matthew's lan-

guage—"He took his wife but knew her not until she had given birth to a son"—does not necessarily imply the couple had sexual intercourse thereafter. They point out that the word "until" does not always indicate subsequent change. For example, one might say to another, "Stay sober until I come," without implying that one is to be drunken thereafter. The argument seems strained and in the interest of dogmatic theology, namely the doctrine of the Perpetual Virginity of Mary. The natural reading of both the Greek and the English seems clear—the couple began a normal sexual relationship after Jesus was born.

16. See Babylonian Talmud *Sanhedrin* 57b. The revered Catholic theologian Jerome, who lived in the 4th century A.D., was so insistent that Mary never had sexual relations that he was willing to say she never married, knowing that marriage within Judaism required sexual consummation. He writes: "But as we do not deny what is written, so we do reject what is not written. We believe that God was born of the Virgin, because we read it. That Mary was married after she brought forth, we do not believe, because we do not read it" (*Against Helvidius* 21) in *The Nicene and Post-Nicene Fathers*, vol. 6, ed. W. H. Freemantle, G. Lewis, and W. G. Martley (Grand Rapids: Wm. B. Eerdmans, 1983), 335.

17. There are New Testament scholars who doubt the historical validity of even this bare outline, particularly the story of Jesus' birth in Bethlehem. They maintain that the Bethlehem story was likely added to provide support for Jesus being the Messiah of the line of David, since Bethlehem was David's city. There is some indication that the question of the location of Jesus' birth, whether in Galilee or in Judea, became a point of controversial discussion among Jewish groups (see John 7:40–44).

18. I will refer to the four New Testament gospels simply by their traditional names: Matthew, Mark, Luke, and John, though most scholars maintain their actual authors are unknown to us. Accordingly, if I write that Matthew or Mark "say" something I mean the book, not the person. A good readable introduction to these matters is found in Bart Ehrman, *The New Testament: A Historical Introduction to the Early Christian Writings* (New York: Oxford University Press, 2004).

19. This is a literal translation of the Greek, rather than the more lofty sounding traditional phrasing "from the Holy Spirit" with definite article and capital letters. In the New Testament the term "holy spirit" is referred to twenty-eight times with the definite article and forty-four times without. Although the meaning is essentially the same, that is, a reference to God's "holy spirit," the use of the article, as in English, does add specificity or em-

phasis to the term. Accordingly, one might expect in a passage dealing with the source of Mary's pregnancy that the definite article would be used but it is not (compare Matthew 12:32, where one finds the article). The practice of capitalizing "Holy Spirit" followed in most translations of the Bible is a theologically based attempt to personify the Holy Spirit as part of the Godhead or Trinity.

20. All translations from the Bible are my own unless otherwise indicated. I have used italics for emphasis in certain places.

21. The Greek translation of the Hebrew Bible known as the Septuagint or LXX used the word *parthenos* in Isaiah 7:14. It does mean "virgin" but the clear meaning in context is not that a woman becomes pregnant *without a male* but that a virgin girl who has never had sex before becomes pregnant. This special child would be born not of a woman who had already had children, but of one who was a virgin when she got pregnant. Since Matthew wrote in Greek and is quoting Isaiah he uses the word *parthenos* as well. When the Revised Standard Version of the Old Testament was published in 1952 the translators correctly used the English "young woman" rather than the traditional "virgin" in Isaiah 7:14. The translation was denounced by many fundamentalist Christians as a devilish communist attempt to undermine faith in the "virgin birth of Christ."

22. One of the most ancient, the "Apostles' Creed," reads as follows: "I believe in God, the Father Almighty, Maker of heaven and earth, and in Jesus Christ, His only Son, Our Lord, Who was conceived by the Holy Ghost, Born of the Virgin Mary, Suffered under Pontius Pilate, Was crucified, dead and buried. He descended into hell and on the third day He rose again from the dead. He ascended into heaven, and sits on the right hand of the Father Almighty, from thence He shall come to judge the quick [living] and the dead. I believe in the Holy Ghost, the holy Catholic Church, the communion of saints, the forgiveness of sins, the resurrection of the body, and the life everlasting. Amen." (Traditional English translation from the Book of Common Prayer.)

23. Some early Christians did debate whether Mary remained a virgin (*virginitas in partu*), with her hymen remaining intact even though she had borne a child. The *Protoevangelium of James* (chapter 20) is our earliest source for this idea. The text recounts how a midwife, examining Mary after the birth of Jesus, found that she remained physically intact through God's miraculous power. This idea never became official dogma and the opinion of most of the ancient Christian theologians was that Mary was "virgin in terms of a man, not virgin in terms of giving birth" (Tertullian *De carne Christi* 23) in

The Ante-Nicene Fathers, vol. 3, ed. Alexander Roberts and James Donaldson (Grand Rapids: Wm. B. Eerdmans, 1986), 536.

24. In Roman Catholic teaching there are four Marian dogmas: the Immaculate Conception, the Virginal Birth (meaning Conception), Perpetual Virginity, and the bodily Assumption of Mary into heaven. The latter was only made official in the 20th century when declared an infallible dogma by Pope Pius XII in 1950. See *Catholic Encyclopedia*, 2nd ed., s.v. "The Blessed Virgin Mary" and "Feast of the Assumption."

25. In 1523 Luther wrote in his treatise "That Jesus Christ Was Born a Jew": "When Matthew says that Joseph did not know Mary carnally until she had brought forth her son, it does not follow that he knew her subsequently; on the contrary, it means that he never did know her," in Jaroslav Pelikan and Helmut T. Lehmann, eds., *Luther's Works*, vol. 45 (Philadelphia: Fortress Press, 1955), p. 212. In his "Letter to a Roman Catholic" Wesley writes, "I believe he was born of the blessed Virgin, who, as well after as she brought him forth, continued a pure and unspotted virgin," in A. C. Coulter, *John Wesley* (New York: Oxford University Press, 1964), p. 495.

2. A Son of David?

1. Although a few modern scholars have expressed doubt about the historicity of Jesus' claim to be either a "messiah" or a descendant of David, the tradition is early and widespread in all our documents, with no one even suggesting otherwise. The earliest texts are Romans 1:3; Mark 10:47; Acts 2:30, 13:23, 15:16; 2 Timothy 2:8; Revelation 5:5, 22:16; *Didache* 10:6; Ignatius *Ephesians* 18:2.

2. Josephus says that John Hyrcanus (reigned 135–104 B.C.), though not a descendant of David, declared himself ruler of the nation *and* high priest— roles ideally intended for two "messiahs," one priestly and the other Davidic (*Jewish Antiquities* 14.14; *Jewish War* 1.120–23).

3. The accounts are found, respectively, in Genesis 38, Joshua 2, Ruth 3, and 2 Samuel 11.

4. Jechoniah or "Coniah" is known in the biblical histories as Jehoiachin (see 2 Kings 24:8–15; 2 Chronicles 36:9–10). He came to the throne at age eighteen and only reigned three months. Nebuchadnezzar carried him away captive to Babylon. He was the grandson of the famous king Josiah.

5. Jews and Christians of that time were well aware of the problem that Jeremiah's declaration created for this particular branch of the royal family. Hippolytus, a 3rd-century Christian, even denied that the Jechoniah condemned

NOTES

by Jeremiah was the same one recorded in Matthew's genealogy. The rabbis, realizing the problem, but revering this royal lineage, speculated that God had later repealed the punishment since Jechoniah had repented of his notorious wickedness in exile—a point not made by the biblical writers (see Babylonian Talmud *Sanhedrin* 37b). Eusebius of Caesarea, the 4th-century church historian, realizing the serious potential for objections to Jesus' qualifications as Messiah had he come from this line, suggests that Luke's genealogy traces his actual bloodline (*Quaestiones Evangelicae ad Stephanum* 3.2).

6. The Greek verb is *nomizo*, referring to what is "thought" or even "assumed."

7. There is in fact a "Mariam daughter of Heli" mentioned in an unflattering way in the Jerusalem Talmud (y. Yerushalmi *Hagigah* 2:2). The translation of her name is disputed and most scholars agree that this Mary, who is punished in Gehenna by being hung by her nipples, has no connection to the mother of Jesus.

8. Josephus *Life* 1.6: "Thus have I set down the genealogy of my family as I have found described in the public records, and so bid adieu to those who calumniate me."

9. Quoted in Eusebius *Church History* 1.7.13–14. Africanus specifically notes that the members of Jesus' clan were concentrated in Nazareth and nearby Kokhaba. There is another Kokhaba east of the Jordan River that some have identified with Africanus' statement but it seems much more likely, since he mentions Nazareth as well, that he has in mind the town north of Sepphoris (Eusebius *Church History* 1.7.14).

10. The spelling of the name of the town Nazareth from the Hebrew *netzer* has now been confirmed by a broken marble inscription found at Caesarea in 1962. It was written in Hebrew and lists the towns where families of priests had settled in the 4th century A.D. See M. Avi-Yonah, "A List of Priestly Courses from Caesarea," *Israel Exploration Journal* 12 (1962): 137–39.

11. The Dead Sea Scrolls, discovered in 1947 in caves along the Dead Sea, preserve the library of an ancient Jewish sect called the Essenes. They will be discussed in some detail later. For example, 4Q 174, a fragment from Cave 4, quotes 2 Samuel 7:14, the promise made to David, and says of the future king, "He is the Branch of David . . . who shall arrive at the end of time." Unless otherwise indicated, translations of the Dead Sea Scrolls are taken from Geza Vermes, *The Complete Dead Sea Scrolls in English* (New York: Penguin, 1997).

12. See Acts 24:5, where the term first occurs.

13. See Dead Sea Scrolls *Damascus Document* 7:18–21; *War Rule* (1 QM) 11:6–7. This designation for the Messiah was based on a prophecy in Numbers

24:17 about a "star" and a "scepter" arising in Israel. Revelation 22:16 desig-
nates Jesus as "the descendant of David, the bright morning star," clearly
linking the two terms.

14. These proud family members called themselves *desposynoi*, which means
"belonging to the Master."

15. Compare Mark 2:14 with Matthew 9:9. Matthew and Levi are the same
person.

16. The clearest statement is in the Dead Sea Scrolls' *Community Rule (IQS)*
9:10–11: "But they shall be ruled by the primitive precepts in which the
men of the Community were first instructed until there shall come the
Prophet and the Messiahs of Aaron and of Israel." See also the *Damascus
Document* B20.

17. As early as Genesis 3:15 we read of the "seed" of the woman Eve. Leviticus
12:2 speaks of a woman "seeding," (RSV has "conceived") with the verb in
the feminine gender.

18. Compare Galatians 4:4 where Paul describes Jesus as "born of a woman,"
with Romans 1:3 where he asserts that he is "the seed of David" according to
the flesh.

3. An Unnamed Father of Jesus?

1. The degree to which a literal interpretation might be taken is best illus-
trated by the claim of the late amateur archaeologist Ron Wyatt to have
located the true site of the crucifixion, to have recovered some of the
dried blood of Jesus, and to have demonstrated by a lab test that Jesus had
no father. According to Wyatt the cells contained only 24 chromosomes—
22 autosomal, one X, and one Y chromosome—rather than the normal 46
(http://www.wyattarchaeology.com/ark.htm). An anthropology colleague
of mine pointed out that although such an idea is a biological absurdity, if
one still wants to imagine it possible the individual would be the most
physically deformed creature in the history of the planet—having just half
the normal chromosomes needed for normal development.

2. For textual examples with some short notes see my academic Web site:
http://www.religiousstudies.uncc.edu/jdtabor/divine.html.

3. Jews were not immune to such ideas, though Jewish texts that relate such
stories invariably affirm that the child, though conceived supernaturally, or
divinely announced, was the offspring of the husband. Most typically a
woman who had not been able to bear children was told she would and her
husband had some type of confirming dream. For example, there is a text in

the Dead Sea Scrolls where Lamech, the father of Noah, suspected his wife
had become pregnant through an angel, but was then convinced by her that
he was indeed the father (*Genesis Apocryphon* 3).

4. Plutarch, *Life of Alexander*, 2–3, Loeb Classical Library, vol. 7, trans. by
Bernadette Perrin (Cambridge, Mass.: Harvard University Press, 1919,
reprint 1999).

5. Translation is my own. The term "whore" (*porne*) in this context is a term of
slander for one guilty of sexual immorality or unfaithfulness.

6. Origen, *Against Celsus* 1.69. In *Celsus on the True Doctrine*, trans. by R. Joseph
Hoffmann (Oxford: Oxford University Press, 1987). The Christian philosopher Origen wrote a refutation of Celsus' work titled *Against Celsus* around
about the year A.D. 248. In addressing the charges that Celsus makes, Origen
quotes long sections of the earlier work, thus preserving it for us.

7. Sikhnin is a few miles from Kokhaba, one of the main centers where members of the royal family lived. It is possible the tomb of Jacob has been
found in modern Sakhnin and there is also a tradition that he was mar-
tyred at Nazareth.

8. There are various spellings of the same name: Pantira, Pandera, Pantiri,
Panteri. The story occurs three times in rabbinic literature but the earliest
account is found in the Palestinian Tosephta *t. Hullin* 2.24. The other versions are in the Babylonian Talmud (*b. Avodah Zarah* 16b–17a) and the
Midrash (*Ecclesiastes Rabba* 1:8:3).

9. Palestinian Tosephta *t. Hullin* 2.22–23. A version is also found in Babylonian Talmud *b. Avodah Zarah* 27b. A somewhat similar healing story is found
in Jerusalem Talmud *y. Shabbat* 14d.

10. The "son of Pantera/Pandera" texts become quite confused and garbled in
later Jewish polemical materials. Jesus gets confused with another figure
known as "ben Stada" who lived in the previous century. Origen answers
Celsus by claiming that Jesus had a grandfather named "Panther." The legendary medieval text known as *Toldoth Yeshu*, which exists in many versions,
completely switches things around. It opens with a story in which Miriam,
mother of Jesus, is engaged to a man of the house of David named Yohanan
or John. Across from her house lived a handsome Roman soldier named
Yosef/Joseph, son of Pandera, who seduced her. So Joseph becomes the
paramour and not the fiancé.

11. Epiphanius *Panarion* (*Adv. Haer.*) 78.7.5 (PG 42:708D).

12. John of Damascus *On the Orthodox Faith* 4.14 (PG 94:1156–57).

13. Adolf Deissmann, "Der Name Panthera," *Orientalische Studien Theodor
Nöldeke gewidmet* (Giessen, Germany: A. Töpelmann, 1906), pp. 871–75.

14. The Latin text reads: "Tib. Iul. Abdes. Pantera. Sidonia. ann. LXII stipen. XXXX. miles. exs. coh I. sagitarriorum. h.s.e." (*Corpus Inscriptionum Latinarum* XIII 7514).

15. Until recently Bad Kreuznach was headquarters to the U.S. Army 1st Armored Division. This important base was closed in December 2001.

16. The slight difference in spelling is insignificant and common with Greek names taken by Semites. On this discovery see *Corpus Inscriptionum Judaicarum* 1211.

17. Cornelius is a prime example. See Acts 10:1–2, where he is described as "a devout man who feared God with all his household, gave charity to the people, and prayed continually to God."

4. Children of a Different Father

1. Epiphanius *Panarion* 78.8–9, and compare *Gospel of Philip* 59:6–11 with *Protoevangelium of James* 19–20.

2. See his instruction in 1 Corinthians 7.

3. The idea of Mary's perpetual virginity was affirmed at the 2nd Council of Constantinople in A.D. 553 and the Lateran Council in 649. Although it is a firmly established part of Catholic dogma it has nonetheless never been the subject of an infallible declaration by the Roman Catholic Church.

4. This is called the Helvidian view, after Helvidius, a 4th-century Christian writer whom Jerome seeks to refute. Eusebius, the early 4th-century church historian, regularly quotes early sources and refers himself to the brothers of Jesus "after the flesh," surely understanding them as children of Mary and Joseph. See Eusebius *Church History* 2.23; 3.19.

5. This is called the Hieronymian view in honor of Jerome (Eusebius Hieronymus, not to be confused with Eusebius of Caesarea), the 5th-century Christian theologian who was its champion.

6. This is called the Epiphanian view in honor of Epiphanius. It occurs as early as the 2nd-century *Protoevangelium of James*.

7. Luke has one later story with Joseph, when Jesus was twelve years old and was left behind after a Passover feast at the temple. This account does mention his father and his mother but most historians question its historical validity. It appears to be modeled closely on typical stories of the time about a precocious child amazing the wise men of his society. (See Luke 2:41–51; compare Josephus *Life* 7–8.)

8. The term *Levirate* comes from the Latin *levir* ("husband's brother"). Jewish authorities differ as to whether the Torah has in mind a deceased brother

who is childless or one who specifically lacks a male heir (*Jewish Encyclopedia*, s.v. "Levirate Marriage"). The practical application of this law within Judaism at various points in history is long and complex (*Encyclopaedia Judaica*, s.v. "Levirate Marriage and Halizah").

9. This is from the 2nd-century writer Hegesippus, who preserves for us some of the most valuable early traditions about the Jesus family (Eusebius *Church History* 3.11).

10. See Mark 3:18 and 15:40.

11. There is a Cleopas mentioned in Luke 24:18 but he does not appear to be the same person and the names in Greek are different.

PART TWO: GROWING UP JEWISH IN GALILEE

5. The Lost Years

1. Establishing the basic dates related to a chronology of the birth, life, and death of Jesus is difficult and historians continue to debate various schemes. See the Timeline on page 319. One major modern breakthrough has been the use of computer programs to instantly reconstruct any date in history based on ancient calendars and astronomical data. I have used such a program extensively, particularly in recounting the chronology, day by day, of the final week of Jesus' life. I have put the birth of Jesus in the fall of 5 B.C. and his death at age thirty-three in April of A.D. 30. Following the gospel of John, I assume a three-and-a-half-year preaching career of Jesus from his baptism by John in the fall of A.D. 26, when he was "about thirty," to his death at age thirty-three in April, A.D. 30. There are difficulties and objections with all the major schemes that have been proposed but I find this one the most convincing. For a detailed treatment of the various proposals see Jack Finegan, *Handbook of Biblical Chronology*, rev. ed. (Peabody, Mass.: Hendrickson, 1998), and for my own proposal in general see John A. T. Robinson, *The Priority of John* (London: SCM Press, 1985), 123–57, on the "Chronology of the Ministry."

2. Origen *Against Celsus* 1.69.

3. See: http://www.salagram.net/JesusLivedInIndia.html and Maury Lee, *Jesus of India* (Philadelphia: Xlibris, 2000). See also Paul Perry, *Jesus in India: Discovering the Secrets of Jesus' Childhood Years* (New York: Ballantine Books, 2003).

4. See http://www.whyprophets.com/prophets/arimthea.htm and E. Ray-

mond Capt, *Traditions of Glastonbury* (Thousand Oaks, Calif.: Artisan, 1983).
William Blake's famous lines perhaps refer to this popular legend:

> *And did those feet in ancient time*
> *Walk upon England's mountains green?*
> *And was the Holy Lamb of God*
> *On England's pleasant pastures seen?*
>
> "JERUSALEM," 1804

5. *Protoevangelium of James* 9:3.
6. It is difficult to translate ancient monetary values into modern equivalents because of the differences between ancient and modern economies and prices. Four Roman sesterces equaled one Roman denarius or Greek drachma. That was one quarter of a Jewish shekel. The stipend for a freed slave was 1,000 sesterces a year. A common Roman soldier earned about the same but living expenses were paid also for army service. To be a member of the Roman Senate one had to have minimum capital of 1,000,000 sesterces. This was also the annual salary of a Roman governor of a major province. See Richard Duncan-Jones, *The Economy of the Roman Empire: Quantitative Studies*, 2nd ed. (Cambridge, England: Cambridge University Press, 1982).
7. *Vita Sophocles* 1.

6. A Kingdom of This World

1. Josephus *Jewish War* 1.148–53; *Antiquities* 14.66.
2. Josephus *Jewish War* 1.659–63; *Antiquities* 17.174, 179.
3. Josephus *Jewish War* 1.656.
4. Josephus *Jewish War* 1.649–50.
5. Josephus *Jewish War* 2.55–65; *Antiquities* 17.271–85.
6. Josephus *Antiquities* 20.102.
7. Josephus *Antiquities* 17.319.
8. See John 6:1; 21:1.

7. The Religion of Jesus the Jew

1. Josephus *Jewish War* 6.423–26.
2. The Mishnah is the oldest compilation of Jewish discussion of the laws of the Torah put together by the Rabbi Judah the Prince around A.D. 200 in

Sepphoris. Until it was written down the traditions and sayings circulated orally. Although written in the 3rd century A.D. some of the material goes back to the time of Jesus.

3. This was commanded in Numbers 15:37–40. Compare Matthew 23:5.

4. These complex issues are thoroughly examined in the masterful work by Louis H. Feldman, *Jew and Gentile in the Ancient World* (Princeton: Princeton University Press, 1993).

5. His main description is in *Jewish War* 2.119–66; he offers a recap in his later work *Antiquities* 18.11–25.

6. See Acts 15:5; 21:20.

PART THREE: A GREAT REVIVAL AND A GATHERING STORM

8. *Hearing the* Voice

1. As explained previously in my reconstruction of events, I am using a chronology that dates the birth of Jesus in the fall of 5 B.C. and his death at age thirty-three in April of A.D. 30. Following the gospel of John, I accept a three-and-a-half-year preaching career of Jesus from his baptism by John in the fall of A.D. 26, when he was "about thirty," to his death at age thirty-three in April, A.D. 30. The precise placement of events reported in both the Synoptic gospels and John, within that three-and-a-half-year span, reflects my best judgment based on various chronological markers such as the age of Jesus at his baptism, the arrest of John, the Jewish festivals that John notes, and other indicators. According to Luke 1:36, John was born six months before Jesus. Shortly before Elizabeth's pregnancy, John's father, Zechariah, was serving as a priest in Jerusalem. The priests lived throughout the country but they were divided into twenty-four divisions or orders according to their ancestral families. Each division served for a week two times a year on a rotating cycle of duty that began in the spring each year. Zechariah was of the "course of Abijah," the eighth division, which put his week of service sometime in May, A.D. 6 (Luke 1:5). If Elizabeth became pregnant in June of that year, then John would have been born in late February or early March, 5 B.C. Mary then got pregnant six months after, probably in December, 6 B.C., and Jesus would have been born in late August or early September, 5 B.C.

2. Acts 9:2; 19:9, 23; 22:4; 24: 14, 22; James 5:20; 2 Peter 2:15

3. Josephus *Antiquities* 18.116–19.

4. Dead Sea Scrolls *Community Rule* (1QS) 8.13–14 and 9.19–20.

5. John 3:23–24.

6. F. C. Burkitt published an English translation of this ancient Syriac text of Matthew in 1904 that is out of print but in the public domain and available on the Web (http://www.trends.ca/~yuku/bbl/aramat1.htm).

7. See Shimon Gibson, *The Cave of John the Baptist* (New York: Doubleday, 2004).

8. Shimon Gibson and James D. Tabor, "John the Baptist's Cave: The Case in Favor," *Biblical Archaeology Review* (May/June, 2005): 36–41, 58. There is a lecture available on a DVD titled "Just Dug Up" by James D. Tabor, "The 'John the Baptist Cave' at Suba: What Are the Facts?" through the Biblical Archaeology Society (www.bib-arch.org)

9. *The Gospel of the Ebionites* as quoted by the 4th-century Christian writer Epiphanius. The Greek word for locusts (*akris*) is very similar to the Greek word for "honey cake" (*egkris*) that is used for the "manna" that the Israelites ate in the desert in the days of Moses (Exodus 16:31).

10. Compare Matthew 11:18–19 and Luke 7:33–34. See also Romans 14:1–4, 21, where Paul characterizes one who follows such an ascetic diet as "weak in faith."

11. There is an Old Russian (Slavic) version of Josephus's *Antiquities* that describes John the Baptizer as living on "roots and fruits of the tree" and insists that he never touches bread, even at Passover.

12. The Q hypothesis, often referred to as the "two source" hypothesis (Mark and Q being the two sources), was first expounded in 1838 by C. H. Weisse.

13. For a reconstruction of Q see www.religiousstudies.uncc.edu/jdtabor/ Qluke.html.

14. George Howard, *Hebrew Gospel of Matthew* (Macon, Ga.: Mercer University Press, 1995). The Hebrew text of Matthew is embedded in a 14th-century Jewish treatise titled *Even Bohan*, written by Shem-Tob Ibn Shaprut of Aragon. Howard has persuasively shown that this version of Matthew, preserved in Jewish rabbinic circles, is not a translation of the Greek Matthew contained in our New Testaments. It preserves independent, and I would argue, more authentic readings in a number of crucial places.

9. A *Crucial* Missing Year

1. See John A. T. Robinson, *The Priority of John* (London: SCM Press, 1985).

2. Josephus *Jewish War* 6.312.

3. Dead Sea Scrolls 11QMelch (11Q13).

4. Testament of the Twelve Patriarchs *Testament of Simon* 7.2.

5. Testament of the Twelve Patriarchs *Testament of Judah* 21:1–2.

6. *Jubilees* 31.

7. See Martin Abegg Jr., Peter Flint, and Eugene Ulrich, *The Dead Sea Scrolls Bible* (New York: HarperSanFrancisco, 1999), p. 477.

8. Dead Sea Scrolls *Testament of Levi* (4Q541).

9. When Jesus finds it necessary to retreat back to Galilee it is "four months until the harvest." This would be sometime around February of A.D. 28 since the "harvest" began in June with the festival of Pentecost or Shavuot.

10. Ushering in the Kingdom

1. Josephus *Jewish War* 2.170–77.

2. *Psalms of Solomon* 17, in R. H. Charles, ed., *The Apocrypha and Pseudepigrapha of the Old Testament*, vol. 2 (Oxford: Clarendon Press, 1913), pp. 647–48.

3. Daniel 7.

4. I have developed this point more fully in a published article, now available on the Web: http://www.religiousstudies.uncc.edu/jdtabor/RUthe1.html.

5. Isaiah 48:15–16.

6. See the remarkable documentation in Michael Wise, *The First Messiah: Investigating the Savior Before Christ* (New York: HarperSanFrancisco, 1999).

7. See Luke 13:16 and 8:2.

8. Dead Sea Scrolls *Community Rule* (1QS) 8.1.

9. Josephus *Antiquities*, 11.131–33.

10. Possibly the Nathanael of John 1:45.

11. Also called Levi in Mark 2:14.

12. He was also known by the nickname "Thaddeus" or "Lebbaeus," meaning "great of heart."

13. There are four lists of the Twelve in the New Testament: Mark 3:16–19; Matthew 10:2–4; Luke 6:14–16; and Acts 1:13, 26.

14. In Mark 3:31–35, when Jesus hears his mother and brothers are outside Peter's house in Capernaum and cannot get in because of the crowds, Jesus says, "Who is my mother and my brothers?—whoever does the will of God." What he is saying implies no rejection of his natural family, but rather an inclusion of all others who would follow God's will. The incident takes place in Capernaum. They are living in the house with him as part of the inner circle. By telling the crowds who were blocking his own family from entering the house, that they too were part of his family, he is showing no dishonor to Mary or his brothers. The other passage similarly cited is

Mark 3:21, where those "by him" try to take him away from the crowds, very possibly to protect him.

15. The Hebrew expression occurs many times in the Bible where it refers simply to a "mortal" or a "human" being (e.g., Jeremiah 49:18; Ezekiel 2:1).

PART FOUR: ENTERING THE LION'S DEN

11. Herod Strikes

1. Dead Sea Scrolls 4Q521.
2. Josephus *Antiquities* 18.119.
3. http://www.jewishvirtuallibrary.org/jsource/Archaeology/boat.html.
4. Dead Sea Scrolls *Damascus Document* (CD) col. 19. This copy "B" was found in Egypt in 1897 among some ancient discarded manuscripts. It has now been linked to the Dead Sea Scrolls found at Qumran with copies of the same text found in Cave 4.
5. The Hebrew word *Sheol* refers to the grave or the realm of the dead. It is similar to the Greek term *Hades*. It was metaphorically pictured as having gates or bars.
6. Psalm 118:10, 17–18, 22.
7. Dead Sea Scrolls *Thanksgiving Hymns* 2.21–24.
8. I base this rough estimate on the inner core group of the Twelve and associates, which likely numbered around twenty or so, and seventy or more others that had become his official delegates as well. Luke roughly confirms the number by stating that Jesus followers who gathered in Jerusalem after his death numbered about 120 (Acts 1:15).
9. See Ezekiel 4:5–6.

12. Last Days in Jerusalem

1. Mark knows a tradition that Jesus went "beyond the Jordan" but he apparently has no details and simply mentions it in passing, as part of his narrative of Jesus "on the road, going up to Jerusalem" (Mark 10:1, 32).
2. John 10:22. Using an astronomical computer program we can determine any date in recorded history within a precision range of seconds using any number of ancient calendar systems—Egyptian, Hebrew, Olympiad, Roman, et al. In the year A.D. 29 the festival of Hanukah began at sundown on December 16, a Sunday, and continued for eight days.

3. The precise dates on both the Jewish and Gregorian calendars are arrived at through computer calculations.

4. Mishnah *Bekhoroth* 8.7.

5. Mishnah *Shekalim* 1.3.

6. Josephus *Jewish War* 6.423–27.

7. The assumption that this area was an "Essene quarter" of Jerusalem seems unlikely. There is a "Gate of the Essenes" mentioned by Josephus, at the southern slope of this western hill, but the name does not indicate that Essenes *entered* the city at this point. This opulent area near Herod's palace would be the last place they would wish to go. The ancient names of the gates in Jerusalem always indicate what is *outside*, not *inside*. For example, the "Damascus Gate" is the gate one exits to go to Damascus, the "Jaffa Gate" in the same way leads to Jaffa. Accordingly, the "Essene Gate" would indicate that groups of Essenes had their camps outside that area, down in the western end of the valley of Hinnom.

8. See John A. T. Robinson, *The Priority of John* (London: SCM Press, 1985): pp. 147–56.

9. Dead Sea Scrolls *Thanksgiving Hymns* 9.23–24.

10. Dead Sea Scrolls *The Messianic Rule (1QSa)* 2.11–25.

11. *The Demotic Magical Papyrus of London and Leiden* 15.1–6, in *The Greek Magical Papyri in Translation, Including the Demotic Spells*, ed. Hans Dieter Betz (Chicago: University of Chicago Press, 1968).

12. *Papyri graecae magicae* 7.643ff.

13. *Didache* is pronounced *did-a-kay*.

14. *Didache* 9:1–3, in Bart Ehrman, trans., *The Apostolic Fathers*, Loeb Classical Library 24, vol. 1 (Cambridge, Mass.: Harvard University Press, 2003), p. 431.

15. Quoted by Jerome, *On Famous Men* 2.

13. The King Is Dead

1. The term used in Greek (*speiran*) normally refers to a cohort that at full strength was 600 men. The word could be used for a smaller "detachment," but by any measure would have numbered 200 or more.

2. Josephus *Antiquities* 20.199. This is further confirmed in Acts 5:17.

3. Babylonian Talmud *Pesahim* 57a; Tosephta *Menahot* 13:21.

4. This magnificent discovery is part of the Wohl Archaeological Museum. It is described with extensive photos and diagrams in N. Avigad's book *The Herodian Quarter in Jerusalem* (Jerusalem: Keter, 1989).

5. Christian pilgrims traditionally venerate two sites as the site of the "house of Caiaphas." The most popular is the Roman Catholic church St. Peter in Gallicantu (St. Peter at the Crowing of the Cock) on the eastern slope of Mount Zion. The Armenians have an alternative site on the summit of Mount Zion near the Dormition Abbey.

6. Philo *Embassy to Gaius* 37.301–03, in *Philo*, vol. 10, trans. F. H. Colson, Loeb Classical Library (Cambridge, Mass.: Harvard University Press, 1962).

7. Josephus *Jewish War* 7.203.

8. Deuteronomy 21:22–23.

14. Dead but Twice Buried

1. Matthew's assertion that Joseph of Arimathea placed Jesus in "his own new tomb that he had hewn out of the rock" is an editorial addition apparently lacking any historical basis. We know that Matthew's only source on Jesus' death and burial was the gospel of Mark. Since Mark says nothing about Joseph owning the tomb, and Luke, who also uses Mark as a source, lacks such claim, it is clear that Matthew added this connection, probably for theological reasons. Decades after Jesus' death, when Matthew wrote his gospel, the Christians were keen to prove that Jesus was the "suffering servant" figure of Isaiah 53. One of the things Isaiah says about this figure is that "they made his grave with the wicked, and with a rich one in his death" (Isaiah 53:9). Apparently Matthew picked up on this idea of a "rich man" and wanted to appropriate Joseph of Arimathea as a way of showing that Jesus fulfilled prophecy. It is a characteristic of Matthew's editing of his sources to try and insert fulfillments of prophecy in Jesus' life. He does this dozens of times. Matthew is apparently so eager to draw upon this quotation from Isaiah 53:9 that he seems to overlook the fact that this text, if applied to Joseph of Arimathea, would characterize him as not only "rich" but also "wicked."

2. Josephus often mentions this tomb, just north of the old city wall, as a landmark (*Jewish War* 5.259, 304, 356; 6.169). Hadrian later built a temple to Venus on the site.

3. This was originally based on Joshua 3:4–6, which warned the people to stay at least two thousand cubits from the Ark of the Covenant so as not to defile its holiness. In the days of a permanent Temple the same basic distance was applied to the Temple grounds.

4. The rabbinic sources uniformly interpret this expression from the Torah, "outside the camp," as a technical reference to a distance at least two thou-

sand cubits east of the Temple (see Babylonian Talmud *Yoma* 68a; Mishnah *Sanhedrin* 6:1).

5. Tosephta *Baba Bathra* 1:2 says that around Jerusalem only the tombs of David and some of the ancients were left, out of respect, but the bones of others were transported and reburied outside the area of sanctity. Some of the most spectacular tombs of the 1st century, such as those of Queen Helena and the High Priest Annas are located well outside this perimeter. The 1st-century "tombs of the Sanhedria" are also more than a mile north of the city.

6. The Bordeaux Pilgrim who toured the Holy Land in A.D. 333 writes of the *monticulus* or "hillock" made of bedrock at the top of the Mount of Olives (*Bordeaux Pilgrim* 595.4–596.1). See www.christusrex.org for an itinerary of this early visitor to the Holy Land.

7. In the 20th century this theory has been revived in many popular books including Michael Baigent, Richard Leigh, and Henry Lincoln, *Holy Blood, Holy Grail* (New York: Dell, 1982).

8. Hugh Schonfield, *The Passover Plot* (New York: Bernard Geis, 1965).

9. The Islamic Ahmadiyya Movement has most recently promoted this theory. Its founder, Ghulam Ahmad, who died in 1908, authored the book *Jesus in India*, now available in English (Islam International Publications, 1989). There is a Web site: (http://www.geocities.com/Athens/Delphi/1340/jesus_in_india.htm) that offers a summary of this view.

10. The idea was first popularized by Baigent, et al., in *Holy Blood, Holy Grail* but has received new worldwide attention as the subject of the bestselling novel by Dan Brown, *The Da Vinci Code* (New York: Doubleday, 2003).

11. Donovan Joyce, *The Jesus Scroll* (New York: Dial Press, 1972).

12. This added ending does not appear in our two oldest manuscripts, Sinaiticus and Vaticanus, dating to the early 4th century A.D. It is also absent from about one hundred Armenian manuscripts, the Old Latin version, and the Sinaitic Syriac. Even copies of Mark that contain the ending often include notes from the scribe pointing out that it is not in the oldest manuscripts.

13. The King James Version, translated in 1611 before some of the more ancient manuscripts came to light, included the later ending and that is how it became so well known and well regarded in the English-speaking world. The most popular modern translation today, the New International Version, includes the later ending, but with a separating line after Mark 16:8 and a note that tells the reader: "The most reliable early manuscripts and other ancient witnesses do not have Mark 16:9–20." This practice is followed by

most of the other translations. The later ending is printed, but with a note indicating that it might not be genuine.

14. Tertullian *De Spectaculis* 30.
15. *Book of the Resurrection of Christ by Bartholomew the Apostle* 1.6–7.
16. All these sites are discussed and evaluated in Jack Finegan, *The Archaeology of the New Testament: The Life of Jesus and the Beginning of the Early Church*, rev. ed. (Princeton: Princeton University Press, 1992), pp. 335–89.
17. Some scholars identify these symbols as Christian while others deny they are of any religious significance. See the discussion in Finegan, *Archaeology of the New Testament*, pp. 359–75.

PART FIVE: WAITING FOR THE SON OF MAN

15. Go to James the Just

1. I accept here the so-called "South Galatian" theory that dates Paul's letter to the Galatians around A.D. 50. His conversion experience would have accordingly been around the year A.D. 36 (the "fourteen years" earlier mentioned in Galatians 2:1), which fits with evidence we have from the *Ascents of James* that puts Paul's conversion around seven years after Jesus' crucifixion.
2. Dead Sea Scrolls *Community Rule* Col. 8.
3. See Acts 3:1–11; 4:13–19; 8:14.
4. The 2nd-century B.C. book of *Jubilees* 7:20–33 enumerates a list of ethical requirements for non-Jews very similar to that of James. The rabbis later summarize what they called the "Laws of Noah" under seven headings, forbidding idolatry, sexual immorality, eating blood, injustice, stealing, murder, and blasphemy (Tosephta *Avoda Zara* 8.4).
5. See the innovative and insightful work of April D. DeConick in *Thomasine Traditions in Antiquity: The Social and Cultural World of the Gospel of Thomas*, edited by April D. DeConick, Jon Asgeirsson, and Risto Uro, Nag Hammadi and Manichaean Studies Series (Leiden: E. J. Brill, 2005); *Recovering the Original Gospel of Thomas: A History of the Gospel and Its Growth*, Supplements to the *Journal of the Study of the New Testament* 286 (London: T. & T. Clark, 2005); and *The Original Gospel of Thomas in Translation: A Commentary and New English Translation of the Complete Gospel*, Supplements to the *Journal of the Study of the New Testament* (London: T. & T. Clark, 2006).
6. This idea is found often in ancient Jewish sources (e.g., 2 *Baruch* 15:7).
7. Quoted in Eusebius *Church History* 2.1.3.
8. Quoted in Eusebius *Church History* 2.1.4.

9. Eusebius *Church History* 2.1.2.

10. Eusebius *Church History* 2.23.4.

11. "Diadexomai," in *A Greek-English Lexicon of the New Testament and Other Early Christian Literature*, 3rd edition–BDAG, ed. by Frederick W. Danker (Chicago: University of Chicago Press, 1979), p. 227.

12. Robert E. Van Voorst, *The Ascents of James: History and Theology of a Jewish-Christian Community*, SBL Dissertation Series 112 (Atlanta: Scholars Press, 1989). Van Voorst has isolated this source from *Recognitions* 1.33–71 and demonstrated its antiquity.

13. Syriac *Recognitions* 1.43.3.

16. The Challenge of Paul

1. The Greek term *neaneas* or "young man," used in Acts 7:58 to describe Paul around the year A.D. 35, usually refers to someone at least under forty.

2. Jerome *De Virus Illustribus* (PL 23, 646).

3. 1 Corinthians 9:1; 15:8.

4. 2 Corinthians 12:9; 1 Thessalonians 4:15; 1 Corinthians 11:23.

5. Galatians 1:16.

6. Colossians 1:15.

7. Colossians 1:16.

8. Philippians 2:7–8; Galatians 4:4.

9. Romans 4:24–25; Romans 8:31–34; Philippians 3:20–21.

10. Romans 3:23–25.

11. 1 Corinthians 11:23–30. Paul says he received this ceremony "from the Lord."

12. 1 Corinthians 15:51–54; 1 Thessalonians 4:13–18.

13. 1 Corinthians 6:2–3.

14. There is a vast collection of such texts, some of which predate Paul, that scholars refer to loosely as the Pseudepigrapha (see James H. Charlesworth, *The Old Testament Pseudepigrapha*, 2 vols. [New York: Doubleday, 1983–85]). The writings of Philo, the 1st-century Jewish philosopher, have more in common with Plato than with the thought world of the Hebrew Bible, though Philo claims to be faithfully expounding "Judaism." The Dead Sea Scrolls reflect an extraordinary interest in the heavenly world.

15. Romans 16:25.

16. He refers to sayings of Jesus only twice in all his letters (1 Corinthians 7:10–11 and 9:14).

17. Galatians 3:19–20.

18. Galatians 4:8–11; compare Colossians 2:16–23.

19. Galatians 4:24–31.

20. Galatians 3:28; 2 Corinthians 5:17.

21. Eusebius *Church History* 2.25.5.

17. The Legacy of the Jesus Dynasty

1. See Bruce Metzger, *The Text of the New Testament* (Oxford: Clarendon Press, 1987), pp. 191–201.

2. Eusebius *Church History* 2.23.24–25.

3. See Peter H. Davids, "Palestinian Traditions in the Epistle of James," in *James the Just and Christian Origins*, ed. Bruce Chilton and Craig A. Evans (Leiden: E. J. Brill, 1999), pp. 33–57.

4. For a restored copy of the Q source see http://www.religiousstudies.uncc.edu/jdtabor/Qluke.html.

5. See Alan Wikgren, "Luther And 'New Testament Apocrypha,'" in *A Tribute to Arthur Vööbus: Studies in Early Christian Literature*, ed. R. H. Fisher (Chicago: University of Chicago Press, 1977), 379–90.

6. See David Capes, *Old Testament Yahweh Texts in Paul's Christology*, Wissenschaftliche Untersuchungen zum Neuen Testament 2, 47 (Tübingen: J. C. B. Mohr/Paul Siebeck, 1992).

7. Several English translations are in the public domain and are available on the Web at http://www.earlychristianwritings.com/didache.html. I have used here the new translation by Bart Ehrman, *The Apostolic Fathers*, Loeb Classical Library 24, vol. 1 (Cambridge, Mass.: Harvard University Press, 2003), pp. 417–43. The Loeb edition has a critical Greek text on facing pages with the English translation.

18. The End of the Age

1. Josephus, *Antiquities* 20.200–1. The parenthetical addition "called Christ" is likely a later Christian interpolation.

2. Eusebius *Church History* 2.23.20.

3. Origen wrote: "Now this writer [Josephus], although not believing in Jesus as the Christ, in seeking after the cause of the fall of Jerusalem and the destruction of the Temple . . . says that these disasters happened to the Jews as a punishment for the death of James the Just, who was a brother of Jesus called Christ, the Jews having put him to death, although he was a man most distinguished for his justice" (*Against Celsus* 1.47). It is unlikely

that Origen would have created this passage in arguing with his sharp-witted and educated critic Celsus. It is more likely that Josephus's account was removed at some point from the later manuscripts of Josephus that have survived.

4. Eusebius *Church History* 2.23.

5. Epiphanius *Panarion* 29.4.1–4.

6. Eusebius *Church History* 3.11.1.

7. Eusebius *Church History* 2.25.5.

8. Eusebius *Church History* 4.5.3–4; Epiphanius, *Panarion* 66.21–22.

9. The case for such an interpretation was first made by Richard Bauckham in his brilliant and groundbreaking study, *Jude and the Relatives of Jesus in the Early Church* (Edinburgh: T. & T. Clark, 1990), pp. 71–78.

10. Eusebius *Church History* 3.31.2–3 gives the sources.

11. Tacitus *Annales* 15.4.

12. Louis Feldman, "Financing the Colosseum," *Biblical Archaeology Review* 27 (July/August 2001).

13. Josephus *Jewish War* 6.312–13.

14. Eusebius *Church History* 3.5.3; Epiphanius *Panarion* 29.7; 30.2.

15. This is according to an ancient Jewish system called Gematria in which words are given coded numbers based on the numerical value of their letters. In Hebrew and Greek each letter of the alphabet has a number (Alef/Alpha=1; Bet/Beta=2; Gimel/Gamma=3, etc.), thus any word be represented by its total. In Hebrew Nero Caesar is written as *NRON QSR* (*Neron Qasar*) and the letters are valued as follows: N=50; R=200; O=6; N=50; Q=100; S=60; R=200. The total is 666, the "number of the name" of the "Beast" that represents Rome (Revelation 13:18).

16. See my discussion of the evidence on the Web at www.religious studies.uncc.edu/JDTABOR/masada.html.

17. Eusebius *Church History* 3.12.1.

18. Eusebius *Church History* 3.19–20.

19. See Eusebius *Church History* 3.20.6.

20. See Eusebius *Church History* 1.7.14.

21. See Eusebius *Church History* 3.32.3–7.

22. The complete name in Latin was *Colonia Aelia Capitolina. Aelia* came from Hadrian's name Aelius.

23. Eusebius *Church History* 3.27.

24. See Hans-Joachim Schoeps, *Jewish Christianity*, trans. Douglas R. A. Hare (Philadelphia: Fortress Press, 1969), for a summary of the basic Ebionite sources that survive and a discussion of their contents.

Acknowledgments

I have dedicated this book to the memory of Albert Schweitzer (1875–1965). The publication of his monumental study in 1906, titled in English *The Quest of the Historical Jesus*, remains a watershed event in the study of Christian origins. He was only thirty-one years old at the time, and he ended up pursuing distinguished careers in music and medicine as well as humanistic philosophy. He spent the last fifty years of his life as a medical missionary in Africa and a passionate and influential advocate of his philosophy of "reverence for life." On this one-hundredth anniversary of the publication of his work on Jesus, I gratefully stand in his shadow, and I continue to find his basic interpretation compelling and relevant to our own time.

I am deeply indebted to a host of my academic colleagues whose contributions to the study of the historical Jesus have informed and influenced my own quest in countless ways. In particular I thank Robert Eisenman, who has done more to rehabilitate the memory of James the "beloved disciple" and brother of Jesus than any other scholar of our generation. I also am grateful to Richard Bauckham who has done so much to remind us of the vital importance of the family of Jesus and to John Painter whose insightful work on James has become a standard for all of us. I am deeply indebted to the contributions of Bruce Chilton, John Dominic Crossan, Bart Ehrman, Paula Fredriksen, John Meier, E. P. Sanders, Geza Vermes, Michael White, and Tom Wright. Through all our differences there is a bond of common devotion to the importance of our task—the quest for the historical Jesus.

I thank my archaeological associates, in particular Shimon Gibson,

Jim Strange, Joe Zias, and Sheila Bishop, the filmmakers Ray Bruce and Simcha Jacobovici, as well as my many devoted students who have worked so hard on the various archaeological projects highlighted in this book. I am deeply grateful to my two esteemed mentors at the University of Chicago, Robert M. Grant and Jonathan Z. Smith, who opened my eyes to the wider Greco-Roman world as more than a mere background for the study of early Christianity.

I particularly thank my colleagues Arthur Droge and Eugene Gallagher for their input and evaluations of this work before publication, as well as various friends and associates who read draft versions, namely Rebecca Christenbury, Chad Day, Joy Beth Holley, Simcha Jacobovici, Ross Nichols, and Lori Woodall. My dearest lifelong friend Olof Ribb read every word of the manuscript along the way, offering helpful and informed feedback. Sadly he lost his battle with cancer before the book was published, but happily I was able to show him the typeset pages a few days before his death.

I thank Doug Abrams, of Idea Architects who so ably served not only as my agent but as a constant dialogue partner on the content of the book as it unfolded. No one could wish for a better and more able editor than the astute and patient Bob Bender at Simon & Schuster. I also thank his highly competent assistant Johanna Li for her untiring work, as well as my skillfully engaged copyeditors Tom Pitoniak and Gypsy da Silva, and all the wonderfully skilled production people at Simon & Schuster. I am grateful to Balage Balogh, whose ten paintings in this book help us imagine the story in a way that takes us beyond words or photographs. His devotion to accuracy in portraying archaeological and historical details in his artwork has distinguished him as the best in our field.

Finally I thank Lori Woodall and our children, Eve Ashley and Seth Alexander, who have cheerfully and encouragingly endured my absence on countless trips abroad and many late nights sequestered away while writing this book.

CHARLOTTE, NORTH CAROLINA
JANUARY 20, 2006

Index

Mary (mother of Jesus), 24, 37, 39, 39–56,
86, 142, 152, 176, 191, 244, 250, 279,
323n1, 324n11, 328n7, 336n14
assumption into Heaven of, 47, 327n24
baptism of, 149
birth of, 39
and burial of Jesus, 224, 229, 230, 235, 248
children of, 75–81, 90–91, 104, 291–92,
308, 331n4
conception of, 46, 327n24
at crucifixion, 77–80, 221, 248
Ebionite beliefs about, 303
enshrinement in Christian theology of,
307–8
genealogy of, 51–56, 58, 65, 164–65,
286
James and, 165
Levirate remarriage of, 76, 77, 164, 289
as observant Jew, 87–89
poverty of, 87, 195
pregnancy of, 41–46, 59–61, 63, 70–72, 81,
88, 151, 326n19, 330n10, 334n1
and sightings of Jesus, 232
tomb of, 24–25, 33, 236, 324n10
virginity of, 16, 46–47, 73–75, 325nn15, 16,
326n23, 327nn24, 25, 331n3
Mary (sister of Jesus), 24, 25, 61, 73, 91, 142,
149, 176, 191
Mary (sister of Martha), 194, 227, 235, 236
Mary Magdalene, 4, 25, 107, 142, 176, 191,
230
at crucifixion, 77–80, 221
and sightings of Jesus, 232–35
at tomb of Jesus, 224, 228, 229, 248
Masada, fortress of, 39, 98, 174, 230, 300
ruins of, 97
Masoretic text, 146
Mass, 200, 202
Matthew, Gospel of, 42–43, 129, 134, 139,
140, 199, 237, 240, 248, 250, 273–75,
289–90, 325n18
apostles in, 163, 165
baptism of Jesus in, 135, 138

birth story in, 44–46, 58–60, 62, 71, 85,
87–88, 324nn11, 12, 15
brothers and sisters of Jesus in, 61, 73, 77,
78, 81
coming of "Son of Man" in, 166
ethical teachings of Jesus in, 275–76, 281
genealogy in, 48–53, 61, 328n5
Hebrew version of, 303, 335n14
John the Baptizer in, 136–37, 180
last supper in, 200, 202, 204
Sidon trip in, 72
sightings of Jesus in, 230–33, 238
social status of Jesus in, 89–92
tomb of Jesus in, 78, 224, 227, 229, 339n1
trial of Jesus in, 212, 214, 215
Matthew the Apostle, 55, 140, 160, 163, 164,
250, 291
Matthias, 102
Menorah, 145
Messianic Movement, 81, 121, 133, 150, 153,
245, 266
acceptance of Gentiles into, 253–54,
266
founding by John the Baptizer and Jesus
of, 70, 262, 265, 307–9
fulfillment of Isaiah's prophecies by,
172
impact of murder of John the Baptizer
on, 175
Pharisee opposition to, 162
Sanhedrin members sympathetic to, 224
see also Nazarenes
Micah, 155
Mishnah, 115, 321, 333n2
Moabites, 50
Mohammed, 315, 316
Moses, 74, 109, 115, 134, 195, 254, 265, 315
Aaron and, 56–58, 125
eating of blood prohibited by, 202–3
Exodus led by, 163
Law of, see Torah
repudiated by Paul, 267–69
Mount of Offense, 235, 236

Photo Credits

All photos not credited below belong to the author, James D. Tabor.

American Vision Collection: p. 295 (top)
Associated Producers, Ltd., Toronto: pp. 25, 57, 213, 236
Balage Balogh: pp. 41, 92, 98, 99, 106, 112, 161, 189 (bottom), 213, 215, 220
Todd Bolen/BiblePlaces.com: pp. 97, 139, 193, 225, 297 (bottom)
Bildarchiv Preussischer Kulturbesitz/Art Resource, NY: p. 39
Jerusalem Archaeological Field Unit: pp. 9, 12, 13 (top and bottom), 17, 21, 29, 130, 131, 132
Amos Kloner: 28
Erich Lessing/Art Resource, NY: p. 45, 47, 263
Mike McKinney: p. 113
Z. Radovan/BibleLandPictures.com: 114, 127, 194, 219, 256
Scala/Art Resource, NY: p. 246
Seth Tabor-Woodall: pp. 66, 68